THE MAGICIAN

John Mulholland's Secret Life

Ben Robinson

Foreword by Dr. John N. Booth

Lybrary.com

ISBN: 978-1-59561-017-0

Published by Lybrary.com
http://www.lybrary.com

First edition 2008.
Second edition 2010.

Cover designed by Dee Christopher

John Mulholland with the Sultan of Sulu, 1923.

After Mulholland began plucking silver dollars out of the air, Dr. Victor Heiser, who witnesses the performance, wrote, "The Sultan's eyes popped so far out of his head that they could have been knocked off with a stick...He was inarticulate with amazement."

CONTENTS

John Mulholland in center with Milbourne Christopher after a TV special taping in New York with many magicians.

SOURCES AND ACKNOWLEDGEMENTS

I first heard the name John Mulholland sometime in the late 1960's after I read his *Book of Magic* shortly after seeing the first magician I had ever seen – Fred Kaps. I originally learned of John Mulholland's involvement with the CIA via my mother Edna Randall Robinson – the best clipping service I ever had. One morning when I was getting ready to go to school in 1977 I found a *New York Times* article sitting on the front table waiting for my inspection along with my lunch money. Twenty years later another Madison Avenue writer would provide me with much more detailed information. That was Maurine Brooks Christopher, noted *Ad Age* writer and wife to my teacher in magic, the great Milbourne Christopher.

Mrs. Christopher graciously gave me the materials John Mulholland gave her husband shortly before Mulholland died in 1970. Milbourne Christopher was the natural successor to John Mulholland in all things historically magical.

Christopher prized secrecy, believing some things should never see print. In fact, when *The New York Times* asked Mr. Christopher if he was aware of Mulholland's involvement with the CIA, he said "no." This could have been true at the time, but obviously Christopher knew and kept his friend's secret until his own untimely death in 1984.

A fine lad named Sam Stashower recently attended a performance of mine. He gently craned his neck, gazed at the back stage enclosures and remarked, "I do not know what is in there." Sam nailed it for all of us researchers.

Therefore deep gratitude is offered to all the researchers, analysts, writers, librarians, collectors, historians, Dr. Sidney Gottlieb, and Sam's daddy – all of whom helped find "what is in there."

Additionally, let the following credits roll noting the grateful assistance of:

The American Museum of Magic, Special Agent A. Anderson, George Belden, Marina Belica, Ted Bogusta – proprietor, Martinka & Co., Dr. John N. Booth – for 25 years of magic, answers and friendship, Bill Bradford, Cary Chalmers – designer of the Triplex at 123 Prince Street, Paul Daniels & Debbie McGee, Dr. Edwin A. Dawes – for the final missing piece of the puzzle, Amy & Adrian Dawes, Jon Dix (HPX.net), Ms. Sidney Eddison, Michael Edwards, Senator Dianne Feinstein, Steve Glassman, Michael Robotham, Benita & Serena Goldstein, Diane & Nancy Gordon, Ray & Ann Goulet, Jim Hammond, George P. Hansen, Richard Hatch for innumerable translation questions answered, David Haversat, the late Michael Hemmes, José Herrera, John Hickey, Woody Howard, Eleni Jaivares – Horace Mann School, Shinyuk Kim, Ken Klosterman, Daniel Laikind, Lincoln Center Library for the Performing Arts, Steven Lowy, Anne Lozier, Smith College, Elaine Lund, Nick Marucci, Dennis McKenna, Bill McCrum, Bill McIlhaney, Dr. Joanne D. S. McMahon, H. Keith Melton, David & Anita Meyer, Kate Milliken, Arthur Moses, the estates of John and Pauline Mulholland, The New York Times Corporation, Karl Petry, Louis Rachow, William V. Rauscher, Blanchette Ferry Hooker Rockefeller, The Rockefeller Archives, Lee Ringelheim, Jessica Roe, David Royce, Steven Saracco – NY Assistant District Attorney, Mark Setteducati, Sam Sloane, Jane Smith, Daniel Stashower, Jim Steinmeyer, Donna Tartt, Ronald Taxe, An R. Trotter, Vancouver Public Library Rare Book Division, Dr. Carl J. Vaughan, Jessica Walter, Cynthia Sablon, Bill Vande Water, Dorothy Stix, Larry White, and Woodlawn Cemetery. And finally to Chris Wasshuber for making it happen.

It is important to note those that did not live to see this published, though their impact is significant to the writer: Jack Flosso, Doug Henning, Terence McKenna, Robert Parrish, and Bob Weill.

Namaste to: Smitty, Stubby, and Dash. You've selflessly put up with this for more than a decade. Maybe having this on your shelves will somehow say thanks, if not erase, all the discomfort it caused. How I wish I could offer more.

This book is dedicated to Milbourne and Maurine Christopher with great thanks.

Finally, to the memory of Dr. George N. Gordon – until we meet again – go get'em kid.

– BR

INTRODUCTION TO THE 2ND EDITION

"A conjuror doesn't have to be of any particular type, nor have any unusual qualifications, but he must have, or develop, a pleasing manner. He should inherently like people and must study group psychology as well as the psychology of deception and presentation. He must acquire a sense of rhythm and a precision of time in order to be able to execute his secret operations invisibly and apparently without effort. Real proficiency in conjuring comes only through experience."

–John Mulholland, *CONJURING*, Encyclopedia Britannica, 1944.

On the second anniversary of this book, this second edition would probably make Pauline Mulholland smile. "Her Johnny" is finally getting the attention and credit he so richly deserves. Not only a performing magician, or writer on magic, but a bonafide patriot. Some have questioned the use of the term "patriot." What exactly does a patriot do? After many years, I have concluded that, the subject of this book, was much more Nathan Hale than Benedict Arnold. In the following pages you will find the shades of intelligence work are made of flannel, oxford cloth and gabardine, but they are all grey.

John Mulholland signed this card utilizing the "J" and lower right the hidden rabbit in hat.

John Mulholland (1898-1970) was born just as the Industrial Age was taking shape. He died just as President Nixon's first term was beginning to combat war protestors. Mulholland, a solid Republican, no doubt sided with the U.S. government's strike against Communist Southeast Asia. Despite history's perfect hindsight, Mulholland had a long history of fighting on the side of good against phony psychics who bilked the bereaved of fortunes, and against pickpockets and luggage lifters. Communism was another formidable dragon to be slayed by his magician's wand. He plied his curious trade around the world, in Burma and even within the folds of the Romanian Secret Service, during the Roaring Twenties. Odd yes; but true.

What drove this man of many faces and talents? There is no one answer. But, there are various facets that made up his six-foot plus frame topped off with protuberant ears, which of course, signal great intellect to some. Throughout his life he charted and analyzed coincidence, and also recognized serendipity when it occurred. He grew without siblings, and sans father (whom he was named after). His growth as a magician seemed blessed to have an inherent understanding of the magician's craft. Because of this, his definitions of the magician's talents well aligned with the necessary talents of the intelligence operative during the Cold War. The first law of illusion: *Just because you don't see it doesn't mean it is not there,* is a wonderful corollary to an edict of war: *You cannot fight an enemy you cannot see.* Mulholland was the perfect man to align both worlds when his country needed him most.

Mulholland continues to fascinate and elude our modern inspection. After the short film of stills from his world travels appeared on the Internet it was discovered that John Mulholland was a guest of the first President of the country then known as Czechoslovakia. Pictures of the magician seated with Tomas Garrigue Masaryk were kept in a special drawer along with leaders of industry in Germany, poets in France and notable scientists in St. Petersburg (now Leningrad). In December 2009, a three-page story was done in the Czech magazine *Tyden*, noting his achievements, and his associations.

Then there was the gold. On page four of this book you will see Mr. Mulholland gently towering over the elegant, if oddly styled Sultan of Sulu, one of the very first modern rulers of Southeast Asia. Mulholland had small leather boxes and containers made for each of his keepsakes. Little did I know when I acquired the small leather box containing the coin he received from the Sultan that the coin was struck in pure twenty-four karat gold.

Mulholland's use of coins is very well known, but his mysteries with coins go beyond his talents with sleight of hand. In 1936, John Mulholland wrote about a coin trick he performed with six 1886 American double eagle twenty dollar gold pieces. The status of his prop was not hard to notice, especially during the Great Depression. The unusual thing about these particular coins was not just their value or rarity at the time, but the fact that these coins were un-circulated. This means that these 90% pure gold coins were never in use as disseminated by the U.S. Treasury Department.

The coin Mulholland used was designed by, **Augustus St. Gaudens**, a premier U.S. sculptor. President Theodore Roosevelt (1858-1919) asked him to redesign this gold coin at the beginning of the 20th century. St. Gaudens' work on the very detailed $20 gold piece is considered one of the finest of all American coins. 11,000+ gold coins were created in 1907. In 2010 these coins are worth approximately $100,000 each. As this second edition was going to press, a vital piece of information came to light: where Mulholland obtained such rare coins.

I had a hunch as to where Mulholland procured his gold coins, but I wasn't sure. Later, I met with the grandson of the founder of Stack's Rare Coins of New York City (residing in the "diamond district" for nearly a half-century). Joseph Stack, the founder, was given these rare double eagle gold pieces as "secret presents" by members of the Treasury Department directly, in exchange for other favors, whether it be selling or trading other valuables. The Stack family maintained several vaults in Manhattan, and the grandson remembers going into the vaults and seeing huge "walls of coins" probably worth millions in their day. He concurred that "...it was my grandfather who sold him or brokered the deal that helped him get the coins...it fits his MO...he worked with many 'prominent' individuals and had access to the highest levels of government through his association with President Harry Truman and a close friendship with Secretary of Treasury John Snyder (appoint. 1946)," the grandson stated. When Mulholland died, it was rampant gossip among magic collectors as to what happened to Mulholland's priceless gold coins. (Were the coins found today, the Secret Service would surely confiscate them as they are classified as "the unlawful transaction of gold bouillon.") The only factual answer is that the coins disappeared upon Mulholland's death. This should have been expected.

Robert Lund, the founder of the American Museum of Magic in Marshall, Michigan, marveled in 1970, after Mulholland's death, that, "we have no modern counterpart." There are magicians who follow Mulholland's lead to define terms on deception and psychic fraud for dictionaries and encyclopedic entry. There are those who have performed before Presidents of the United States. But, Mulholland was the first to elucidate terms for standard definition, bringing erudition to conjuring. No one has approached his record of eight performances at the White House for Franklin and Eleanor Roosevelt. He verily invented the first magic-lecture platform show mixing education with entertainment. Many followed Mulholland's trail, including, but not limited to: John Booth, Harlan Tarbell, J. Elder Blackledge, and Milbourne Christopher.

*His 1940 lecture brochure featuring the famous photo from Vanity
Fair at the height of his fame.*

In Washington DC on F Street stands a very old building with many
secrets inside. It is called The International Spy Museum. In October
of 2009 an austere group assembled to hear one retired intelligence
operative and a famous intelligence historian and teacher discuss
Mulholland. Sitting with the former CIA Acting Director John
McLaughlin, a dedicated magic hobbyist, just prior to his magic
presentation, I offered a few words of advice directly from Mulholland
to Mr. McLaughlin. He took the advice, and thanked me afterward
saying it made his short presentation better. John Mulholland
continues to influence the intelligence community as he did sixty years
ago.

While his famous long essay *Some Operational Applications of the Art
of Deception* has now been reprinted in full by the aforementioned
speakers, Robert Wallace and H. Keith Melton, Mulholland would
have laughed that his clandestine essay is now popular reading! In July
2002, during a phone interview with Mr. Melton, I told him for the
first time about Mulholland's essay. I had read the copious essay, in
the magician's handwriting and hand-corrected typescript in the late
1980's. A copy was included in papers Mulholland left to my teacher,
Milbourne Christopher. Mulholland's insights into human perception,
carefully culled over many years, remain as salient and intriguing

today as when Mulholland first wrote on this topic for the U.S. government in 1953.

So rabid was the interest in the manual Mulholland created to teach field agents the art of deception (misdirection and sleight of hand), the CIA allowed their name to be used on a book titled *The Official CIA Manual of Trickery and Deception* (HarperCollins Books, 2009) edited and with a new introduction by H. Keith Melton and former CIA officer Robert Wallace. Though, typical to the world of governmental paradox, the inside cover disclaimer clearly states that the CIA avows that the material in the book does not represent their stance. The press surrounding authors Wallace and Melton led to certain greater interest in the book you hold. This book preceded theirs by a year, and Melton told me he was astonished at my find of Mulholland's "dope coin" as it corroborated a technique previously used in spy "tradecraft." It would seem reading the CIA "Official" book that all Mulholland did for the Agency was write one manual on deception and another on clandestine signals. This is hardly the case. After all, his larger manual was submitted in May of 1954, and his last CIA pay stub in my collection dates from *four years after that.* Mulholland was no government sinecure. (I was aware of his second, less known volume, but Information Officers at the CIA told me *not to* describe it, because some of the precepts were still being used in foreign surveillance, said officers at Langley.)

John Booth told me quite candidly that he did not accept the job Mulholland agreed to, because he knew that once inside the Agency, one never really left. As a friend of the wife of Bill Donavan, the first Agency chief, Booth was courted before the Agency was actually named. Still in the days of the OSS, Booth treasured his freedom outside of government scrutiny more than analytic work. His travels to meet world leaders (particularly in the Mid-East) and his facility with languages made him an ideal candidate to be, as he put it, "exploited." He would have none of it.

Others *directly associated* with Mulholland told me that John Mulholland was employed by the CIA in a variety of capacities in the 1960's. Some of his writing was heard on Radio Free Europe selling U.S. propaganda during later conflicts. Given this nugget, his final book with Dr. George Gordon takes on new and different significance. The war he fought was not won with bullets and bombs, but with the fact that if you repeatedly tell someone something, they will start to believe it. Here Mulholland took a page from the Houdini promotion book and succeeded with the master's plan; the message was simply different.

To gain an understanding of John Mulholland I encourage the reader to read all his books, in all their incarnations. His 1944 volume *The Art of Illusion* was released nary a year later by an entirely different publisher as *Magic For Entertaining* and also as a wartime pocket book. While the obsessive researcher might believe reading different editions of the same tome reasonable, the casual observer may not. Here is where the Cheshire Cat grin of Mulholland lives. Throughout the thirty-plus years I have spent inside John Mulholland's private world, I have come to realize that his lifestyle typified a magician's platitude: *The larger action hides the smaller.* John Mulholland was a physically impressive man with size sixteen shoes, wing-like ears and less than perfect teeth. He knew that later versions of his books might offer opportunities for tidbits and details either he missed originally, or pearls he'd enjoy hiding in plain sight.

Looking carefully at his sixty-year output, you will see one constant. He reworked material repeatedly, when possibility presented and when he wanted to make something happen. The fact that his entire book with Cortland Fitzsimmons *The Girl in the Cage* was released by the *Philadelphia Inquirer* as a tabloid-sized newspaper insert toward the end of the Great Depression tells you something about the authors, their need for money and the bounty they realized with such significant publicity.

The sensational cover of the Philadelphia Inquirer edition of his novel with Cortland Fitzsimmons.

Mulholland once asked a friend of mine how her book was going, during the writing process. She replied that she was enjoying the research and looked forward to finishing. He barked his reply: "Don't give me that 'enjoying business' I know that writing is like carrying a baby; it's tough work. It's Hell on Earth sometimes and getting through it might kill lesser souls." She recoiled and smiled at the famous editor's moxie and truthfulness. The glad hand of professional comradery was being offered with a sandpaper grip. His chain-smoking demeanor did not suffer professional politeness well when it came to hard work. Mulholland was no stranger to this type of hard work – just look at the bibliography of material he wrote!

The Vanity Fair photo, circa 1939, which Mulholland reprinted with a New Yorker profile of on the back.

John Mulholland was the art of magic's popular ambassador for more than forty years. His platform was that magic was a fine art; like opera or drama. He repeatedly offered that Servais LeRoy's or Cardini's performance would stand up to the finest intellects as first-rate entertainment. There were other famous performing magicians who stood on stages during his life, but none who received as much attention. Houdini greatly influenced Mulholland's thinking in this regard.

Perhaps the oldest advertising card known of a young 19 yr. old John Mulholland. He appears in the forefront at this Sideshow photo wearing a skimmer.

I have been able to track most of his movements from the time he was in high school through his death. One can plainly see that he was written about or he wrote an article that appeared in the media every two weeks throughout that time. It's an amazing fact, and one worth the inspection by any intelligence scholar to find out who this scion of the history of deception was. John Mulholland was being truthful in 1946 when he responded to a Horace Mann alumni questionnaire writing that he'd aided police and governmental agencies for "thirty years." I did not believe it when I first came across this document. I thought the magician was perhaps exercising a bit of showmanly revisionist history. Yet, the truth was available, if I just looked hard enough for it. The dates matched up with his earliest ghost-busting work for Houdini.

The actual mock up John Mulholland used to create his most famous icon.

Magic, as an art form, might be in a much different place were it not for John Mulholland. Today, at the end of the first decade of the twenty-first century, we can see most any magician who ever appeared on film or video via the Internet. In part, the art of magic has grown into broad popular entertainment because Mulholland convinced our fathers and grandfathers that magic was important as an intellectual pursuit or serious avocation. He would have delighted in the investment house that took an entire page of advertising in *The New York Times* in 2009 that showed the white ears of a rabbit just peering over the edge of an inverted black top hat to signify that science was at work, not magic.

HAPPY NEW YEAR

PAULINE & JOHN MULHOLLAND

The final product used here as a Christmas card.

Do we realize just how famous the icon of the rabbit in hat is? Manufacturers spend billions in advertising attempting to cement icons in the mind of the consumer. The name John Mulholland rarely appeared without his small bunny sitting in a high hat deftly indicating his profession. One of the rarities Mulholland left behind, possibly to document his precise methods, were the photos taken of a rabbit in a hat used by artist Henry Hering. He created the original 14" square bronze image that adorned Mulholland's stationary, books, manipulative copper and brass coins, and the impressive plaque to his private office door.

Mulholland collected seminal references to the rabbit in hat and doled them out in the fortieth anniversary issue of the magazine he edited for twenty-three years, *The Sphinx.* Given that *Collier's* magazine and Chesterfield cigarettes were convinced to take out expensive advertising in that thick issue, it was obviously editor Mulholland who pressed the point: rabbits in hats greatly aided sales.

*The uncooperative rabbit was straightened out
by the artist for his first brochure.*

JOHN MULHOLLAND

*John Mulholland's very first lecture brochure, without picture of him,
by the Feakins Agency of Fifth Avenue. Extremely rare.*

Perusing my working magician's library of several thousand titles, I am often amazed while researching in the wee hours when I come upon either an influence to the tall, always well-dressed conjuror, or someone who credits him. In England, in the early 1930's his performance, particularly close up with coins, was compared to the brilliant qualities of a diamond. Yet, in France months later, some of his writing was accused of being misogynistic. One great find was fulfilling Milbourne Christopher's directive that I should deduce "where Mulholland got it." Christopher was referring to Mulholland's definition of magic being an "agreeable" art of illusion. The 1899 text, *Isn't It Wonderful?* written by Charles Bertram, showed me where the young John Mulholland had avidly taken notice.

Another great surprise came in understanding, perhaps, one of his biggest illusions. Arriving at his summer home, I was convinced, having seen the entire space, it was a ranch house; one floor artfully designed and decorated. Six years later I was invited once more, and I discovered John Mulholland's work fooling me again. An artful tapestry hung across a small closet door. Actually it was an entrance to a staircase leading to a full second floor complete with bedroom, storage and other display areas. Surely the magician's tricky architecture was at work, delighting me as I imagined the clever magician standing on the lawn chortling at my initial misperception.

The land Mulholland's summer home was created on was a wedding gift from his wife's parents. Her father, a U.S. Army General was related to Franklin Pierce (1804-1869), the 14th President of the United States, who had owned the land, in a much larger parcel during the 1860's. The Mulholland property was initially 70-acres and then divided by Pauline Pierce Mulholland after her husband's death. A significant portion was given to a wild life preserve so it cannot be built on. The Mulholland property borders this preserved land and now rests on eight acres, complete with babbling brook. Recently, I visited the property for the last time and coordinated the moving of something John Mulholland loved.

*The Mulholland book cabinet he built in the 1940's
to hold the rarest of volumes.*

The Art Nouveau bookcase he built in the 1940's to hold his most valuable books (one priceless volume from the late 1400's) was taken to rest elsewhere. It was an honor to be asked to instruct the moving team as to who made the bookcase, when, and why. Given that the magician created this large glass cabinet, it tells us something about his needs, skills and tastes when you see what he built. It is very similar to the cabinets he made to house his materials, which were later sold to his beloved New York club The Players on Gramercy Park South. (One of the reasons his collection was sold in 1965 and was then moved in full *three years later* was due to the size of the material, and the fact that the magician's arthritis prevented him from the necessary woodwork he felt needed to properly house his treasures. Once completed, Mulholland stated in a letter to his friend Dr. John Henry Grossman that his collection would be looked after much like the JP Morgan Library. Unfortunately, history has not honored his wish.)

Like the WWII story, *The Man Who Never Was*, by Ewen Montague, the tales of Mulholland and his Cold War work for Gottlieb's MK-ULTRA project are genuinely fantastic. In both cases, there was an enemy, a timetable and the possibility things could go terribly wrong. Of course, my Chapter VI explains that early practices of the CIA had some flaws (gently put). John Mulholland, being aware of the problems attendant to the work he was involved in – early police investigations into clandestine work did not help – was didactic that none of his writing be changed at any time while he was working with Dr. Gottlieb and crew. Having worked with master magicians Harry Kellar, John William Sargent, Dr. Hooker and Houdini, Mulholland knew the importance of the slightest details, which can be seen in all of his writing.

The MagiCIAn: John Mulholland's Secret Life is only the tip of the iceberg for my passion for the man who has guided me since I was seven, along my own path as a magician. This volume was mostly created with original, unseen materials that have never been published before this book. Other researchers and writers have taken the material from this book, as if it were common knowledge. If this tome is incomplete in not telling the "whole story" at points, it is because I sought the absolutely irrefutable truth from original documents that I held in my hand. These documents were acquired from either the people who created them, or the people who previously owned them after their creation. When I quote a letter from Sidney Gottlieb to Mulholland, I own that letter with Gottlieb's original signature. If there is a quote, I heard it directly from who said it, or I was told about it from someone who was there when it was uttered. To tell the proper story of John Wickizer Mulholland (exactly his correct name given at birth – to silence the misinformed) I have been fortunate to have the guidance and friendship of three people who knew him very well (in some cases, for decades). All three are now gone, but their legacy lives on in this book along with John Mulholland's.

MULHOLLAND, John, magician; b. Chicago, Ill., June 9, 1898; S. John
and Irene May (Wickizer) M.; ed. high school and spl. cources Columbia and
Coll. City of N. Y.; m. Pauline Pierce, 1932. Began practicing magic at
5 years of age as a hobby, and entered field professionally while in sch.;
teacher of industrial arts, Horace Mann School for Boys, New York, 6 yrs.;
formerly identified with the World Book Co.; editor of The Sphinx (magicians
mag.); has given exhibitions of magic and lectured upon magic in principal
countries of the world. Owner of a notable collection of books on magic.
Mem. Soc. Am. Magicians, Inner Magic Circle, British Magical Society,
Magicians' Club (London), Magicians' Club (Japan), and many others. Republican. Protestant. Clubs: Players, Town Hall, Authors, Dutch Treat (New York).
Author: Magic in the Making (with Milton Smith), 1925; Quicker Than the Eye,
1932; Story of Magic, 1935; Beware of Familiar Spirits, 1938; Girl in the
Cage (with Cortland Fitzsimmons), 1939. Contbr. to mags. and newpapers.
Address: 130 W. 42nd St., New York, N. Y.

*The biography John Mulholland submitted to the Chicago Registry,
the actual typed copy misinterpreted, setting off the controversy
about his last name.*

Informally, I studied with **Milbourne Christopher** (1914 - 1984).
He was Mulholland's contemporary, competitor, fellow writer and
recipient of many of his most treasured materials (including his
private CIA file). I knew him from 1979 to 1984 and was at his hospital
the day he died. A comprehensive biographic portrait is my Chapter
Four in my book *Twelve Have Died*.

Dr. John N. Booth (1912 - 2009) knew, worked with and also
competed on the celebrity lecture platform with Mulholland for fifty
years. He became one of my closest confidants. His eloquent Foreword
adorns these pages, as his last original published writing. He and I
worked on four books* over a twenty-five-year period. Booth plainly
admitted in his famed autobiography *Memoirs of a Magician's Ghost*
that he patterned his first career after Mulholland. When death was
near Booth, at age 97, in May 2009, with a shaky hand, he directed me

---

* *Twelve Have Died*, *The John Booth Index*, *The MagiCIAn* and the
unpublished *The John Booth Reader*.

to his final thoughts about Mulholland that he felt important to impart despite his frail state.

Similarly, under the dictum, "Get here soon. I am dying." I met **Dr. George N. Gordon** (1926 - 2003). He was Mulholland's last literary collaborator and dear friend of many years. Dr. Gordon told me via many phone calls, one six-hour in person meeting, and many emails, like Pauline Mulholland, that he felt that Mulholland never received "his rightful due" during his lifetime. I countered that Mulholland's travels to forty-three countries, numerous books and articles, thousands of shows and work for the CIA yielded "success." Yet, Gordon replied, "John knew, as Pauline and I did, that it was the harder road. He was an unconventional magician."

The 1926 Smith College yearbook photo of the elusive
Pauline Nell Pierce who shunned photography.

It would take an unconventional magician to help the United States government fight an unconventional war in the 1950's and 60's with a plan that involved a certain reinterpretation of legality. Challenged by an audience member in Maryland, during a lecture-demonstration of Mulholland's methods, I explained that in wartime, the MK-ULTRA team felt certain measures were necessary, regardless of human life.

While that is not a popular stance, war simply breeds death. Testing their radical methods of drugs mixed with electro shock "therapy" and hypnosis *on themselves* and other "unwitting subjects" was the only way to get the knowledge to win that silent, international conflict.

May those unwitting individuals forgive the deeds of our past society. They too contributed to the cause to fight the Cold War. Sixty years later, the record clearly shows that John Mulholland applied artful deception for the U.S. government challenge to Communism for the greater good of democracy and peace.

As this second edition goes to press with rare, previously unpublished images and updated, corrected and noteworthy bibliographic references, it is important to recognize the continuing contribution and important research of the following: George Hansen, Ted Bogusta, Bill Vande Water, Robert Stack, Bill McCrum – executor for the estate of Michael Hemmes, Ted Chapin, Diane Gordon, Jennifer Gibbs; Irene Conrad, Roy McDonald and rock steady engineer Travis Ruscil at the Production Plant (L.A.Digital/NY) for their expert production of the audio version of this book, multiple Edgar award-winning author Daniel Stashower for his vigilance, Editor/Publisher Stan Allen at *MAGIC* magazine and Dodd Vickers at *The Magicians Newswire* for their unswerving support, Jim Steinmeyer for shouldering the good fight, Ken Klosterman for his great trust with rarities from magic's past, Ray Goulet, Denny Haney, Marc DeSouza, world champion magician Johnny Ace Palmer, Allan Smith–President of the Los Angeles Adventurer's Club, Harrison Kaplan, my agent Ms. Ricki Olshan at DBA, Bill and Barbara Marx and the MAB10's – you know who you are. I tip my top hat to you all.

Ben Robinson
New York City
August, 2010

THE PLAYERS

16 Gramercy Park, New York

Pipe Night, Sunday, March 7th

A NIGHT OF MAGIC

JOHN MULHOLLAND, *Pipe-Master*

Our guests will be

FREDERICK EUGENE POWELL

ELMER P. RANSOM

HARRY ROUCLERE

NATE LEIPZIG

and

AL BAKER

The magicians appearing have a total of two hundred and fifty years experience in the art of mystifying.

Dinner will be served at 7:30 sharp, and the cost will be one dollar and a half per plate.

Please respond immediately by return card.

Reservations not cancelled before Saturday noon, March 6, will be charged.

Guest privileges will necessarily be suspended for this evening.

This undated program flyer (pre-1939) from the famous club, formerly actor Edwin Booth's mansion on Gramercy Park South, was printed on very heavy paper, and shows an incredibly brilliant line-up of talent, hosted by Mulholland.

FOREWORD
By Dr. John N. Booth

In the late 1920's, *Tarbell Course in Magic* advertising graced a full page in a number of pulp magazines. Testimonials boosting it were printed from Howard Thurston, Harry Blackstone and an unknown (to me) John Mulholland. Why was this mysterious person linked with two great illusionists as worth quoting?

The passage of years more than proved to me the justification for a Mulholland recommendation. And Ben Robinson's latest book demonstrates the lasting imprint on magic and the public created by the thinking and contributions of this tall, professorial master of conjuring.

Although I met John Mulholland superficially at magic conventions, it wasn't until I invaded New York City as a full-time professional performer that I began to converse frequently with him in the *Sphinx* office or visit the Players. It became evident that every action of his life was organized, pre-examined.

Lighting a cigarette was a ritual, starting with the graceful removal of a silver case from his pocket. Closing the case, tapping the cigarette tip against it and the striking of a match for a light were not ostentatious or dramatic but one couldn't help watching them happen; the timing, the movements, the suaveness, were an unspoken, underplayed exhibition we enjoyed.

He once asked me how I prepared for a newspaper interview. "I know my business so I don't; the interviewer leads the way," I answered. "That is a mistake," he said. "In your mind make a list of significant, appropriate achievements and occurrences that you would like to come out in the write up. Work those into your interview replies." This simple, obvious advice has served well all my life. It was the inner, unvarnished John Mulholland speaking.

Appearing in the prestigious NYC Town Hall nearby, he presented his memorable lecture-show in which he flung his long arms in a wild circle to vanish a small Hertz birdcage. This was the only low point in a staid program with numerous high touches of subtle humor and skill, especially with the Linking Rings. I did not realize then that soon I would be his and Doc Tarbell's congenial competitor nationally on the celebrity lecture platform. Both accepted me as gentlemen.

In this scholarly volume, Ben Robinson has probed and expanded upon Mulholland's documented influence in lifting the public's image of magic and magicians. An undeniable new respect and concern for the meaning, history and performance of the conjuring arts was engendered by his writings and presence.

Living in New York City, Mulholland was easily accessible to the media as editor of America's #1 magic magazine, *The Sphinx*. It could obtain immediately, trustworthy information in depth for any aspect of our art. Producers of dictionaries and encyclopedias, magazines and books, received deathless statements that time has not dated or undermined.

Ben Robinson has thoughtfully and beautifully synthesized the pile of personal notes and documents which is the legacy passed from John Mulholland to Milbourne Christopher, to Maurine Christopher and finally to author Robinson. No better foundation exists for learning what made John Mulholland into magic's most influential voice in the 20th century. This book tells that story.

John Booth
California, 2004

The Magician

And ye shall know the truth and the truth shall make you free.
John VII - XXXII

The words on the forefront of the CIA building in Langley, Virginia

PROLOGUE

Millionaires don't believe in magic.
Billionaires do.
– J. P. Morgan

As the world has turned its attention to the use of biological weapons by the Iraqi army in the late twentieth century, the reader may be surprised to learn, via recently discovered documents from the 1950's, that the U.S. has been engineering biological, chemical and bacteriological weapons for warfare since 1943, and at an accelerated pace since the end of World War II. In the 1950's government agents carried deadly bacteria from rain forests to Washington labs. Those same labs also manufactured drugs to be used as a policeman might use a nightstick and handcuffs.

Incredibly enough, one of the consulting agents involved in this covert activity was an internationally famous stage magician and historian. Fifty-four pages of letters, ledgers, bills, phone records, handwritten notes, and reports stored for decades in the famous Milbourne Christopher magic collection, and now the property of this writer, provide a story of this remarkable man's involvement significantly more detailed than anything previously imagined.

From these recently uncovered documents[1] a better picture of the CIA's use of such unusual consultants—described by former CIA Director William J. Casey as "bankers and tycoons, safecrackers and forgers, printers and playwrights, athletes and circus men"—now comes to light.[†]

When one learns to be a magician, one learns secrets dating back to 2,500 BC. Some of these secrets have been orally passed down from master to apprentice since the Renaissance.

In the 19th century, the French government employed their greatest magician, Jean Eugene Robert-Houdin to help repel a rebellion in French-controlled Algeria. "The Father of Modern Magic" employed a cunning blend of psychology and forward looking technology, using a powerful electro-magnet to make it appear that the Marabout chieftains, who found themselves unable to lift a delicate wooden chest, had been robbed of their strength.

[†] Character actor Eddie Albert, best known to TV audiences for his role opposite a pig on the comedy *Green Acres,* allegedly worked in a one ring touring circus as an aerialist and clown while gathering intelligence about Nazi activities in Mexico in the late 1940's.

A century later, the magician Jasper Maskelyne, the third generation scion of a British magical dynasty, was employed in World War II to outwit the Nazi Desert Fox, General Rommel, and succeeded brilliantly. Maskelyne hid Alexandria harbor from the Luftwaffe, and saved thousands of lives. He made tanks appear, battle ships appear and disappear and created a fireproof paste. Some of his work is still classified as Top Secret by the British War Department. Magicians have been called upon for service to their country many times since.

John Mulholland, unpublished 1930.

Some recount the notion of a "Manchurian Candidate" as fiction, however; in light of the events of 9/11, no scenario in warfare seems too far-fetched. In fact, such unusual thoughts as hiding tanks, and making armies appear might also be thought cartoon fiction, but in fact such feats were executed by the famous illusionist Jasper Maskelyne in North Africa when the magician left the family's historic Egyptian Hall to fight in the Egyptian sands. The genuine fear of Rommel was that he had a "sixth sense" for battle.

The Allied forces were beat so often by his panzer division and mighty Luftwaffe that a disorderly wave of opinion was fearfully discussed in the ranks: Rommel was believed to have genuine prescience. While hard to accept, the concept was carefully guarded against in the ranks, and field commanders were often reprimanded for expressing any such belief. Though the silence of the upper command often spoke volumes of frustration. It was one of the great myths of the second World War that this general had a "gift."

John Mulholland, published 1930.
(from William V. Rauscher collection)

Maskelyne hid Alexandria Harbor during night raids, created a false battleship called the Houdin and hid the Suez Canal in a "whirling spray" of light generated by arc beams refracted intensely by rotating mirrors mounted on moving trucks.

Such secrets are rarely printed and some become popular conversation.

"It's up his sleeve" more than one magician has heard children yell out at a birthday party. "It's all done with smoke and mirrors" many an audience has believed, even if they don't exactly know to what they are referring.

Perhaps the most pervasive doctrine of the illusionist's trade is: *Just because you don't see it, doesn't mean it is not there.* The conjuror's corollary is defined: Hide in the obvious.

This means that the world of illusion thrives on that which is hidden. This is conspicuously different from most other arts.

Consider the ballet dancer. When the dancer leaps, or turns on point, her technique, however effortlessly displayed, is right in front of you.

The magician's art is exactly the opposite. The great comedic British magician Paul Daniels – a veteran of 40 years on the stage – says, "Magic is the art that conceals art."

What you see, such as a floating body, or a talking, decapitated head might be fascinating. But, often, the secret is much more fascinating.

Magic historian Milbourne Christopher defined magicians as "the scientists of show business." This is the world of hidden wires and secret mechanisms that are not just unseen, but completely alien to the perception of the uninitiated.

However intriguing these magical effects might prove to a lay audience, the inner workings – the hidden wires and trap doors – came to hold an even greater fascination for a smaller, more elite audience, one obsessed with secrecy and deception: the covert agencies of the United States government.[2]

The result, played out against the upheavals of the embryonic Central Intelligence Agency from 1953 to 1958, forms one of the most bizarre chapters in the history of the intelligence community, an uneasy balance of illusion and *realpolitik*, and at center stage stands an internationally famous New York scholar-magician known as John Mulholland.

I. OVERTURE

The Eden Musee on lower Sixth Avenue was an intimately-seated wax museum with stage attractions.

Variety acts had played there since the late 1800's and the wax figures cast a spell on audiences, as did one magician who was making his second visit in a dozen years.

"He looked like a trained bear deftly moving about the stage" wrote one critic. However, the bear was also a true beacon of magical invention; other conjurers' reputations were beholden to his creativity. The intimate stage was perfect for the heavy set conjurer. Making scarves disappear from his hand and wind up between two soup plates previously shown bare was just a warm up.

"The Greatest of All Living Sleight of Hand Conjurors" was born Joseph Buatier in 1847, and performed on stages throughout Europe as the celebrated Buatier DeKolta. Flowers appeared at his fingertips – a somewhat dainty manifestation for this full bearded Ulysses S. Grant type. Cards rose from a narrow glass, and then after the chosen card floated to his fingertips, an unexpected surprise came in the form of all the cards rushing high into the air as if transformed into a gushing fountain!

DeKolta was just getting started. Water changed to wine; flag staffs appeared and a button hole suddenly sprouted a flower. The crowd was impressed, but the final mystery would leave their mouths ajar.

Spreading a newspaper on the stage, the French magician placed a simple wooden chair atop the day's papers. His wife entered and sat wearing a floral-patterned silk gown. A large silk sheet was placed over her head and completely covered her body, though her form was clearly visible to the audience. Her hands moved beneath the silk sheet. He spoke a few words of humorous French, and suddenly the mighty DeKolta whipped aside the sheet and his wife was gone. It took the audience a moment to also realize that the silken covering *also disappeared!* Only the chair sat center stage; empty as it was brought to the stage.

For a finale, DeKolta claimed his wife had somehow gotten inside a small die, barely the size of a small watermelon. Suddenly the black die with white spots grew fifty times its size and his wife stepped from the confines of the peculiar enclosure. Gasps permeated the small hall, followed by thunderous applause. The conjuror was held over, as he had been many times before.

DeKolta was an inventor of many feats still seen in the performances of great magicians. Balls that multiply between the fingers and a small cage holding a single canary that dematerializes were DeKolta hallmarks. Along with such later renowned mystery workers as Hertz, Kellar and Blackstone. DeKolta influenced several generations of magicians and audiences.

This eccentric conjuror, who, when not on stage, habitually wore many pairs of pants and jackets at the same time, did not know that night in the Eden Musee, that it would be the last performance of his career in New York. And he would never imagine he would also set in motion a career that would also influence magicians the world over for the next sixty years.

That evening, in January 1903, as the French master magician made things disappear and received cheers, a little boy of five sat cradled in his mother's arms. He had survived rheumatic fever, and the mother was trying to distract her son from the recent abandonment of his father. Conjuring has always served as a respite from emotional pain, and DeKolta's performance created a deep obsession in the young Johnny Mulholland.

John Mulholland, 18 months old.

As the boy grew, he would also master the "flying cage" where DeKolta's canary magically disappeared, and his deep-seated interest would even take the illusion one step further. Mulholland would take DeKolta's cage to the stage of Radio City Music Hall, and in front of 6,000 patrons whisk the small cage from view.

34

Shortly after the century turned, the magic bug had bitten young Mulholland hard. He became passionately interested in conjuring, to the point of influencing his mother to spend a whopping two dollars and fifty cents on a beginner's magic set. He practiced with diligence that would be emblematic of his career.

By age ten he had befriended celebrated stage magicians, amateur illusionists who made hefty sums practicing medicine and chemistry, and a relatively new breed of collector enthusiasts. He saved his pennies to take formal lessons in sleight of hand and study the magician's deceptive psychology. He poured over books written by the first magicians to place conjuring among the theatrical arts.

A goateed magician living nearby, named John William Sargent, became his formal teacher. Young Mulholland elaborated on his teacher's "lecture show" and blazed a new trail combining scholarship with illusion. Again, Mulholland filled vast auditoriums with shows unimaginable to his 19th-century predecessors.

JOHN MULHOLLAND
Lecturer, Entertainer and Performer of Magic

By 1939, John Mulholland had traveled to forty countries and entertained royalty and presidents. His birdcage vanished at his fingertips bringing him wide acclaim. He now fictionalized himself in a book called *The Girl in the Cage* with a noted fiction writer. Mulholland's fictional character Peter King was to take the stage in a comeback show, a cat walking between his legs as he made his introduction. King walked forward embracing the mystic unknown. King's plight was not far from Mulholland's experience. Mulholland admitted later in life that employment as a teacher, salesman, woodworker and editor helped pay the bills when Post Depression America provided little opportunity for the performing magician.

Mulholland despaired that he was unable to lend his talents to help his country during both world wars. He knew magicians all over the world, had supped with Lord Mountbatten and Nelson Rockefeller, and confided to each that he wished magic could be used to fight Hitler.

By 1965 the magician was esteemed as a celebrity, writer and intellectual who frequently appeared in the papers. He was invited to appear on a radio program called *The Lively Arts* on the CBS network as both an artist and expert in his field. He walked into the radio station on West 53rd Street one late Friday afternoon and announced his arrival by stating declaratively, "I am John Mulholland."

For the next thirty minutes the conjurer explored every avenue of his profession. However, he did not speak of his greatest achievement while alive. That remained a secret the magician would take to the grave.

This is Mulholland's amazing story, and only the players themselves have changed a few of the names.

STATE OF NEW YORK
DEPARTMENT OF TAXATION AND FINANCE
BUREAU OF MOTOR VEHICLES

LICENSE NUMBER—DATE OF IS

663624 SEP 16 43

OPERATOR'S
LICENSE

ISSUED BY THE
STATE OF NEW YORK
BUREAU OF MOTOR VEHICLES
(Do not write in this space)

EXPIRES SEPTEMBER 30, 1946

SPACES BELOW TO BE FILLED IN BY APPLICANT

Print Full Name	John Mulholland
Give Legal Residence	Street and No. 600 West 115 Street
	City or Post Office New York 25 State N.Y.

ANY ALTERATION VOIDS THIS LICENSE

Date of Birth			Color	Sex
Mo. Ju	Day 9	Yr. 1898	W	M
Weight 180 Lbs.	Height 6 Ft. 3 In.		Color of Eyes Blue	Color of Hair Brown

Sign Your Name in Full — Not Initials

NOT VALID UNTIL DATED AND NUMBERED BY ISSUING OFFICE
LIST CHANGE OF ADDRESS ON OTHER SIDE

M.V. 2

37

John Mulholland in 1945.

II. THE WORLD'S MASTER MAGICIAN: JOHN MULHOLLAND
(June 9, 1898 - February 25, 1970)

"A marvelous magician, Mr. John Mulholland, performed seemingly impossible feats before our very eyes."

– Eleanor Roosevelt

John Mulholland[3] was born in Chicago, Illinois on June 9, 1898, and came to New York City when the century turned. It has been suggested by Robert Lund, the founder of the American Museum of Magic, that Mulholland was not the birth name. However, a Marshall Fields birth announcement in this author's collection confirms that the child was indeed born to Mr. and Mrs. John Mulholland of 445 Elm Street. The birth announcement with its ornate ribbon, and the child's booties made of red leather that button up the side, indicate that the family was well to do. These were accoutrements of a fashionable family, and the fact that they still exist over a hundred years later also indicate that heritage was a value impressed upon the child from a very early age.

John W. Mulholland,

Born June 9th 1898.

Mr. & Mrs. John Mulholland,

445 Elm Street.

The only known copy of his birth announcement, certifying his given name.

The future mystifier's mother was born Irene May Wickizer in 1867. She was a teacher by trade, a profession her son would also practice. An accomplished violinist, she studied at the Chicago Conservatory, holding a card dated April 14, 1894, giving her entree to entertainments in the recital hall. She graduated with a teaching Certificate of the First Grade from the Caldwell Academy in Sumner, Kansas, on September 1, 1888. She was also an active photographer who held a Guest Photographer card from the New York Zoological

Park, dated 1942. On the back of her card, her daughter-in-law Pauline wrote (long after Mrs. Mulholland's demise): "Rennie (short for Irene) actually got into the cages with animals – learned to imitate the keeper's call. Quite a gal!" Mrs. Mulholland died after suffering with Tourette's Syndrome in New York City in 1951. Her maiden name became her child's middle name.

Mulholland's father, John Mulholland Sr., was born in 1852 and died on December 22, 1910. The elder Mulholland was a dapper man.

In a series of unpublished interviews given by the younger Mulholland a few weeks before his death to his friend and compatriot Milbourne Christopher, the magician described his father as a "six-foot, one-inch promoter of sorts" who came into nearly two million dollars when he sold land he owned (which was occupied by a toy manufacturer on West 30th Street) in Manhattan on which the original Pennsylvania Railroad Station was constructed during the early 1900's. "Promoter" is used here as a "stock promoter."

The conjuror went on to describe how his father lost his fortune. In 1903, the elder Mulholland was sued for 1.4 million dollars in a financial dispute that was reported in a *The New York Times* report titled *Say John Mulholland owes $1,400,000 -- International Finance Development Company Admits Charges, Promoter Said to be Missing, Creditors Want Ancillary Receiver...*

According to records reported in the *Times* – and analyzed in 2003 by high finance banker Samuel Sloane – it appears that the elder Mulholland operated a "pyramid scheme" beginning in 1901 that eventually ended up in court proceedings in August of 1902. Although Mulholland Sr. claimed offices in seventy-five locations nationally, it was discovered that shares of preferred stock the company offered in the prospectus (incorporated in Delaware, with the "object" to "promote business and commercial enterprises") against bonds of the company, did not exist.

Six months after an initial offer to investors to redeem their investment at a profit of 6% to 8% (depending on the sum invested) Mulholland was sued by a man named William Muirhead (of New York) for his initial investment of $86,300 of common stock and $56,000 of preferred stock. Another man named Hugo Eyesell brought suit for monies lent of approximately $127,500. A third complaint against Mulholland Sr. was filed by a man named H. H. Field who provided operating capital of $17,500.

When investors went to redeem their shares at the New York office at 428 Broadway, Sloane reports, "the investors were met with smoke and mirrors. There was nothing there." The notes upon which the bonds were apparently secured in Mulholland's "scheme" (a word used in the *Times* and admitted to by the company) never existed. Only a letter describing the bonds, dated 1898, provided any substance upon which the loan of millions was based.

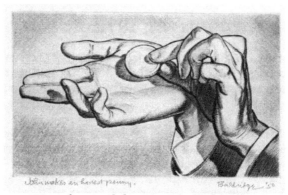

One of several drawings by Baldridge.

The illicit "game" seemed complete when, eight months later, William Muirhead, the man who brought the initial complaint transferred his interest in the suit (his settlement money to be received) back to Mulholland! In other words, he who yelled loudest at the onset of this impropriety proved to have been acting in collusion with Mulholland Sr. In bringing suit against the company, Muirhead seems to have served as the "shadow" needed to actually gain the most from a suit, to guard against other investors attaining their rightful return on their money.

In the course of the investigation, the elder Mulholland was found to have documents suggesting that this "operation" was in the planning stages in 1898, also the year his son, and namesake, was born. Mulholland resigned his position as president of the company on August 15, 1902, and was succeeded by Hugo Eyesell. All told, the elder Mulholland seems to have survived the complaint, allayed his creditors and "disappeared," according to the *Times* with 1.4 million dollars in 1902. That money was due in outstanding payments by the company in November of 1903. It was never paid.

It is somewhat fitting that John Mulholland Sr. should have been able to commit a perfect disappearing act. For the mysterious Mr. Mulholland was not to be found, nor was he assumed dead. He was simply, and conveniently, "gone."

Mulholland's 1.4 million dollars would be roughly the equivalent of thirty million in today's terms. It is unknown what portion, if any, of this money was recovered after John Mulholland Sr. disappeared.

41

John Mulholland Sr. died in 1910, leaving behind enough money for his young son and widow Irene May to live comfortably on Manhattan's Upper West Side, and to provide the son with a first class education.

FIRST INTEREST IN MAGIC 1903

Like many professional magicians, Mulholland suffered the absence of a father from early on, and it is significant that the son of a successful con man should himself have become a professional, if more legitimate, deceiver.

At age five in 1903, just after his father successfully outfoxed his creditors and the law, the young boy saw his first live performance by a magician, an event that would echo throughout the rest of his life. He is quoted in *The American Magazine* in 1931 as saying, "Mother gave me a 'child's-complete-assortment-of-parlor-tricks-price-two-fifty-cash'" and his life course was set. While held in his mother's arms he saw the French illusion inventor, Bautier DeKolta[4] make a living canary, in a small hand-held cage, disappear. This was a feat Mulholland featured throughout his fifty-year career, even utilizing the exact same apparatus used by the famed British magician Carl Hertz (who was once ordered in front of Parliament to prove that his canary wasn't injured during its rapid matinee and evening disappearance).

Mulholland later improved upon this piece of conjuring by adding a subtle touch to the illusion. While only magicians would appreciate this touch, it did make the illusion more remarkable. In Mulholland's hands he was able to pick up the cage from a table before its disappearance. Having inspected the Hertz/Mulholland apparatus personally, this writer can attest to the ingenious, yet typically simple change in the construction that John Mulholland made to this famous illusion. Clearly, the thinking of the illusionist was edified in that changes he made provided that the illusion became just a touch more practical, *and sensational.* In 1937 Mulholland wrote an article, in a magazine edited by his friend, noted literary personality Lowell Thomas, that laid bare the history of the celebrated feat detailing who had performed the feat before him. Mulholland was careful to note that the inventor of the feat was always misplaced with the current performer – a concerned, detailed and gentlemanly point of view rare among magicians. Once when his cage was stolen, he noted, the theft made the front pages of New York newspapers! In 1939, Harry Hansen wrote in *The New York World-Telegram* that "No one is smoother than John Mulholland when he makes the canary disappear in mid air, and his tricks are getting better and better."

While the influence of DeKolta is undeniable, Mulholland occasionally gave conflicting reports of his early influences, even offering contradictory accounts of the first conjurer he saw live. Sometimes he claimed it was Harry Kellar, whom he befriended in 1910 – the year of his father's death. Another interview, given shortly before Mulholland's death, clearly states that the first magician he saw was an authentic Chinese conjurer, Ching Ling Foo.

Despite his growing interest in magic, the young Mulholland also followed more common boyhood activities. As a youth he played baseball for the "Roosevelt Oysters" while living in the 80's near Riverside Drive. Having already shown a serious interest in magic during his ball playing years, his coach cautioned him not to catch fly balls because he felt the boy might injure his precious magical fingers. Mulholland switched to running track, later becoming a coach in this field at his preparatory school.

GREETINGS

FROM

JOHN WILLIAM SARGENT

JOHN WILLIAM SARGENT

As a teen Mulholland studied sleight of hand with magician and book collector John William Sargent, known as "The Merry Wizard." The magician's looks resembled the famous 19th century magician Alexander Herrmann, slender with a goatee that was well kept and commanding. Known as "the devil in evening clothes" the Herrmann image has become the stock portrayal of a magician with top hat, cloak, mustache and goatee. Sargent's brochure offered "modern magic, Oriental Magic, Japanese Magic, and Chinese magic." As a precursor to Mulholland's later exploitation of the lecture-performance, Sargent's brochure from 1917 claims that his entertainment is suitable for: "opera house, lecture course, or church or drawing room." Sargent offered two different programs: "The Children's Hour," and "A Lesson in Magic."

A young John William Sargent.

Given that Mulholland lived at 507 West 113th Street and Sargent lived at 313 West 120th Street, the young conjuror did not have more than nine blocks to walk to study the intricacies of the magician's art with one of the first presidents of the Society of American Magicians. In fact Sargent held membership card #9 in the august society, which today is the oldest society of conjuring in the western world, having celebrated its centennial in 2002 in New York City.

Their first meeting demonstrates the depth of the young Mulholland's devotion to magic. Though only ten years old, Mulholland boldly approached Sargent on the street, not far from their homes, after seeing his performance. He asked the older magician, "Can you teach me about the psychology of magic? What would it cost?" The magician replied, "Fifteen dollars for three lessons – in advance."

After lesson number three, Mulholland resigned himself to saving another fifteen dollars for more instruction. The gentlemanly older illusionist adopted his protégée by saying, "Why Johnny you are a slow learner, you haven't finished the first lesson yet!" Sargent also counseled the fledgling magical practitioner, "I want you to perform your own way. I want you to understand how the audience is deceived and then apply this knowledge in your own style." He went on to advise his student that the professional was never at a loss for words; other magicians agreed that John Mulholland was never, ever lacking for a descriptive phrase over the next sixty-one years.

John Mulholland at age 17.

Young Mulholland followed in his teacher's footsteps by joining the Society of American Magicians, becoming, at the age of 16, the society's youngest member in a special exception to the organization's bylaws. By his early 20's he was the club's Vice President, though it must be remembered that he was VP of a club with barely fifty members at the time. He stayed a member for fifty years, and would come to hold a number of important roles in the society and its sister organizations.

Along with his dedication to the Society of American Magicians, John Sargent imbued the young Mulholland with a passion for collecting magic, particularly rare books. Sargent, whose annual Christmas card illustrated a fondness for composing light verse, expressed their shared bibliomania in a special bookplate he made for his young student:

"My gathered store of magic lore
was incomplete tis' true.
But I am glad
that what I had
is cherished, John, by you."

Sargent also instilled in young Mulholland a love of genuinely brilliant sleight of hand – the guts of a magician's being. On June 22, 1909, Sargent, always in the thick of current magical doings, witnessed the set-up of the Thurston show and wrote to his friend Oscar Teale that "it is a big job." Sargent and Teale had both aspired to being touring magicians in their day. Each knew that Thurston began his career as a top sleight of hand man. Thurston, in fact, was a celebrated "King of Cards" at the London Palace Theatre at the turn of the century. Sargent, a fellow sleight of hand man, was amazed at Thurston's transition to becoming a pioneering world-touring illusionist.

Mulholland noted in his 1927 book *Quicker Than The Eye* that John Sargent called the eyes the "faithful servants of the brain," but added that they "were only a combination of lenses that function mechanically," and that the brain had to translate the images. He then gave an example of the "translation" where a person sat on a train and became deceived when the train across the track began to move believing that it was his own train that was moving. For, if a person could be so easily deceived into perceiving that his train was in motion, when actually it was still, then this indicated the fallibility of the senses. Sargent was perhaps the first magician to detail what neuro-sensory relationship existed to feed the brain misinformation. Sargent imparted how to fool the eye, and *why* the brain was deceived by what the five senses delivered.

Mulholland later wrote of his teacher, "In all probability, John William Sargent did more research than any other magician into the mental processes of audiences. He was the first magician, at least in America, to correlate the work of academic psychologists with the magician's wide but indefinite knowledge of the psychology of deception. He formulated many rules whereby magicians could know more definitely the responses they might expect from audiences faced with any given trick."

Mulholland also had high praise for another of his early mentors, Dr. Saram R. Ellison – a medical examiner for the City of New York, who also had the distinction of holding the first membership card in the newly-formed Society of American Magicians.

"Dr. Ellison was born in St. Thomas, Canada, on January 17, 1852," Mulholland later wrote. "As a boy he was shown several feats of magic by a traveling performer." Mulholland went on to quote Ellison's reaction: "The tricks were pretty and ingenious, and they interested me. But I found the magician still more interesting. He had led a life full of adventure." From this early inspiration Dr. Ellison went on to amass one of the first important collections of magical literature, now owned by the New York Public Library. Many of Ellison's volumes were acquired from William E. Robinson who later became known as "Robinson, the Man of Mystery." Still later, Robinson became world-famous as the ill-fated Chung Ling Soo, who died on stage attempting to "defy bullets." Mulholland would note that there had been magic collections before Ellison's (Adolph Blind known as "Professor Magicus" in Switzerland comes to mind) but the doctor's was the first very large collection of its kind, even pre-dating Houdini's massive theatrical, criminal and occult collection of books and ephemera. Ellison's collection of magician's wands was also unparalleled. (In fact, at the 2002 centennial convention of the Society of American Magicians in New York, the Ellison wand collection was the most visited exhibit.)

As a boy, Mulholland would regularly call on the good-natured doctor on Sunday mornings at his home at 118 West 103rd Street, not far from the Mulholland residence in upper Manhattan. The doctor would show him rare volumes about magic, describe tricks and then give his impressions of what type of man that magician was. Mulholland recalled these weekly sessions as a crucial element of his magical education.

At age twelve Mulholland was given entrée to an exclusive circle of magicians at Clyde Power's magic shop on West 42nd Street. Once, he was introduced to Ching Ling Foo (born Chee Ling Qua), who held the title of Conjuror to the Empress Dowager of China. Powers suggested to Ching that Mulholland was the son of the President of the United States. Later, Mulholland was apprised of the hoax, though he was pleased that Ching had shown him the best of his repertoire because of his false assumption. Ching Ling Foo was also a juggler, pantomimist, dancer and famous for producing a large basin of water followed by the instantaneous appearance of pigeons and ducks, and then his baby son. After igniting tissue paper and ingesting it, he spit sparks and colored smoke from his mouth. Such a difficult endeavor as the fire spitting prevented him from more than a twice-weekly demonstration. From his fiery mouth he also brought forth unburned colored tissue streamers. Foo ended his long touring stage career with great wealth, owning several motion picture facilities.

When Powers introduced Mulholland, Foo would surely have been at his mannered best from his prior associations with people of power. Mulholland alludes to his height being abnormal for his sixteen years. The Chinese magician might have also been impressed with Mulholland's uncommon height, powerful hands and unusual dexterity. Mulholland frequently demonstrated the latter by rolling five coins simultaneously across his fingers.

Mulholland, a serious collector of old books on conjuring since the age of ten, knew all of the great collections intimately. Having had access to the best collections of magic by Ellison, Hooker, Houdini and his teacher John Sargent as well as the accumulations of William E. Robinson, Dr. Milton A. Bridges, Charles Larson and Earl F. Rybolt, he taught himself the history of an art. He also learned the detective work needed to acquire his own growing collection, which would become the single largest collection of rare books, posters and ephemera on conjuring extant. As reflected in a letter from 1930, he sought to purchase an exceedingly rare volume from the seventeenth century for four dollars. To a rare book dealer in Prague he expressed interest in acquiring "any and all titles pertaining to the conjuring art from the 17th century."

MULHOLLAND'S EDUCATION (1915-1919)

Mulholland was educated at New York's Trinity School and the Horace Mann High School for Boys, possibly on a scholarship. During his time as a student at Horace Mann, Mulholland was exceedingly busy in extra curricular activities: Editor–in-Chief of the school newspaper *The Horace Mann Record*, chief performer of the Dramatic Club (where his "prestidigitatorial feats and illusions" were noted); he was on the Board of the Yearbook, on the Board of *The Quarterly*, Manager of the Track Association, and of his work with the Soccer team, it is noted, "John Mulholland deserves by far the most credit for the success of this year's team, for while he was captain and star half back, at the same time he coached."[‡] Yet, while this busy student is acknowledged a whopping fifteen times, with a dozen pictures of his staff positions at the famous school, he did not receive a degree! It seems that Mulholland's penchant for learning overtook his desire for accreditation. He always confided to others that his teaching career was born because "the shop teacher did not show up."

[‡] The "Horace Manniken of 1919".

48

While noted as a member of the class of 1919, he is not mentioned in the Commencement brochure. In his yearbook, like his teacher Sargent, he states in rhyme:

> He's a Jack of all trade, and a squire of maids,
>   A mechanic he is without peer,
> He tinkers with magic, manages plays tragic,
>   Which fellows come flocking to hear.
> He transmutes any metal to brooch or kettle,
>   His talk is convincing and clear;
> Which proves he has brains, but the sad fact remains,
>   His place in the class is the rear.

Interestingly enough, without a degree, Mulholland was offered a faculty position, teaching "industrial arts" or drawing, from 1920 to 1925. In the Horace Mann School *Mannikin* of 1924 he is credited with having taught drawing at the Barnard School for Boys in 1923.

On January 11, 1924, Mulholland gave a short program at his alma mater. He opened with his favorite thimble routine simply titled The Magic Thimble, where thimbles appeared on all of his fingers and then melted away into nothingness.

He moved on to The Cantonese Card Trick and the Curious Handkerchief, a routine generally referred to as the "Sympathetic Silks" where scarves replicate the actions of other scarves. He finished with Spirit Writing, a phenomenological apportment of supposed spirit activity. The last was a variation of an effect he'd feature for the rest of his life. Mulholland's signature trick, besides his coin magic, was having ghostly messages appear in a variety of places.

Shortly after his teaching career ended, there was a short term where his income was derived from selling books of the World Book Company. In a biographical statement he later submitted to his friend Will Goldston's *Who's Who in Magic* he identifies this brief stint as a salesman. As an example of his practical approach to life and conjuring, he realized he could make more money from selling the *World Books* than by teaching from them. But he soon tired of this as well and in 1925, he became a full time magician.

During this period he lived at 306 West 109th Street in the Columbia University district. His personal collection of materials relating to magic, by this time, were inclusive of rare volumes from the 17th and 18th century and contained exactly 334 volumes; the oldest from 1691 was called *Mathematical Majick* and written by F. Wilkins[5]. Later he would own an authentic 1584 edition of Reginald Scot's famous book *The Discoverie of Witchcraft*, which exposed the secrets of conjuring and provided an important definition of the craft behind them. Years later, when placing his vast library at the Walter Hampden Memorial Library at the Players club on Gramercy Park, Mulholland noted that Scot's book "was used by The Bard as a source book in the writing of both *Hamlet* and *Midsummer Night's Dream*. This fact alone should be ample proof that the juggler's hanky-panky has a direct connection with both Tragedy and Comedy."

Drawing by Baldridge.

At the age of only 26, Mulholland had a scholarly polish that Houdini greatly admired. Though the younger man did not possess any formal degree, Mulholland was nevertheless an educated man. He had attended and taught at the Horace Mann School for Boys, Columbia Preparatory School (also known as the Barnard School for Boys), the Teachers College of Columbia University, and The Trinity School. The Honorable Judge Giles S. Rich, a '22 graduate of the Horace Mann School spoke of Mulholland as a teacher:

> *Let me read you what the 1950 Columbia Encyclopedia says about him: Born in 1898. American magician. While still a schoolboy, he established a*

reputation for his skill in magical tricks, and he came to be one of the most celebrated of stage performers of magic. He also wrote with simplicity and charm on the subject and on spiritualism.

That's who he was. But what you are not told is that back in the early 20's when I was at HM, John Mulholland was the manual training teacher...In other words, we had our resident magician and he delighted in practicing his skill at the school. He was always collecting little crowds in the locker room and pretending to pick ping-pong balls out of some boy's mouth. He had marvelous large hands and was the ambidextrous prestidigitator par excellence, sometimes letting us in on some of the magician's secrets, or possibly pretending to while tricking us further. John was a frequent performer at school assemblies, one of his favorite displays of manual dexterity being to tear the pages of an entire Manhattan telephone book in two.

Mulholland made it a habit to ensure attendance at his classes by offering an incentive: Were each child present for the weekly lessons, the class would receive a magic show at the end of the week. Only once was the show called off because of truancy and the others laid in waiting for the delinquent and, as was said in the day, "soundly gave him what for." That boy never missed a Mulholland class again. A rare artifact from this period still exists. In Mulholland's pencil scrawl he outlines a lesson, and the major points to be stressed. He writes at the bottom: "Successful class and attendance begets the wine and roses trick to illustrate the spoils of learning!"

HOUDINI & MULHOLLAND

From the age of two, John Mulholland and his family had lived at 507 West 113th Street on New York's Upper West Side. Four years later, in 1904, another magician moved into the neighborhood, just four tree-lined blocks from the Mulholland residence. His name was Harry Houdini.

Born Erik Weisz in Hungary in 1874, he was the middle child of six children. Erich, as he came to be known in the U.S., was devoted to his mother after his father died when the boy was in his teens. Harry "Handcuff" Houdini, as he often penned his signature, was an icon of the oppressed masses liberating themselves from industrialization. Early in his career it became fashionable for the press to use his name to describe an impossible situation or a politician getting out of a tight squeeze. But the power of Houdini was not as a magician per se. While most people understand that "Houdini equals magic," the heartbeat of Houdini was that his behavior astonished because he bordered on the supernatural. He presented not only an enigma on stage, but an odd proposition to law enforcement.

Primarily, he was an escape artist. He got out of things. The drama that made headlines was how difficult, or life threatening, the escape might be. While short in stature, he was larger than life. Houdini convincingly implanted on the popular consciousness that he could enter or leave any building. If caught, he could not be restrained. Biographer Raymund Fitzsimons wrote, "He could have been the master criminal of all time. He would have to be mutilated, his hands and feet cut off, but even that might not stop him. Society would have to kill him, for his powers were beyond its control."

In 1900, Houdini had just begun to make an impression on audiences and those who booked the Orpheum chain of theatres. His salary rose with his popularity. Then, he decided to sail for England without a booking. His gutsy move paid off. His European success flourished, legend has it, when he defied Scotland Yard by unlocking handcuffs binding him in less time than it took to bind him. Houdini excited publicity by hurling challenges to the police; if the law failed to challenge Houdini, Harry challenged them. Consequently, Houdini, by 1904, had been working as a star attraction in Europe for four years. Beating challenges, including poverty, was nothing new to the great Houdini.

Having been poor most of his life, he spent his kingly salary on conjuring and other ephemera – glorious lithographic posters, rare books, the first electric chair and Edgar Allan Poe's portable writing desk – and returned to New York, needing a residence that could accommodate a lavish library and offices.

As young John Mulholland's interest in magic blossomed, he was enthralled to have the celebrated Houdini just a few doors down the street, across Morningside Park. Houdini was a hero to Mulholland, as he was to many young boys. Apparently Mulholland lost no opportunity to learn from the world-famous showman. Once, as a boy of twelve, Mulholland, along with several thousand others in a New York theater, found himself baffled by a particularly impressive chain escape. Something about the effect seemed familiar to Mulholland – it resembled a trick that he himself, a magician of only seven years experience, had discarded as too simplistic. With his curiosity getting the better of him, Mulholland boldly walked backstage to visit the master mystifier. He asked Houdini if the trick was indeed the same one he himself had discarded. Houdini showed him the apparatus. Muholland's eyes widened at the revelation. Houdini put an arm around the young boy and said, "Always remember Johnny, it is not the trick which impresses the audience, but the magician." It was a lesson Mulholland would never forget.

There would be many other lessons learned from Houdini as Mulholland matured and honed his skill. As Mulholland grew tall and lanky, the short, stocky Houdini counseled him on how to use his size and ungainly feet to his advantage when forcing a card. The great escape artist advised Mulholland simply to step on someone's foot when the card the magician desired to be selected ran by the hand of the spectator. In all likelihood, the subtle contact would prod the spectator into selecting the desired card. Mulholland was impressed, and confided to friends years later that it was "nerve" that made Houdini a great showman. Houdini also scolded the boy magician for not making better use of his "peculiarities," Mulholland stated in 1934. "Johnny, I can't understand why you don't think up some trick for those great big ears of yours," Houdini said.

Many years later, Mulholland would write that Houdini was the most knowledgeable magician he had ever met. If Mulholland benefited from Houdini's vast knowledge, however, occasionally the young magician also had to endure the brunt of the escape artist's famously volatile temper. On one occasion, Mulholland would recall, Houdini tossed the young magician out of his home, insistent that Mulholland was lying about something. When Houdini found that Mulholland had, in fact, been telling the truth, he attempted to make amends. He stopped a boy messenger on the street and handed him a rare volume on magic to be delivered to the boy conjurer.

When Mulholland received the rare volume wrapped in old butcher paper, tied with ratty string, the boy messenger claimed, "Some guy in a rumpled shirt, and kind of smelly-looking, paid me a whole dollar to give this to you."

The next time Houdini and Mulholland met, Houdini asked why Mulholland had not acknowledged the gift. Mulholland replied that he had had no idea who sent the book. Houdini replied, "That's just like you, Johnny, to hold a grudge." The literary treasure Mulholland received had passed from the first English collector, James Savren, to Henry Evanion and then to Houdini.

Houdini, Mulholland once observed, was a mass of contradictions: a devout Jew who loved ham sandwiches; an exceedingly generous man who could also be frugal to the point of making his wife cry, a showman loved by audiences the world over, but hated for his unethical treatment of fellow performers.

Many years later, Mulholland would return to the theme, describing Houdini's "diverse attributes and interests" at length.

"Houdini was a practically unschooled boy who grew into a man whom the world admired and paid millions of dollars to watch," Mulholland wrote. "He was ruthless to competition and yet a sentimentalist who would pay any price to indulge his emotions. While often an opportunist, he devoted untold hours throughout his life to making certain he was the world's outstanding authority on locks and various forms of human restraint. Even though he feuded with some magicians, he spent much of his time and money to better magician's organizations. He was a great physical athlete, particularly in the water. He never drank or smoked, but in other ways he took poor care of his health. Houdini was an innovator rather than an inventor."

Perhaps so, but Mulholland was only too happy to make use of Houdini's innovations. When the writer Laurence Stallings praised him as "the Prince of Prestidigitateurs," Mulholland eagerly reprinted the accolade in his promotional materials. Over the years, however, Mulholland decided to make a slight improvement to the quote, sacrificing alliteration for hyperbole as he changed the word "prince" to "king." Houdini, the master self-promoter, would undoubtedly have approved.

MULHOLLAND'S EARLY CAREER

John Mulholland made three extensive trips around the world between 1921 and 1933. This was in the tradition of the magicians he admired, studied, and in most cases, knew.

John Henry Anderson, the Scottish "Great Wizard of the North" traveled to all five continents in the 19th century and survived many theatre fires in a life of romance, intrigue and sorrow. Herrmann the Great arrived in town with his own railway car or by a coach drawn by white stallions. Each appearance of the great Herrmann was ablaze in satanic images filling the sides of buildings. It could not be missed that Herrmann, the devil in evening clothes had arrived – in England, France, the U.S., Havana and China. Kellar, traveled the world as a tough-nosed showman in search of the greatest mysteries. Kellar lived through hardship and at other times with great wealth having toured fifty countries. Like his predecessors Mulholland wanted to see the world, to see what they had seen, and to feel what they had felt, as a magician.

Practiced in the customs of forty-two countries before his 40th birthday, this fact alone prepared him for government work. The combination of world travel and being a performing magician was the perfect cover for a perfect consultant.

By his early 20s, Mulholland had adopted a scholarly, almost professorial appearance both onstage and off. The young magician stood six-foot, three-inches tall, had brown hair, star sapphire blue eyes and a prominent nose. Perhaps his most distinguishing feature, according to one description, were the "generous ears" that protruded like jug handles. He favored a dignified bow tie and three-piece suit, with the chain and fob of his pocket watch displayed across the vest. The watch had belonged to his father, and inside was a picture of his mother. He dressed in this manner when he made his professional debut in 1915.

In Prague, 1923.

In 1921, at the age of 23, he traveled to Europe for his first time, visiting Vienna's Kratky-Baschik's long-running magic theatre, spending time in France with technical magic author Dr. Jules D'Hotel, and joining the London Magic Circle. He also spent time backstage at London's Egyptian Hall, the home of the famous Maskelyne family of magic. Maskelyne's mysteries, first at the Egyptian Hall in London was an institution that lasted for sixty years. Opening in 1873 they were put out of business when London was bombed during the Blitz of World War II.

There were many firsts on Maskelyne's intimate stage known as England's Home of Mystery. The first person to float horizontally and to have a hoop passed completely around the floating body was presented on the famous stage. "The tricks ought to astonish scientific London" roared a headline in *The Daily Telegraph*. DeKolta's woman had vanished from this stage, and Herrmann had spent a thousand fabled nights surrounded by the plush velvet curtains. Master conjurer David Devant made a woman, dressed as a moth, vanish in the flicker of a candle. Motion pictures were first exhibited there shortly after the introduction of the "picture-throwing magic lantern." The founder, John Nevil Maskelyne (1840-1917) and the fame of his "Maskelyne's Mysteries" began the family's career by challenging spiritualist England to a veritable duel. He thought the spiritualists were charlatans and said so from the stage. Three generations of Maskelynes would entertain from the family stage over a period of sixty years. Maskelyne's was always a place where things were sure to be exciting!

Photo by Irene Mulholland of Indian street magicians – the jadoo wallah – in Bangalore India, 1921.

Beginning in 1925, Mulholland's mother joined him as he launched an ambitious, nine-month sight seeing and performance tour of Japan, Korea, Manchuria, China, The Philippines, North Borneo,

Java, Malay, Siam (now Thailand), Burma and India. Photographs of that world tour show him making a knot disappear for a Manchurian guard, and sitting with the elite of the conjuring world in Vienna and Prague, with Ottokar Fischer and the heads of the Czech Magifcher Birkel; upon his return back to New York he entertained the literati of the Algonquin in the 1920's. Alexander Woollcott led his gang of zanies with the impresario power a big New York theatre critic could command. According to Maxine Marx, when her uncle Harpo, and such literary luminaries as Harold Ross, Robert Benchley, Dorothy Parker and Franklin P. Adams all conjoined in a Mulholland miracle at close range Woollcott could not resist having the final word. Mulholland asked the burly Woollcott to choose a coin. Mulholland pushed the coins forward and said, "Name one." Woollcott cocked an owlish stare, deftly extended his forefinger and touched one of the gleaming dollar coins. He said, "Very well, I name this one Elmer." Everyone appreciated his wit, and this story was repeated many times in the Algonquin dining room.

Drawing of photo by Mrs. Mulholland.

"Rennie" Mulholland took a series of photographs to document her son's travels, including a rare shot of Indian street magicians performing the Indian Basket feat in an outdoor performance. Later, these photographs would be made into a series of illustrations to adorn the dust jacket and interior of *Quicker Than The Eye*, Mulholland's book about magicians of the world.

Mulholland joined a pantheon of world touring illusionists by performing in China. One spectator wrote that Alexander Herrmann's (1844-1896) magic was thought to be influenced by opium fumes. Harry Kellar's cast members died of a plague while touring China. Charles Carter had an audience member die in his seat during the performance. Howard Thurston encountered the fact that the audience delighted in discussing each feat before the next commenced. He waited in the wings and had a smoke while the audience discussed the stage show.

Irene Mulholland

Mulholland ran into some trouble too, even though he prided himself on being one of the few to capture an Asian audience's attention. He labored to learn a few lines of "magician's patter" in the native tongue and the audience unexpectedly (to the magician) reacted by bursting into laughter. Instead of learning the proper patter he desired, the interpreter taught him to boast of his own accomplishments and what a wonderful fellow he was! Like Thurston, Mulholland never forgot his experience in China.

Many years later, the celebrated magician John Booth, who was only in his teens when he met Mulholland, would remark that Mulholland was the best "suitcase magician" he had ever seen. This meant that he could fit a full hour's performance into a single suitcase. While this description may seem like faint praise to those unfamiliar with the magician's craft, actually Booth was paying his friend an enormous compliment. That John Mulholland could carry his entire show – for the stage – in a small suitcase was a true achievement of planning and organization. The author is in possession of several of

58

Mulholland's props and they speak to his craftiness and craftsmanship. Everything he carried had its own case. He made a majority of his props himself. A small paddle, similar to a tongue depressor was used to make miniature cards appear. The item was carefully constructed out of cherry wood, and covered by felt adorned with small mirrors, providing the magician with the natural quip that, "it's all done with mirrors" in the presentation of the small wonder.

Irene May Mulholland, with unknown girl, photo by Gus Fowler, probably 1930's. Note the physical resemblance to her son.

To hold a special coin he procured in China, he had a small leather case made in New York. The same manufacturer made a case used to hold his shirt studs. However, he carried his shirt studs elsewhere. This case would forever protect his magician's "thumb tip," a piece of magician's paraphernalia. His wand, now part of the Society of American Magicians Ellison Wand collection, is scarcely bigger than an average pencil, but weighs considerably more, being made out of solid ebony. A seemingly innocent pencil he had made as a promotional gimmick featured a magnet at one end instead of an eraser. This facilitated a lightening-fast change of a penny into a dime. Altering such common items would aid his government work in the future.

He was careful to carry a deck of cards at all times. Often the backs bore the logo of whatever club he was performing in at the time. In the author's collection are several decks of cards – gold gilt, and arranged for tricks – bearing the imprimatur of the Cunard Line, the extremely wealthy, conservative-based Union Club, and the Princeton Club.

He knew that using familiar, if elegant household items, as props would diffuse patrons' suspicions. Likewise, he often obtained a bookplate from each club at which he performed at. These plates would be put into *his own* texts and then he would opt to "borrow" a book from the premises, making his deception all the more impenetrable. Several of his silk scarves are made of the best materials, adorned with tasteful patterns, yet bold enough to be seen in the largest performance halls. A hidden stage property that replicated the size of a bridge pack of cards was engineered, no doubt by the wizard himself, out of solid copper. The device aided his apparently impromptu feat of making selected cards rise from the deck. It was also built to last a lifetime, and it did.

Perhaps the prop most characteristic of Mulholland is the "pull" used to make his birdcage vanish. While the description of secret workings of magician's illusions is not the aim of this narrative, it can be said of this very simple prop that it was made out of military strength cord, an ivory ring and the most common of watchbands. True to form, the magician used nothing but the best – his watchband was made by the Swiss company, Bulova.

Mulholland always counseled other magicians that the titles of tricks should have no bearing on what was to happen, so as to preserve the surprise, and that the illusions should be representations of much larger stories. The silent flight of a powerful eagle was illustrated by fifty-cent pieces stamped with the American eagle traveling from hand to hand without notice. A small Buddha named Ho Chang disappeared while held on a book, as if on a tray, only to melt into nothingness and reappear in a small brass temple the magician had shown empty moments before. In Mulholland's presentation, the small idol was returning to his prayer site. Mulholland methods were simple, but his stage presence was bold and his showmanship was erudite. His literary skill made the show better. One trick flowed into another naturally, like sentences in a book.

Mulholland had a slow and deliberate manner of speech, which sometimes led to criticism. Once, during a series of USO performances in 1944, some of the men in his audiences even went so far as printing calling cards touting the services of "Dullholland – World's Most Boring Magician" and noting his references as "U.S. Sleep Society, the "Unconscious Society" and "Regurgitate, Inc." Happily for John Mulholland, few of these cards exist today.

By 1933, Mulholland was coming into his own as a professional in New York City. Records in the Museum of the City of New York certify the population of Manhattan at this time as a solid one million. Five professional magicians were prominent in the public eye: Paul Rosini, Nate Leipzig, Fred Keating, Cardini and John Mulholland. While there were others, these five men were the most publicized and highly paid entertainers in Depression-ridden New York. A careful look at the books of private clubs from Boston to Baltimore show a remarkable trend: John Mulholland appeared at all of them.

Even as a rising young performer Mulholland had already developed an intensely practical and orderly turn of mind. He stressed organization, preparation and consideration in all aspects of his life; qualities that defined his work as a magician, writer, and editor, and would later serve him well in his work for the CIA. Mulholland valued preparation to such a degree that he even had stock replies to questions and propositions made to him by hecklers. He later listed his replies to audience's jabs in *Stage* magazine. Then as now, it was fairly common for an audience member to say "I will hold onto my wallet" in the presence of an evidently light-fingered magician. Mulholland would invariably reply that he had already put the wallet back because it wasn't worth bothering with in the first place. To the common question heard by most magicians – "Would you make my wife or husband disappear?" – Mulholland's reply was a masterpiece of gentle one-upmanship: "I hope I don't seem to have such bad taste."

HOUDINI HIRES MULHOLLAND, 1924

That Houdini was home much on 113th Street cannot be chronicled, but no doubt his possessions largely remained in his town house. Houdini's secretary from 1919 to 1921 was Mulholland's mentor, John William Sargent. Later, former Society of American Magicians President Oscar Teale succeeded Sargent, and also became a close friend of John Mulholland. Via these two connections, Mulholland knew the inner workings of the Houdini library and what projects the escape king had on his desk. It was Teale's job to armor

Houdini against the death threats, dire predictions and lawsuits that came in weekly from those Houdini angered in the Spiritualist world.

Houdini had been lecturing to law enforcement groups since 1921. The emergence of his book *Miracle Mongers and Their Methods*, Kellar notes in a letter to Houdini, that his book was "most cleverly done. It is complete. It is artistic and ingenious." These were the standards by which Houdini waged his untiring attack against fraudulent mediums, and he needed someone who could provide content and writing that would live up to Kellar's praise. While Houdini purchased and sifted through thousands of documents related to his anti-spiritualist cause, and stayed up late writing, Houdini biographer Kenneth Silverman writes that, "But he did so with no understanding of how scholars assemble, judge, and organize evidence."

In 1922 Houdini had met with Sir Arthur Conan Doyle who positioned himself as a supporter of the Spiritualist movement. By 1923 Houdini was in the throes of his very public battle with the Boston psychic Mina Crandon, known in the press as "Margery." The mountain of information Houdini had amassed on fraudulent mediumship was worthless unless he recruited cultivated people to help him use the information in his public attacks. Mulholland was perfect for the job of helping to shape Houdini's public pronouncements against such celebrities as Doyle and Margery.

In 1924 Houdini hired the budding professional magician to design a course of lectures that would help to dispel the public's growing belief in the paranormal, and spiritualism in particular. Mulholland was no stranger to working with big league magicians. In 1924 he wrote the foreword to Howard Thurston's *Easy Pocket Tricks*, published no doubt by Thurston in 1924 to sell at his shows for a quarter. He also appeared in a half dozen of the booklet photos with his eyes appropriately widened.

Douglas and Kari Hunt write in their 1967 book *The Art of Magic*, "He (Houdini) realized that his formal education was poor and he was afraid that his poor grammar would dull the effect of his lectures. . . he contacted Columbia University and asked them to recommend someone who could teach him how to lecture. The University recommended Mulholland and the two men spent much time together exchanging information. Muholland's influence not only helped shape Houdini's lectures, but helped shaped the entire present day world of conjuring." It was actually Oscar Teale, Houdini's secretary, and a part time Columbia teacher, who recommended Mulholland. Houdini was only too happy to have recommended someone with whom he already had a fifteen year relationship.

While John Mulholland sometimes despaired that he was not making a living solely as a performing magician because he was teaching, he realized that being an educator ultimately brought him one of his most important assignments. For the next six months Mulholland would write copy and suggest concepts Houdini could use against phony psychics. While the exact dictum prescribed by Mulholland is unavailable, one paragraph from Houdini's 1924 campaign has a distinct Mulholland touch:

> "The effect of the fraudulent mediums are far more dangerous than is thought by the public; in fact it is astounding when it is considered that millions of dollars were fraudulently attained yearly in America alone, homes are wrecked, wills changed. I would say without the slightest fear of contradiction, the neurotic believer in Spiritualism is safely on the way to the insane asylum, without a return ticket."

Such writing seems conspicuously similar to thoughts expressed in Mulholland's later writing:

> "We need only read our daily newspapers to realize how pernicious it [Spiritualism] may be. Just a few weeks ago, for instance, a twenty-six year old mother of two children jumped to her death from the ninth floor of a Chicago hotel after a fortune teller had informed her that her son would go blind and her husband would leave her."

Houdini's assault on mediumistic fraud was made up of inventive technique. Mulholland counseled Houdini to carry very organized, portable, accordion-pleated files of clippings; have clipping services on both sides of the Atlantic feed him current information, and to end each show with a question and answer session where the audience was encouraged to prod Houdini with written questions. Every touch, gaffe and psychological manipulation from sideshow crystal gazers, medicine show mediums and the lecture platform was explored to give Houdini's wrath credence and clarity.

Mulholland's material would be used in, and to promote, the final show with which Houdini would tour. The Houdini extravaganza was comprised of three parts. Part I was a spectacular magic show where, in one sequence, an eagle appeared. Part II was Houdini's legendary Chinese Water Torture Cell – his most incredible death-defying escape. Finally, after an intermission, the master mystifier became a star lecturer, explaining how slates bearing messages from the dead were the result of having been switched for blank slates in darkened sitting rooms. This lecture accompanied a series of fifty glass slides exposing the charlatan's methods. Some were posed in the Mulholland house on 113th Street.

Houdini met the charlatan seers with an army of informers and stooges. A matronly nurse, Rose Mackenberg, led the way in reporting back to Houdini. Ferreting out the con involved was child's play for Houdini and his team. At times, his virulent lecture caused near rioting in the theatres. This was attributable to Houdini's magnetic showmanship and the damning expose of unscrupulous pseudo-psychics, prescribed, in part, by John Mulholland. The rough edge of the challenger Houdini was made more smooth and polished and therefore more penetrating to an audience.

No doubt the money Mulholland made from Houdini helped fund his 1925-26 world-wide travel that brought him back to the U.S. just before Halloween.

After nearly a year on the road with the show Mulholland helped script, Houdini died of peritonitis in Detroit on Halloween, 1926. Almost immediately Mulholland took up where Houdini had left off. If Houdini was the circus barker stomping on fraudulent mediumship with sensational claims, Mulholland took a more subtle, less bombastic route by expounding on the details of charlatanism in the popular press. In *The New York Times, The Boston Herald, The Philadelphia Inquirer* and *The New York World Telegram* there were twenty-five articles that mentioned Mulholland's erudition on the subject between 1927 and 1937. In the *American Magazine* from January 1932, he stated his claim quite perfunctorily by writing, "These are the boom times for the fortune tellers who prey upon other people's troubles. [This is] the story of a $125,000,000 racket."

In 1938 Mulholland would publish a great deal of his ghost-busting research in his authoritative *Beware Familiar Spirits* aided by the young writer and magician, Barrows Mussey. The two men had a vast archive on which to draw. In his introduction to his friend Gerald Kaufman's 1938 book *How's Tricks?* Mulholland categorically states that his personal collection "while not complete, comprises about forty-five hundred volumes."

KELLAR & MULHOLLAND

John Mulholland prided himself on being able to work miracles with whatever materials happened to be at hand. Once, while performing at a mountain resort, he took a stroll along some nearby railroad tracks and picked up a handful of small green lizards. That night, Mulholland's performance featured a novel and somewhat hair-raising "multiplying lizards trick" that sent most of the audience screaming out of the hall and into the night – all except one patron who could not leave his wheelchair.

This sort of versatility was one of the many traits that Mulholland admired about the legendary Harry Kellar, whom he had met many years earlier at Clyde Powers Magic Shop on 42ⁿᵈ Street. Mulholland later wrote that he had thought of Kellar every day for five years up until the time they met in 1910, when Mulholland was twelve. Apparently Kellar took a shine to the young man. "John," he said, "I like you. Let's go in the back and talk about magic." Mulholland, already shrewd about the habits of professional magicians, impressed the master by not asking him how any of his tricks were done. At the time, Kellar was renowned as the first Dean of the Society of American Magicians, having visited nearly 50 countries to present a full evening magic show. Now in the twilight of his career, the legendary performer had just finished his farewell American tour, bringing a former vaudeville "King of Cards" named Howard Thurston onto the scene as his successor.

Kellar knew talent when he saw it, and he saw it in abundance in the twelve-year old John Mulholland. Kellar's high opinion of Mulholland was borne out when the boy gave him a valuable insight into the mysteries of an eccentric colleague, Dr. Samuel Hooker.

DR. SAMUEL COX HOOKER (1864-1935) & MULHOLLAND

There probably isn't a person alive today who saw a very select series of performances by a little-known amateur magician with a walrus-style mustache named Samuel Cox Hooker. Hooker, born in Kent, England, was the director and one of the chief technicians for the American Sugar Refining Company. As an industrial chemist he synthesized the molecules of the sugar beet veritably creating some of the first bio-engineered commerce. During the 1920's he worked for Rockefeller University in New York. Among other innovations his work extended the range of the sugar beet and the shelf life of packaged sugar, setting the pace of biotechnology. His work was later assessed by technical journals in his field as "eighty years ahead of its time."

Consequently, we can see that Doctor Hooker was a trendsetter and this talent was evident in his passion for conjuring. Dr. Hooker gave the impression that he could make anything float in the air.

Anything.

He proved this to some of the world's best magicians in a series of 20-person soirees titled "Impossibilities" at his home in Brooklyn at 82 Remsen Street. Houdini scratched his head. Servais LeRoy clapped his hands in astonishment. John Northern Hilliard wrote in his magnum opus *Greater Magic* of Hooker and his conjuring: "All in all I can only report that this exposition of the Rising Cards is the nearest approach to real magic that I have ever witnessed, or hope to witness."

Kellar knew how it was done only because it was he who provided an essential missing element to the mystery . . . an intelligent twelve year old boy named Johnny Mulholland.

Mulholland and Hooker became acquainted in 1910 and worked together as late as 1924. In fact, when Hooker died in 1935, his equipment for his "Impossibilities" went to Mulholland and his friend, professor of physics, Dr. Shirley L. Quimby (also a *Sphinx* magician's magazine executive) who guarded the secret. Interestingly, the complexity of the illusion prevented both men from ever reprising the doctor's invention for paying customers, though they attempted to with weeks of practice. A perfect, yet intricate mystery, Hooker's floating objects have only been presented twice since all the essential parties have passed on. Mulholland showed such prowess for conjuring at an early age that the doctor was able to rely on the boy for aid when presenting the uncommon feats. Split-second timing was essential for the successful performance, and the backstage boy magician needed to be quick on his feet; in charge of secret devices that perpetuated the perfect mystery.

In fact, Mulholland's involvement in the illusion was kept "pure." He entered before the audience arrived and left well after the last had departed. Hooker insisted on this to protect the secret of his young off stage assistant. Once, Mulholland related to drama critic Brooks Atkinson, he almost blew his cover to Harry Blackstone Sr. who was visiting Jean Hugard at Luna Park in Coney Island. Mulholland wanted to approach Blackstone near the Hooker residence, but realized his presence would belie his oath to Dr. Hooker and his "Impossibilities."

Hooker and Mulholland shared the love of performance, and the passion for rare books. Dr. Hooker, like Mulholland's friend Dr. Ellison, amassed a huge collection of rare conjuring literature, which he donated to The New York Public Library upon his death.

The depth of their relationship is exemplified in that when Dr. Hooker died, John Mulholland was the only other magician mentioned in Hooker's obituary in *The New York Times*. In Mulholland's final hours, he reviewed a letter from 1906 to Dr. Hooker by an obscure magician. This letter, along with materials of other seminal characters of Mulholland's past was found in his bedside table.

In 1925, one year after his stint as a writer for Houdini, he made his book-writing debut with his Columbia colleague Milton A. Smith as co-author of the book, *Magic in the Making,* published by Charles Scribner's Sons and subtitled "a first book of conjuring." Smith was a Mulholland contemporary at both the Horace Mann School and Columbia University. Smith had also written a book on dramatic deportment that Mulholland gravitated to and from which he admitted that he learned his first lessons in stagecraft. As small income teachers, even at the prestigious private school, it seems natural that he and Smith should combine literary forces to increase their income and enhance their resumes for further employment in the academic field. Although Mulholland attended a first class school, he had to work hard teaching, selling textbooks, doing magic shows and writing to make a living. As Bob Lund said of Mulholland "He wasn't born to the velvet."

A TYPICAL PERFORMANCE

Returning to New York from his world travels shortly after Houdini's death Mulholland called a press conference in his house on 113th Street (just as Houdini would have done at *his* 113th Street home). Now styling himself as a "leader of the younger school of magicians," the 29-year-old Mulholland performed the following wonder for the reporters of *The New York Sun.*

A pack of unopened, factory-fresh cards was selected at random from a gross of such decks in a beat up cardboard box.

One man selected a card, signed his initials on the back of it, and put this signed card in his pocket. Everyone saw that the card he selected was the Two of Diamonds. This was not a secret, and his choice of this card was fair and free, and all of the remaining fifty-one cards were shown to be different from one another.

Another man supplied four rows of four-digit numbers. Again, these numbers were chosen randomly by the reporters themselves.

Mulholland and the reporters added these numbers and came up with the sum of 25,396.

The magician now instructed the man with the numbers to open a New York City phone book to the 253rd page, and read the name and address of the 96th person listed.

The name was "Mary Giles, phone number 887-1576."

When the reporter removed his selected card from his pocket, Mulholland asked him to verify that the initials on the back were genuine. The reporter readily did so. While the card had been in his pocket, however, it had undergone a small, but important transformation.

On the face of the card was now written in blood red, dry ink: "Give my regards to Miss Giles at 887-1576 signed Beelzebub Jr."

The reporters might well have run screaming into the night had it not been for a wry final comment by the confident young magician: "Yeah, believe that, and I got another for ya."

While not typical, John Mulholland contributed this pet effect – magician's jargon for "trick" or "feat" – to the massive thousand-page classic volume *Greater Magic*, by John Northern Hilliard. He abided by the compiler's request to give professional material and the two feats he offered packed the same punch of extraordinary mystical qualities, spirit writing and a degree of sophistication, as numbers had to be added, books read and directions followed to the letter. Classically Mulholland, both feats utilized his favorite card, the Two of Diamonds.

While Mulholland was usually reluctant to publish pet secrets, he offered a similar effect to a little known booklet of magic titled "CIGAM." Here, the magician relates how he adapted this feat to a performance he gave for the New York State Photographer's Association. In this performance he had the image of a photograph appear on a piece of cardboard that had previously been signed by someone from the audience. Characteristically, the magician ends on a professional note: "The cost of this trick in all is about fifty cents a performance, but it creates many dollars' worth of notice."

While this man of a thousand wonders was clearly dedicated to the magic arts, he was judicious in doling out secrets when he would not directly benefit. In the massive eight-volume *Tarbell Course on Magic*, John Mulholland appears only twice in over three-thousand pages. He is mentioned once for a trick from his first book, and the other for being prominent in the lecture field. Perhaps the fact that Tarbell was an arch competitor in this field had something to do with the brevity of Mulholland's involvement. In addition to performing, Mulholland's other full-time occupation was as Editor of *The Sphinx*.

The Sphinx was the most prestigious conjuring periodical in the western world. Combining exciting pictures, historical tidbits and professional advice, its reputation stretched across the globe. The slim magazine was founded just after the century turned by Bill Hilliar and was later edited by Dr. A. M. Wilson. Mulholland joined the staff as a lad of fourteen assisting Wilson. He gained full control as Editor upon Wilson's death in 1930. The magazine ran continuously until 1953.

When it came to *The Sphinx*, magician Mulholland was far more prolific. Mulholland's explanation for his decision to publish his own secrets was tempered in *Our Mysteries*, a publication of his friend Al Flosso. Mulholland wrote in his introduction: *"Professional magicians, because they are being paid for their performances, are in a very different position from those to whom magic is only a hobby. The magic of the professional must not only work, but must interest an audience to the point where each member feels that he has received full value for his money."*

As a leader in the conjuring field and a famous editor, Mulholland was in constant demand by the conjuring fraternity to offer opinions, reviews and common sense for marketed items by brother conjurers. To Robert Sherms at Grand Central Magic Co., he wrote, on August 6, 1927, that he liked Sherms's "effect" very much. He noted the portability, attractiveness and ease of presentation that accompanied the minor miracle called "Chink-A-Chink" an entertaining assemblage of coins or sugar cubes under impossible circumstances. He was judicious in praising other creators of coin magic, always taking into account the practicality of the magic and the affect it would have on an audience.

Mulholland was a unique combination of talents. He was a writer who could clearly elucidate his views on the conjuring of others. As a professional he knew the practicality of marketed tricks and how audiences were likely to respond. Given this combination of talents, his friend Milbourne Christopher labeled Mulholland's later *Book of Magic* as more "thorough in the preparation, logic and presentation of its feats *than any other text on the subject.*" (Italics added.) Given that there were over ten thousand titles concerning the conjuring arts when Christopher wrote this, it is distinctly high praise.

On the fiftieth anniversary of *The Sphinx* Mulholland enlisted Christopher to edit what he felt were the best selection of tricks from the pages of *The Sphinx*. This small soft bound book copiously titled as if on a sideshow banner: *Fifty Years of Great Magic, The Golden Years (from the Sphinx Golden Jubilee Book of Magic)* was later published by Al Flosso. Mulholland penned the Introduction and wrote of the thrill he received as a young man of seventeen who eagerly awaited each issue. He credits this publication with turning his "casual interest" in magic into a "deeply rooted interest."

His deep interest combined with his various other titles in magic organizations, and his associations with such famous writers as Fulton Oursler, Dorothy Parker, Alexander Woollcott, and actors Jean Harlow, Eddie Cantor, Jimmy Durante, Harold Lloyd, and Orson Welles, made John Mulholland a very talked about magician on both coasts. Like his mentor Houdini, Mulholland used his associations with famous people to garner press for himself. Power through association is classic show business and as Houdini paraded his friendship with Arthur Conan Doyle, so did Mulholland make sure he was known to be fast friends with the creator of *Citizen Kane*.

The difference was that John Mulholland scored success as a magician who lectured on his topic and his travels. Though Houdini's gifts as a showman and self-promoter helped to make his escape act a worldwide sensation, he never really made a big splash as a magician in his lifetime. It is a great paradox of Houdini's life is that he became known as the greatest magician ever after he died! As a contemporary of Thurston the Magician, who presented "The Wonder Show of the Universe" Houdini paled in comparison. History will probably never be corrected in this regard.

Like Houdini, Mulholland debunked fraudulent psychics by creating more impressive wonders than the phonies. Mulholland's sculpted eloquence set him apart from others who attempted to pick up Houdini's mantle as an anti-spiritualist crusader, though, ironically, Houdini's success in this arena had owed in part to Mulholland's initial efforts! In 1931, Rebecca Hourwich wrote a lengthy article in *The New York Times* titled *Forecasters of the Future Who Flourish in New York*, noting the paradox that the popularity of fortunetellers seemed to be in direct ratio to the rapid progress of science. She quoted Mulholland saying:

> *"We are living in a mechanistic age, with the tangible evidence of scientific progress all about us. Automobiles, radio, the wizardry of electricity, are just so many magic symbols to the untutored mind. Lost and oppressed in our modern world, people seek the solace of something personal, comforting, more akin to their understanding. Accustomed to the terminology in current use, they yet seek fortune telling in the guise of science. That accounts for the present vogue of pseudo scientific fortune tellers, the astrologers and numerologists."*

It must always be remembered that a Mulholland miracle was always laced with subtle touches that kept audiences guessing. For just a brief second perhaps, the onlooker would be moved to wonder if they had actually seen something from another, magical realm. Like great fiction, his performances were well written and inviting. John Mulholland's performance always heeded his own definition of conjuring that "Magic is the art of creating illusions agreeably." The notion of "agreeability" indirectly included the audience's acceptance on that basis. He may have also gotten this idea from the 19th century conjurer, Charles Bertram. The burly conjuror mentioned in his first autobiography in 1899 that a conjurer should be "agreeable and entertaining."

His magical education is seen in his preferences as a conjuror. Early in his career he noted his favorite magician of the time as Horace Goldin, his favorite author as Robert-Houdin, his favorite trick as the multiplying thimble trick, and his favorite journal as *The Sphinx*. He also noted that his hobby was the history of magic. Unlike most people, if Mulholland had a favorite performer, he knew them. If he had a favorite trick or illusion, he performed it. And if he had a favorite author, he probably had every book by the writer. In the case of Horace Goldin, he knew the master conjuror well, as their correspondence attests. Goldin made his vaudeville mark by embracing a whirlwind pace that left the audience breathless to the "blink and you'll miss a trick" style. In 1937, Goldin wrote to Mulholland from England. In a very newsy letter he also enclosed dues to be delivered by Mulholland to the Society of American Magicians. As well, Goldin related how excited he was to be presenting his newest version of the fabled Indian Rope Trick in an act that ran fifty minutes. Goldin also wrote that he was to perform outdoors during the Coronation Week in Hyde Park, but that the authorities had stopped his performance.

From the first, delivering lectures on the art of magic was an important component of Mulholland's career. In 1927 he gave his first lecture-demonstration in Boston. "I saw John Mulholland's first appearance in Boston," wrote his friend Silent Mora (Louis Jerome McCord), the vaudeville magician. "He carried as few things as possible, and collected three times the fee I would have for working a week." Nearly twenty years later, always one to return a compliment to the magical fraternity, Mulholland wrote equal praise of Mora by noting that "(he) never makes a motion that lacks complete certainty, and never a posture that does not make an attractive picture...He has devised innumerable slights (sic), and while many of them demand great skill none of them seems to be manipulative, but rather natural emotions of a man who is performing amazing wonder." Mulholland's careful dissection also gives a clue into what he considered important about his own show and how he viewed the best attributes of magical performance.

During his early lectures, Mulholland displayed an illusion for every country he visited on his round the world trip. Mulholland is generally credited with being the first magician to present a lecture-demonstration of this kind. The distinguishing factor of his lecture was his polish as a teacher, which set him apart from the bogus snake oil salesman who lectured from the back of wagons in the late 19th century. The word "mountebank" is often used to describe the itinerant magicians from the 19th century. The word literally means "to mount a bank" or to "attain a higher ground" as a performer would be likely to do in order to command the attention of an audience. Though it would be inaccurate to say that a mountebank was an early form of lecturer, it is fair to say that the performances relied as much on elaborate verbal dexterity as any other form of manipulation. In this regard, John Mulholland was a natural successor of his marketplace mountebank predecessor. He took the next evolutionary step via his formal education and the social class his upbringing afforded him.

JOHN MULHOLLAND

MAGICIAN LECTURER

In all ages and in all lands there have been a few persons with genius to mystify, amaze, and to entertain—adepts in the art of magic. • The greatest of these is John Mulholland, since he accomplishes surprising wonders seemingly without effort.

His GREAT CHARM is an easy, friendly, conversational manner—an invited guest who brings into present company Old World mysticism and his own rare contributions to magic. There is more than entertainment, more than an intellectual treat in John Mulholland's appearance. His easy companionable presence makes him a welcome guest in any company—large groups or intimate gatherings.

Mulholland has the great gift of enter-taining others without the intrusion of cumbersome, dominating equipment. The accessories he employs are simple as his own gentle manner.

John Mulholland lectures, too, on occult subjects. The fascinating history of different phases of the mystic arts he relates in a series of lectures which include demonstrations. His talks are palatable and instructive and informative and entertaining.

Exclusive Management
WILLIAM B. FEAKINS, Inc., 500 Fifth Avenue • New York
SAN FRANCISCO OFFICE: MRS. M. J. STEVENSON, MGR., 1700 Taylor Street

One of the greatest magicians.—*London Evening Standard.*
Roi des Prestidigitateurs.—*Patissair.*
Chief Magician.—*The Manchester Guardian.*
De los Illusionistas mas famosos del Mundo.—*El Universal Grafico, Mexico, D. F.*

Vastly entertaining.—*Ottawa Journal.*
One of the most adroit sleight of hand performers in the world.—*New Yorker.*
United States magician number one.—*The Oregonian, Portland, Ore.*

Interior of a lecture brochure.

Mulholland made magic an intellectual art that was appreciated by curators of scholarly materials. One case in point is his studious stewardship of the Society of American Magicians collection donated to the New York Public Library shortly after Saram Ellison died. A letter dated May 3, 1928, from the Assistant Director of the Library, Harry Miller Lydenburg, suggests that Mulholland had some qualms about revealing secrets to the general public: "The Library appreciates the interest of the Society in this connection, and wishes to emphasize the fact that it is not trying to secure for future competent and qualified students of the art and practice of magic documentary material that will enable the next generation to understand what the present generation did, and how it did it." Apparently the two men came to an agreement on the subject. Many years later, in 1943, Mulholland would contribute a chapter on the art of collecting old books on magic to Lydenburg's book titled *Bookmen's Holiday*.

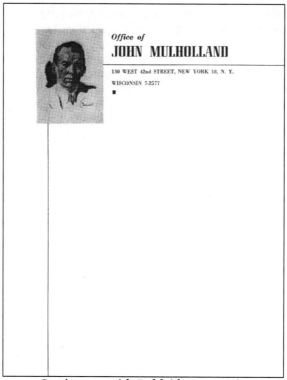

Office of
JOHN MULHOLLAND
130 WEST 42nd STREET, NEW YORK 16, N. Y.
WISCONSIN 7-2577

Stationary with Baldridge portrait.

1928 was a full year for the thirty-year old magician. In addition to having an exhibition of his rare volumes from his ever-increasing collection at the Grolier Club on 32nd Street, he also returned to Europe and performed for the eight-year-old King Michael of Romania in the palace at Sinaia. As well, he authored a companion piece to the exhibition of conjuring books from the Hooker and Ellison collections at the New York Public Library, "Behind the Magician's Curtain."

Given that his office was on 42nd Street, *The New York Times* was on 43rd Street and the Library was equidistant between the two, Mulholland had a cozy arrangement of professional endeavors in midtown Manhattan beginning in 1928. His contributions to magic were observed by older historians such as Henry R. Evans and his many decorations and awards from many international magic societies show how involved he was in worldwide magic fraternities.

Mulholland had a penchant, it seems, for being the authority on magicians who passed on, and for being quoted in their obituaries.

His office was at 130 West 42nd Street. *The New York Times* is located at 229 West 43rd Street. Because he was an editor of the most esteemed magicians' magazine *The Sphinx* it is very likely that when his contemporaries Nate Leipzig, Will Goldston, Leo Rullman or Dr. Hooker died, that it was Mulholland, the brilliant magazine editor and performing magician, who led to the mention in the venerable New York newspaper. After all, he had less than one full city block to walk to deliver hard copy of some burning activity in the magic world. Such activities led to his own publicity in *The New York Times* being enhanced. Between 1929 and 1932 Mulholland prominently appeared in at least ten articles about the general state of pseudo psychics and his condemnation of such practices. He also made sure to align himself with the fraternal powers of the Society of American Magicians, appearing with Houdini's brother on the official 1929 Christmas card!

Beginning in 1921 he joined the Magicians Club of London at 14 Green Street, having paid a membership fee of eight pounds (the equivalent of eighty-four dollars today). His membership was signed by the club's honorary Treasurer, Will Goldston. In the 1930's he would be offered a lifetime membership.

On July 1, 1928, Mulholland also obtained membership in Germany's Magischer Zirkel (Magic Circle). But perhaps his most elegant memento from this period is the green leatherette passport-like membership card to the Syndicat International Artiste Prestiditateurs of Paris. His Carte Identite at the club at 11 Place D' Hotel de Ville (no.1ve) was described by Maurine Christopher as being "from another era, when better quality things were done at a fraction of the cost that would not even be pursued today."

Mulholland's accomplishments also secured his place as the second magician ever admitted to the august Players club on Gramercy Park in New York (the first being his childhood mentor, Harry Kellar). He was brought to the club in 1930 by Columbia University professor Brander Matthews (whom Mulholland always called "Beloved" and who seconded Mulholland's candidacy to help Houdini with his anti-Spiritualist endeavors). Matthews' essay *The Method of Modern Magic* concerning the magician as a comedian still stands as a deep insight into the art of conjuring. Matthews also wrote (in 1888) a three-part story in *Harpers Young People* about Robert-Houdin, noting that the conjurer was often the quickest witted of people. Mulholland liked this description. Mulholland formally joined The Players in 1935 after many years of attending and performing at social functions.

Mulholland's celebrity during this period is perhaps best shown by a pair of pot-boiler thrillers – *Shivering in the Dark* and *Ghost Girl* – in *The Illustrated Detective Magazine* in May and June of 1932. The stories appeared under the byline of one Anthony Abbott, which was actually a nom de plume of the celebrated writer Fulton Oursler, author of *The Greatest Story Ever Told*. Oursler had become acquainted with Mulholland, correspondence shows, when the writer contacted the magician in 1929 requesting a rare book that later helped a theatrical production in Paris, which Oursler had written, concerning the magician Cagliostro. Oursler later situated Mulholland in a series of "mystery parties" thrown by the wealthy during the heights of the Depression. The magician became the focal point when a woman was murdered during his act. (Commensurate with the themes of magic and murder, he featured his largest illusion, a "floating coffin" as a one-time wonder for another magazine piece.) In one story, he was paired with one of the biggest stars in Hollywood, Jean Harlow. Oursler described Mulholland's act in glowing terms:

> *"The magician, John Mulholland, most brilliant of the young practitioners of an ancient art, set out his props on a little square table and proceeded to amaze the visitors with his dexterity. He performed the birdcage trick, in which a canary as well as cage disappears inexplicably when thrown into the air. He linked and unlinked a series of apparently solid metal rings. He filled a cup with water plucked from the air. Calling upon Arthur Garfield Hays and W. Adolphe Roberts, the writer, to act as magician's assistants, he performed marvels such as no one present had seen or dreamed of, with a pack of playing cards."*

Mulholland was depicted as performing "East Indian magic," while not being East Indian, and Oursler further inflated his reputation by writing that he was a professor of chemistry at Columbia University! Clearly Mulholland's familiarity with chemistry came from his association with the chemist Hooker, and his ease with this subject would benefit him later while dealing with the CIA.

In October of 1932, a visiting magician from England named Stuart Drayton Raw wrote in *the Magic Wand*, a periodical for magicians, that "John Mulholland is probably doing more to advance magic in America than any other one man. Hardly a week passes without some article by him being published in a newspaper or magazine – not exposures of tricks, but articles that are likely to interest the public in magic."

Three years later, Mulholland was profiled by the great Max Holden, owner of a chain of magic stores across the Eastern seaboard. Holden records a fine description of a typical Mulholland performance including costumes and masks, instantaneous rope magic, the unexpected growth of flowers, manipulations with thimbles, silk scarves, playing cards where extreme strength was casually exhibited, and mercury-like wizardry with coins, cigarettes and then concluding with making it snow paper flakes in the auditorium. "Mulholland presents a clever show that holds interest throughout," Holden wrote.

Generally, as depicted in a show from 1937 in Albany, New York, he performed for an hour and twenty minutes without an intermission, spoke eloquently of his travels, and demonstrated a trick that was indigenous to each country he discussed. For example, having been to Czechoslovakia, then spelled as Czech-Slovakia, he demonstrated "The Stolen Apple" concerning a well-known apple fair where choice apples were threaded on ribbons. In Mulholland's magical hands, the threaded apple seemed to melt through its bonds, much to the delight of his audience. Mulholland appeared as a sophisticated gentleman and an effortless sorcerer rolled into one.

By his mid-thirties, Mulholland had learned a great deal about the business of being a magician. Though he had been a superb performer for many years, he had now acquired a comparable degree of skill in the art of self-promotion. In addition, he learned to maximize the income and exposure from his writing by recycling the same articles and essays over and over.

He alluded to the expertise he felt comfortable with by stating in his 1937 introduction to his friend Keith Clark's *Encyclopedia of Cigarette Tricks,* "To be a real authority on magic means that there must be a wide background of experience by one who has been successful not only in entertaining his audiences but so successful that managers were willing to pay large salaries for the privilege of featuring the performer. Besides knowing all about the history of the subject, he must also be a deep student of psychology, or art, of acting, and above all be possessed of that rarest of all gifts – common sense."

John Mulholland was a writer who constantly made use of everything he ever learned. This was certainly true regarding his relationship with his friend Keith Clark. Just five years after his professional alliance with the cigarette tome, Clark penned another opus, this time about sorcery with silks, and once again, in 1942, Mulholland rode shotgun with an Introduction. While reiterating his feelings of professionalism from his earlier essay, Mulholland probably learned a lesson that he used twenty years later. At the back of the Clark silk magic booklet, the name "Keith Clark" is repeated to cover the entire back of the 6" x 9" pamphlet. When Mulholland finally expanded his *Art of Illusion* to become *John Mulholland's Book of Magic* he used the repeating name example, but featured his own on the cover.

He was a living example of "anything one learns can help you do anything you want to do." The adage of using what he knew to further his career is well illustrated by tracing his publications and understanding what happened to his writing. Material that was first published as a series of syndicated articles for *The Boston Herald* and *The New York Times*, was later published in 1932 as his second book *Quicker Than The Eye*. An essay called "Peddlers of Wonders," which had originally formed a chapter in his book *Quicker Than the Eye*, got a second airing in *The New York Herald Tribune* under the title "The Trade of Trickery" in April of 1932. His essays "Conjurer and Pedagogue" and "Magic in America" were also reprinted in many forms. One series of articles that appeared the week of his marriage paid him enough to afford an extensive honeymoon during the heights of the Depression.

His 1935 book *John Mulholland's Story of Magic* became the basis for his booklet ten years later *The Early Magic Shows*. His 1944 opus *The Art of Illusion* was printed three times, first as a hard back from Scribner's and then as a pocket size War Department edition. Finally this treatise on simple tricks was reprinted one year later as *Magic For Entertaining* (Magic Men Can Do).

His 1945 article *The Christmas Conjurer* featuring children's reactions (aped later by many but never with the meaning) became a pamphlet he used for the purpose of booking shows. One year later it became an article he sold to *The New York Times* under the title *The Old Old Magic*. All of his technical writing on magic (since 1925) ultimately wound up in some form in his extremely successful 1963 tome *John Mulholland's Book of Magic* (still in print in 2005). While his writing remained constant, it always developed. When he traveled to Peking, for example, he substituted that city for his previous exotic reference of Bombay, a city he visited a decade earlier.

As a former school teacher, Mulholland undoubtedly appreciated the value of being paid to teach the same lesson more than once. While other writers were paid by the word, Mulholland learned early on of the advantages of a flat fee, which often exceeded the per word rate.

234 WEST 44TH STREET, NEW YORK CITY Kansas City, Mo., June 11, 1932.

Mr. John Mulholland,
507 West 113th Street,
New York City.

Dear John:

Glad you want and did it. Never say the
first cross word and never hear the first
cross word and you will be happy.

Every good wish to you both.

Cordially,

Thurston's congratulations to Mulholland on his marriage, 1932.

MULHOLLAND'S MARRIAGE 1932

Mulholland had good reason to watch the bottom line. Since 1924 he had been actively courting an attractive young woman named Pauline Pierce, whom he had known since his teaching days. Like the magician, she lived in the Columbia University district. With his income from writing, lectures and performance giving him a small nest egg, he was able to demonstrate to his prospective in-laws that he was not a run-of-the-mill starving artist.

John Mulholland and Pauline Pierce, age 29, were married on May 17, 1932. While his gentlemanly demeanor and her society affiliations made them a dashing couple, one factor of their union was most uncommon. When John Mulholland asked Pauline Pierce to marry him, one broad condition applied. The magician told his wife-to-be that she would have to accept his ongoing love affair with a woman he had met in New Hampshire the summer before meeting her – Dorothy Wolf. Later in life, Pauline Mulholland would say, "Johnny was so much a man, one woman's love could not satisfy him."

With his future wife in New Hampshire, 1927.

Born October 17, 1903, Pauline Nell Pierce was a student at the Barnard School for Girls next door to Columbia University where Mulholland taught at the Barnard School for Boys in 1923. He claimed that they met because she was a student at Barnard; she said they met when he chaperoned a group of Horace Mann students to a social mixer with Barnard students.

Ms. Pierce was a graduating member of the Horace Mann class of 1922. She was later graduated as a member of the Smith College class of 1926. She was a cousin of the 14th President of the United States, Franklin Pierce. Pauline was a second cousin to Barbara Pierce, who married George Herbert Walker Bush, the 41st President of the United States. The Pierce family was wealthy and her father was a General in

79

the U.S. Army. For their wedding, the family gave them seventy acres of land in Newtown, Connecticut, on which to build a summer cottage.

*John Mulholland with Dorothy Wolf
in New Hampshire, 1926.*

Shortly after his marriage, he and his wife spent time in Virginia, then Atlantic City and finally Mexico. There the newlyweds were joined by Mulholland's doting mother, which seems to have caused the young bride a certain amount of angst. Shortly before he traveled to Mexico, Mulholland broke his collarbone while playing with his friend Julien Proskauer's children in Westchester. His mother felt compelled to join the young couple so that she could help look after "her Johnny." In Mexico City, when Mulholland gave a performance for the President of Mexico at Chapultepec Palace, his mother received something of a rude awakening. Upon being told that he could bring only one guest to see the performance, Mulholland brought his new wife. It should be noted, however, that Pauline Mulholland was not a magic fan, having fallen asleep at magic shows she attended in New York.

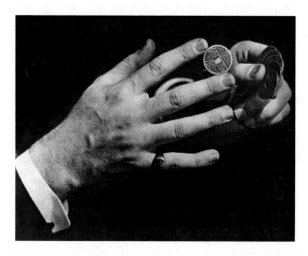

As Mulholland's collarbone healed, he was able to resume his sleight-of-hand work. Throughout his career he maintained the ability to make four or five coins roll over his fingertips like horses running a steeplechase. He invented the Mulholland Coin Box, similar to the magician's standard prop, the Okito Box. He also is noted for having invented a sleight (a hidden movement of the hands) called The Slide Vanish. Inventing a sleight of hand move is admirable, but Mulholland's achievement is a thousand times more astonishing given that he developed this sleight at age twelve. This particular sleight involves a sophisticated understanding of the neuro-muscular activity of the eyes and the psychology of audiences; something he instinctively grasped at a very early age. He would use his knowledge of the eyes and the deftness of the hands in his future work for the U.S. government.

Mulholland would remain fascinated by coins and coin magic throughout his life, amassing a collection of 175 priceless coins featuring images of magicians, some of which dated back to the early eighteenth century. The image of Mulholland's hands manipulating coins was a recurring feature of his advertising matter. To emphasize his mastery of coin sleights, he had a special coin minted for him by the President of the Numismatic Society, Howland Wood. The coin featured Chinese characters and words that sounded like "John Mulholland." The coins also lauded Mulholland as "Controller of the devil's knowledge and skill." A brass token he commonly made appear had his face in profile on one side, the other bearing a rabbit in a high silk hat surrounded by the words he used to describe his profession. Sometimes these were handed out in aluminum stamped on only one side.

One of Mulholland's signature effects, written up in his *Book of Magic*, seldom seen today, combined his coin expertise with card manipulation:

> *A handful of coins were proffered. A pack of sealed cards was opened and shuffled. A coin was selected; the cards were placed on the table face down. The top four cards were dealt face up. An ace. The Nine of Clubs. The Three of Hearts. Another ace. The coin was looked at. Nothing special seemed to happen. Then John Mulholland, with his devilish sense of humor asked the holder of the coin to read the date aloud. "1931" was the response and all of a sudden the audience realized the impossible: the cards that were randomly shuffled matched the date on the coin!*

Some people were known to quite literally pass out when he did this! In his thirty-eight years as the regular magician at the Union Club in New York City, generation after generation passed along the myth of "Mulholland's Curious Coincidence with Coins and Cards."

At the equally impressive Union League Club (also in Manhattan) John Mulholland set a standard still adhered to by the club. One magician found, during an audition in 1984 that he was introduced to his "audience": a 6-year-old little girl with a bow in her hair – the daughter of the club President. After the audition, the club President told the magician, "We had a fellow years back – John Mulholland. Tall fellow – always kept the youngsters enthralled – that's what we look for."

A Mulholland brochure from this period promised "a diverting intellectual experience...delightful and completely mystifying." He also offered a definition of magic as "the art of creating illusion agreeably," while he left it to others to say that "he knows magic more than any other man alive." Years later, in an introduction to his friend P.C. Sorcar's book on magic, Mulholland returned to the theme, describing his colleague in terms that might readily have been applied to himself: "His performances have always been artistically and financially successful. He is a man of agreeable personality possessed of a keen and trained mind, and having the capacity for an inordinate amount of work. He has the none too common attribute of never satisfied with today's effort, excellent though it be, and has the consistent determination that tomorrow will find him doing even better."

At the time of Mulholland's marriage, sixty-three year old Howard Thurston was touring America with an hour-long show presented in conjunction with one of the new "talkie" motion pictures. For nearly thirty years Thurston had toured the world with the three-hour

Wonder Show of the Universe, where women were sawn in half, floated all over the stage and even vanished in the theatre dome above patrons' heads. In 1932, a one-week gross of Thurston's Pittsburgh theatre engagement was $15,604.32. In the early 30's Mulholland and Thurston each charged $1, $1.50 and a gigantic two dollars per seat to their shows. Mulholland's show was conspicuously smaller in scale and he received criticism from amateur magicians for charging equal sums to Thurston, whose advertising heralded "The Greatest Mystical and Scientific Problem in the History of Magic."

Both Thurston and Mulholland were billing themselves as "The World's Master Magician," but apparently Thurston felt no resentment toward the younger performer. Thurston disbelieved that Mulholland could achieve front-page publicity in each town where he appeared. Mulholland proved Thurston wrong by explaining that his method was to spotlight the local star magician in each town he visited, which naturally gave him space as an expert on home town news. Thurston was envious of his friend's guile. They had been introduced years earlier by Kellar who declared, "Thirsty, this is Johnny – he's going to be one of the good ones."

Though Thurston's hectic schedule had him on stage three or four times daily, he managed to find time to drop the young bridegroom a congratulatory note:

Dear John:

Glad you went and did it. Never say the first cross word and never hear the first cross word and you will be happy. Every good wish to you both.

    Cordially,

        (signed) Howard Thurston

Thurston knew of what he wrote; he had been married three times – his last wife nearly forty years his junior.

THE SCHOLAR COLLECTOR

Like other big league magicians, Mulholland devoted a great deal of his time and resources during this period to presenting himself as an anti-Spiritualist crusader. This was just one of the many ways in which he sought to carry on Houdini's legacy. In January of 1932 he began spinning out a series of hard-hitting magazine articles to expose the "racket of fortune telling." He noted there were 25,000 fortune tellers plying their trade in New York City alone, and that some of them were "raking in $100,000 annually," costing the American public $125 million annually. (Keeping in mind these are 1932 dollars!)

"It is amazing and to me appalling," Mulholland wrote, "that the American public has yet to be aroused to this growing evil." He concludes, in a clear echo of Houdini, "I have yet to observe one trick in the fortune teller's bag which a skilled magician cannot do."

Mulholland's articles on phony mediums would culminate, in 1938, in his authoritative *Beware Familiar Spirits*, in which he wrote, "The more intelligent victims are, the harder they fall." Mulholland cited "the great American surgeon" William J. Mayo, to support his conclusions: "Anyone dabbling in the occult, deliberately depriving himself of vision, man's chief means of getting information, injures himself mentally." Mulholland concludes in perfect 1932 vernacular, "It's all the bunk."

In many articles castigating the charlatans he would use the word "trickster" to describe those who fleeced the "victims" who could least afford their losses. The word is important to note because he would use it in later writing when describing acts of trickery prescribed for CIA clandestine operations. His vast knowledge of trickery was paralleled by his widespread associations with big time magicians and is illustrated by his appearance on a variety bill in 1934.

On November 12, 1934, Mulholland appeared at the Hotel McAlpin in a program billed with all the hoopla of a circus program:

METAMORPHOSED INTO A PSYCHOMANTEUM!

ONE NIGHT ONLY!

MIRACULOUS MYSTIFICATION MARVELOUS MAGIC

Mulholland appeared with no less than fourteen different acts that featured: Walter B. Gibson (noted ghost writer for Houdini, Blackstone, Thurston and Dunninger), Houdini's brother, Hardeen, The Dean of the Society of American Magicians Frederick Eugene Powell, the magic dealer Frank Ducrot and comedic magician Al Baker. The evening finished with a recreation of Houdini's Water Can Escape by the Master of Ceremonies, Julien J. Proskauer. Oddly, on the single sheet poster that advertised the acts, the running time of each was also noted. Mulholland was given four minutes.

His live appearances and his reputation as an intellectual were lauded by his student Barrows Mussey, who later wrote that "Neither can anything I write about magic be dissociated from the friendship and learning of John Mulholland." In fact Mussey later wrote that he worked a great deal on *Beware Familiar Spirits*. He stated, in his seminal masterwork *The Amateur Magician's Handbook* "John was a New Yorker and spent the greater portion of his life globe trotting within a block or two of the place." What did Mussey (writing under the nom-de-plume Henry Hay) mean? The conundrum is worthy of the man about which it is written.

When Mulholland's mother died at the age of eighty-seven, she lived at 507 West 113th Street. Her son kept a large portion of his magic collection at this address conveniently near his home at 600 West 115th Street. He globe-trotted via his recollections of his adventures while he ensconced himself with the historic magical treasures he had picked up all over the world.

Mussey was a student of Mulholland's at Columbia University. Ten years later, as a publisher, Mussey published Mulholland's 1935 opus *John Mulholland's Story of Magic*. Given that this book was largely about the history of magic from the 18th century on, and published in the first third of the twentieth century, it would have been somewhat audacious of the author to include himself in his own history. But, his former student, and now publisher, thought otherwise. Once Mulholland handed in the manuscript, in 1934, Mussey added the pictures of the author in his three stage personas, and made sure the reader was aware that Mulholland was not glorifying himself in the last two pages. Mussey wrote, "Mulholland is ingenious, skillful, and a superb showman; but the most striking feature of his work is its perfect effortlessness." Truthfully, he slyly added later: "If it's magic, he's done it; if it's a magician, he knows him; if it's been done, he can explain it (but won't)."

By 1935, Mulholland had been Editor of *The Sphinx* magazine for magicians for five years. He succeeded Dr. A. M. Wilson in 1930, whom he said bequeathed the editorship to him on his deathbed. Mulholland used his editorship of this publication effectively to further position himself as an authoritative scholar in the public eye.

Ultimately, the magazine was largely a labor of love for Mulholland and he often complained of losing money on the venture. At the same time he always made sure that articles about the magazine included the note that non-magicians were not able to obtain copies of *The Sphinx*. His dedication to the magazine he edited for twenty-three years is seen in a letter he wrote in 1935 to Baltimore magician Phil Thomas. Mulholland is positively testy over the president of the Society of American Magicians (S.A.M) getting his column in late. He writes, "I see no reason why the entire Society should be made to suffer for the procrastination of any individual no matter how high his office."

In fact, five years later, in the robust and heavily illustrated 40th anniversary issue, Mulholland barked at the club he had so enthusiastically joined at age sixteen. After lauding the venerable club and mentioning how *The Sphinx* had generously allotted pages to the Society as a non-profit corporation, he writes, "*The Sphinx* has never made a single cent of profit from the S.A.M and for many years the association has cost *The Sphinx* money." It seems that the magician was somewhat a victim of his own celebrity when it came to favors for magic associations. While the amateurs loved the mystery and mastery of Mulholland, he often had to turn down dates at magic conventions that paid nothing. He often opted to compromise by offering to speak for a few minutes, as long as his appearance was not announced. Because of his editorship of an international-publication, he was also in demand to write forewords for magic texts. While the pay was probably minimal at best, a Mulholland foreword put the seal of scholarship on many a tome. It assured the reader that the scholarly man of mystery, world travel and successful author himself had found it worth his time.

As time passed, and Mulholland entered his forties and fifties; his youthful enthusiasm was replaced by an awareness of the realities of non-money making favors for "the club." He grew angry when the disciplines he applied as a professional were not adhered to by the clubmen. If he was stern with Phil Thomas, he toned down his admonitions somewhat to Thomas' boyhood magician partner, Milbourne Christopher in a letter from 1950. Christopher, age forty-six, was already a world-traveled wizard and a magic collector who showed signs of rivaling Mulholland. *The Sphinx* editor upheld the strict deadlines by underlining the date and noting repeatedly that timeliness was everything and that printing costs were to be observed. Christopher complied, but this was the beginning of the end for *The Sphinx*.

Unlike most clubmen, Mulholland respected Christopher's efforts, including Christopher's paying a hefty portion of costs involved for the Society of American Magicians printing. He also realized that Christopher was an upcoming competitor in the lecture arena with similar credentials.

Mulholland first met the younger magician in 1935 after Christopher wrangled an appearance for the Roosevelts at the Easter Monday egg rolling festivities on the White House lawn. In July, 1936, Mulholland featured Christopher on the cover of *The Sphinx* applauding him for disseminating articles to the popular press, much like he did. In fact, when Milbourne Christopher went to Europe in 1936 as the comedic foil for the pantomimic comedian Freddy Sanborn, it was John Mulholland who wrote letters of introduction to magic societies on behalf of the young magician.

The Society of American Magicians news had appeared under the aegis of *The Sphinx* since the Society was founded. However, in 1951, Christopher took over the editorship of the Society of American Magicians news, and after a unanimous vote to depart from *The Sphinx* the S.A.M started their own magazine called M-U-M. The loss of revenue and subscriptions was crippling to *The Sphinx*.

Mulholland ceased editing and publishing the beloved *Sphinx* magazine in March of 1953. In an open letter to the subscribers issued in June 1953, Mulholland noted doctors' orders confining him to other work. He referred to the magazine's "indefinite suspension." It is very likely that in addition to his new duties for the CIA that the Sphinx Corporation was having financial difficulties, teetering on bankruptcy. Trouble had been brewing for three years. When the S.A.M pulled out of having *The Sphinx* as its monthly magazine (and beginning its own in June 1951), *The Sphinx* lost important subscription revenue. Records from Dorothy Wolf's ledger often show Mulholland making cash disbursements to the company, sometimes without reimbursement. Advertising dollars often came in later than expected and printing costs escalated yearly while subscription price was seldom increased. His ongoing work at a lucrative fee from the CIA may also have weighed in his decision to cease publication.

Mulholland's editorship of *The Sphinx* afforded him the opportunity to come into contact with magicians all over the world and to obtain ephemera germane to their careers, expanding his already massive collection of magic. Mulholland learned "big collecting" from Houdini, Dr. Ellison, Dr. Bridges, Dr. Hooker, and his primary teacher John William Sargent, but in time he eclipsed them all as a collector and went on to influence a new generation of historians, collectors and hobbyists.

Amidst his massive collection, his advertising memorabilia was distinct from other magicians in that it always was emblazoned with his definition of conjuring as "the art of creating illusions agreeably." Coins, playing cards, stationary, business cards, his wallet, cigarette case, cufflinks and curved walking stick bore his logo of the rabbit in a hat sitting next to black and white balls. He often drew his icon of a rabbit in a hat with two small balls near the hat when inscribing his books, and autographing playing cards. This icon even adorned his fireplace in the hamlet of Newtown, Connecticut where he and his bride Pauline built their "Hide-A-Way." The famous logo reflected Mulholland's considerable skills as a draftsman and layout artist. The original rabbit in hat was photographed by the magician and later turned into line drawings that even adorned a special serving tray and doorknocker to the summer retreat. One curiosity was always attendant to this ubiquitous symbol of Mulholland's trade. The rabbit's two long ears were placed strategically near the double "l's" in the name "Mulholland." But, graphically, the two ears could have replaced the double "l's." It tells us something about his notion of advertising his name with clarity that he did *not* use this graphic offering but chose the more subtle offering. Clearly, John Mulholland approached his advertising with originality and a magician's eye.

The magician carried a solid silver ornate cigarette case made for him by magicians in Japan also adorned with his logo of a rabbit in a hat. Set for a day out, cigarette case, coins, business cards and playing cards in his suit, along with his heavy pocket watch, the magician was ready to entertain anywhere, anytime and always to leave a lasting impression.

Unfortunately, his addiction to filterless Philip Morris cigarettes burdened him with lasting emphysema in his later years. Upon his death he left his cigarette case to a friend who framed it as a reminder of the man he referred to as "the magus." A large bronze plate of a rabbit in a hat, emblazoned with his definition of magic, adorned the entrance to his Times Square office. This also went the way of the cigarette case. Always one to use everything at his disposal, Mulholland's cigarette smoking created the opportunity in the 1930's for his participation in a national advertisement promoting cigarette smoking. The ad also featured magicians Nate Leipzig, Elmer P. Ransom and "Believe it or Not" creator, Robert Ripley. Mulholland was a man who never got rid of anything. Consequently, in 2004 a discovery was made in Michigan. A small magician's "feke" was discovered containing two of Mulholland's cigarettes. The prop, no doubt made by the magician himself, speaks volumes about his mechanical precision.

The advertising brochure distributed in the 1930's by his agent William B. Feakins stated "John Mulholland has developed an original place for himself both in the world of magic and on the lecture platform." In 1936, during the height of the Depression, Mulholland decided to inform the readers of *The Sphinx* on his thoughts concerning originality. He wrote in his *Editor's Notes*:

> *"The best trick is nothing but an idea or two and a few props until it is performed. The performer gives life to the trick. It is comparatively easy to copy a trick that one has seen performed. It is much more effort and much more difficult to get a trick out of the printed page, for then it is necessary to supply all the little details of presentation."*

In 1939, Mulholland partnered with fiction writer Cortland Fitzsimmons to create a detective thriller. The result was *The Girl in the Cage*, featuring a master magician as one of the central characters. One of the themes of the novel was the odd nature of coincidence, a subject that fascinated Mulholland throughout his life. In the opening pages, Mulholland wrote:

> *Peter King is a magician. He is more than a showman; he is a scholar in the field of magic, because magic is his one and only passion. He is an educated man, but more than that he has made use of his education. He is well informed on practically every subject, knows a great many surprising things and has a fine active intelligence. A glance at him gives more than a hint of that. There is nothing of the dark, sinister, piercing-eyed master of the black arts about him. He is tall and professional in appearance, except when he is on the stage; then he is all showman. He has a broad kind face and wide pensive eyes. His voice is rich and full, hypnotic when he wants it to be. Most of the time his speech is rather slow and deliberate except at those times when he is trying to hoodwink an audience. Like most of the people in the theater, there is a little of the Jekyll and Hyde in Peter.*

What is also particularly noteworthy about this passage is that he synthesized it from a passage written about him by Lowell Thomas, the celebrated newscaster and author, from a 1930's article titled *The Master Magician*:

> *He is, moreover, a scholar in the field of magic. A glance at him gives a hint of that. He is by no means the mestophlian figure with piercing eyes and a slight black mustache. He is tall and rather professorial in appearance with a thoughtful academic kind of face and a pensive studious manner of speech.*

Clearly Mulholland was a man who paid attention to his press clippings. A few years later, John Erskine, a noted author and educator, would echo Thomas's appraisal when he described Mulholland as "A trained scholar as well as a superb practitioner of the art."

Mulholland's fees reflected his growing status. By 1942 his secretary Dorothy Wolf was answering inquiries about the magician's availability with the information that the fee to engage Mulholland was $250. The fee covered either a 90-minute lecture demonstration involving magic, or a straight magic show, usually geared for children. This is the equivalent of nearly $1700 in 2005 currency.

Dorothy Wolf in Sphinx office.

A typical issue of *The Sphinx* from 1941 gives some idea of Mulholland's demanding schedule. In the space of a single week he appeared at New York's Barbizon Hotel for a Society of American Magicians program, did a run of five nights at Radio City Music Hall appearing with his Chinese magician's impersonation, and finished the week in Rhode Island at another S.A.M show. In his Radio City shows he made a large basin of water appear, and at the S.A.M shows his cage and canary vanished as they had many times before.

In 1943, Mulholland contributed to a collection of essays honoring his old friend Harry Miller Lydenburg, the former President of the New York Public Library. Titled *Magic in the Library* the erudite showman tells the circuitous story of the Library's magic collection. He cites the lineage of the books from William Ellsworth Robinson, to both Dr. Hooker and Dr. Ellison. Typically, he delved into the idiosyncrasies of each individual, rather than just noting the age of each volume and the unusual contents thereby creating more interest in the books.

Mulholland concludes with appropriate camaraderie by stating that Mr. Lydenburg appreciates the magical bibliophile's thirst for knowledge and that Lydenburg has scorned the view of those who felt that volumes of magic were, as described in the seventeenth century, "but a darke composition of words to blind the eye of the beholder." Mulholland kept up his scholarly association with the New York Public Library and would later have an exhibit of his own rare volumes there. Later in life, he wrote a lengthy article for the *Library Journal* in which he discussed the problems of cataloguing books on the art of magic. After a mostly stinging essay concerning how confusingly the books were catalogued he wrote, " I hope that readers of this piece will not think that I am critical of librarians. My complaint is merely with some of the details of library cataloguing. Some of my best friends are librarians...or were." The wry Mulholland never let go of bibliomania. In 1962, he published an article on the obscure topic of ""Unpublished Magic Books" adding, "Will the readers please send him (the editor) notes about magic books which, while announced, ain't."

Concerning his own library, it is interesting to note that the number of books in his massive collection is specified as 3,500 in 1933. Five years later, he writes in his foreword to his friend Gerald Kaufman's book *How's Tricks?* that his book collection boasts 4,500 titles. Consequently, we can assume that between 1933 and 1938, John Mulholland collected one thousand books! At a rate of two hundred books a year, we can surmise that this man of many wonders was also collecting an average of sixteen books a month or four books per week! Unlike today's collectors, Mulholland was not known for acquiring large amounts of books at once. His collection was meticulously put together piece by piece and often, when he did come into a large quantity of materials, it was because someone had died and willed it to him. He was the natural repository for many magicians' materials, and this, plus his editorship of *The Sphinx*, is another way his magnificent collection grew.

The important thing about Mulholland's *Library Journal* essay is not only the message he imparts, but, as he somewhat pointedly states, the nature of who is the messenger. As perhaps one of the few living familiar with the genesis of the S.A.M. collection he is precise in naming the paradoxes inherent to performing and collecting magic. He further states that while the practice of collecting may insure one's knowledge of conjuring techniques, such knowledge does not make a conjurer.

Knowledgeable of what did make a conjurer, Mulholland by 1944 had explored almost every avenue of his profession. One fact nagged at him however – he did not have any formal degrees. So, when an alumni questionnaire was offered by his alma mater Horace Mann, he sought to impress the school with his various accomplishments. The 46-year-old Mulholland noted that for "30 years City Police and governmental agencies have engaged me as a consultant."

He added that he had undergone "several prolonged sessions in the hospital complete with surgery" in the last few months though did not write precisely what ailed him. It is likely that his over-acidic stomach had created ulcerous conditions. He referred to his *6,000 books* on conjuring and was prideful of his volume from 1584. Concluding, perhaps feeling the passage of the years, he wrote that he saw less of his classmates, but more of their grandchildren who had been told of his magic by their grandfathers.

Noted American theater critic Edmund Wilson wrote[6] in *The New Yorker* magazine in 1944, "It was not until Mr. Mulholland appeared that this department of human activity was explored in all its aspects and branches by a scholarly and critical intelligence which knew how to express itself." Wilson went on to say, "The articles in *Encyclopedia*

Britannica have always been unsatisfactory...when further encyclopedia articles have to be written, Mr. Mulholland ought to write them."

Article on magic for Compton's Encyclopedia, 1950's.

With characteristic thoroughness, Mulholland did just that, eventually contributing the entries on conjuring, showmanship, psychic phenomenon and the occult for the *Merriam-Webster Dictionary, Encyclopedia Britannica, The World Book, Compton's Encyclopedia* and *Funk & Wagnels*. His four-page essay, simply titled "Conjuring," for *Encyclopedia Britannica* was hailed as the standard work on the conjurer's art for forty years.

In his *Encyclopedia Britannica* essay it is one of the first times we see Mulholland breaking a word into parts, and then spelling the word backwards. This provided the distraction for the eye to confuse the mind. It was also the perfect example to teach the deceptive ways of the conjuror. This was a tactic he would use in at least three more books over the next twenty-five years. Of course, for the encyclopedia, he wisely broke apart the word "Britannica," and leveled the reader with: Acin nat irb.

It is characteristic of Mulholland's exacting standards that he gave credit where due, citing Frikell as the first to wear evening tails and noting that Robert-Houdin became known as the "Father of Modern Magic" because he absorbed the knowledge of every other conjurer before him. Houdini is written about with respect, but as no more than a specialty act in vaudeville.

Copious dates are given and texts dating back to the 15th century are cited with panache and erudition. It is the final seven hundred words where Mulholland sews up almost two thousand years of history. He details the rudiments by which the modern magician presents his mysteries as entertainment. Setting aside historical texts, Mulholland speaking from his own practice, writes:

> *A conjurer does not have to be of any particular type, nor have any unusual physical qualifications, but he must have, or develop, a pleasing manner. He should inherently like people and must study group psychology, as well as the psychology of deception and presentation. He must acquire a sense of rhythm and a precision of time in order to be able to execute his secret operations invisibly and apparently without effort. Real proficiency in conjuring comes only through experience. A conjurer must present all his tricks in a manner fitting his own personality, so he also has to be original.*

His most eloquent phrase closes the second to last section: "In conjuring, one of the oldest and most delightful arts, the best of the old is kept and added to the best of what is new." This essay had the widest circulation of anything he had ever written. The great achievement of this essay was that it established the art of magic as one of the fine arts; Mulholland's lifetime goal. *Conjuring* also excited the imagination of scholars, newsmen and educators around the world. It gave a new light to conjuring and the specifics of the essay paid silent tribute to his teacher Sargent, as many of the concepts discussed were originally his. Advertisers took notice and in *Colliers Magazine* in the late 1940's the magician was invited to write a series of explained feats and tricks that were used to increase readership.

Mulholland would reiterate many of the same points to novice deceptionists twenty years later when consulting to the CIA.

The history of magic had been written about before his essay in *Encyclopedia Britannica*, but never with so much insight, historical

93

reference and showmanly guts. John Mulholland was a professional magician who wrote professionally, like Robert-Houdin and David Devant before him. The difference was that John Mulholland wrote with the advantage of having read his six thousand books on conjuring and possessing the professional experience to experiment with history as a chemist might use materials in a lab. Mulholland was a purist, but also wise to the ways of show business and the myths inherent to theatrical ways. He doesn't pick apart myth in his essay; he merely labels it appropriately and supports the art he represents with integrity and love.

THEATRICAL PROMINENCE

Mulholland's prominence as a theatrical figure was noted by another theatrical critic, the esteemed John Mason Brown. Writing in *The Saturday Review*, Brown notes that the great American actress Laurette Taylor's performance on Broadway in the Tennessee Williams masterpiece *The Glass Menagerie* was as pronounced as Mulholland's tightly woven relationship with his props. "Anyone, for instance, can list John Mulholland's props." Brown wrote. "But it takes Mr. Mulholland to perform his tricks. Even then, they cannot be followed or explained. The same thing is true of Miss Taylor's art. Although Mr. Mulholland is a known as a professional magician and Miss Taylor as a professional actress, she makes us realize once again that, regardless of what a magician must know about acting, the actress and the magician, can be, indeed should be, one."

Mulholland's theatricality and scholarship was also evident in his performances. After a "Pipe Night" performance by Mulholland at his beloved Players club on Gramercy Park South (formerly the home of the great 19th century Shakespearean actor Edwin Booth), *The New York Times* theatre critic Brooks Atkinson told another member that Mulholland's style was as "everyone's uncle," putting up with errant actions of small children. Atkinson later wrote, "His public stance was one of modesty and forbearance. He seemed to suggest that he was so used to his superior skill that he was resigned to being the one unobtrusive genius in a room full of blockheads."

Mulholland's stature as a magician is perhaps best illustrated by the esteem in which he was held by his colleagues. William W. Larsen Jr, editor of *Genii - the International Conjuror's Magazine* would write that "John Mulholland is the most knowledgeable magician on Earth." Henry Deane, Jr. wrote of Mulholland in *The Linking Ring* (the periodical of the International Brotherhood of Magicians): "All through his life, John Mulholland has made it his business to meet and learn all he could about great magicians, both in this country and in the forty-three countries of the world in which he has visited and studied magic." The legendary Walter B. Gibson, the prolific author

94

perhaps best known as the creator of *The Shadow*, wrote that Mulholland knew practically every magician on earth.

LITTLE THEATRE
KING EDWARD AVENUE

T. D. deBlois

Presents the

World-renowned Wizard, Magician and Wonder-worker

John Mulholland

John Mulholland is the best magician in hand and voice and manner I have seen in ten years.—Albert Payson Terhune.

TWO

NIGHTS

ONLY

Representative of this new generation of magicians— John Mulholland, who taught at Horace Mann before becoming a professional magician. Mulholland has taken up magic as he would any academic subject. He traveled through Europe and Asia in the study of magic and performed as he went along.—Editorial in The New York Times.

Thurs. Nov. 21 - Fri. Nov. 22

ON THURSDAY NIGHT MR. MULHOLLAND WILL PRESENT

"Magic of the World"

with demonstrations of marvels, which he has collected from the farthest corners of the earth.

FRIDAY NIGHT

"The Science of Soothsaying"

In simple detail the tricks of the crystal gazer, the palmist, the trance medium, and other pretenders to power are explained. Mr. Mulholland gives such convincing demonstrations that he is apt to be conceded the power he denies.

Tickets $1.00 and $1.50

Box Office now open.   Phone R. 2792

When the celebrated vaudeville magician Nate Leipzig (1873-1939) died, his widow, Leila, printed a formal notice introducing Mulholland as Leipzig's theatrical successor. This was an especially meaningful honor to Mulholland who had considered Leipzig the best natural sleight of hand magician in the world. Magician and Broadway star Fred Keating – a confidant of Leipzig – often felt overlooked for this honor, as noted in letters between Keating and Mulholland. Yet, a letter from 1952 details Keating's enduring feelings of friendship and respect. He wrote, "As his true protégé, I say that for meritorious service and gallantry far beyond the line of duty to his tradition, you may forever honorably wear the medal bequeathed to you by Nate

95

Leipzig." Keating and Mulholland, in Mulholland's words, were "pals since boyhood" and while they may have had their differences, sometimes their fractious attitudes were parlayed into entertainment. In 1956 their constant "dueling" at The Players was turned into a night of friendly barbs and good-natured magic where each seemingly topped the other's wonder. Though in actuality, the audience realized "the fix was in" toward the end of the contentious performance.

For a number of years, my husband, the late Mr. Nate Leipzig, regarded Mr. John Mulholland as a delightful entertainer and most skilful prestidigitator. It was his wish that Mr. Mulholland be recommended as his successor.

Leila Leipzig

At the time of Leipzig's death *The New York Times* quoted Mulholland as saying: "Nate Leipzig was a cultured gentleman, a clever raconteur, a most loyal friend, and the wise and helpful advisor of countless young magicians. He never spoke either ill or in an unfriendly manner of anyone. He was never too busy to give his valuable services to a worthy charity, nor aid and counsel to one in need. In short, he stood as a model of conduct for magicians to follow."

Few did. Like Leipzig, Mulholland's work at close quarters smacked of real magic. His technique was invisible and his presentation was that of a common man who performed miracles, not mere tricks, with disarming ease and gentlemanly humor.

JOHN MULHOLLAND

130 West 42nd Street, New York City

Mulholland epitomized the magician's desire to "pack small and play big." He was the focus of articles in many countries spot lighting such intimate wonders as tearing a deck of cards in two and then into fourths as a nonchalant demonstration of superhuman strength. He received significant press for passing through a coin-operated turnstile without depositing a coin; correctly divining the sum total of numbers merely thought of by strangers; sometimes noting thoughts before newsman had them. The Hindu Mango Tree Trick, which Mulholland performed as a blooming rosebush that grew instantly from a seed, was an early creation depicted in sequential photos in national magazines. It was Mulholland's ability to fool magicians with their own tricks that brought him praise from his peers around the world.

The turnstile trick was a favorite of Mulholland's at home as well as abroad, as noted in New York newspapers. It was reported that Mulholland magically used a nickel repeatedly for himself and friends when entering the New York City subway system until the train booth operator became upset. Mulholland placed the magical nickel he somehow retrieved from the turnstile for each person and gave it to the token seller. When the subway booth operator opened his hand he found a stamped aluminum coin with the name "John Mulholland" and a rabbit sitting in a high silk hat, the news reported.

Historian David Price, writes of Mulholland's performance, "The author...can attest to the remarkable impression Mulholland made with his close-up work, particularly with coins. Several stage performers, though not many, have been seen who could imbue their performance with an aura of magic. Mulholland is the only one seen who could do the same with a close-up bit of magic. The effects occurred as if by true magic without any semblance of sleight of hand or hanky panky."[7]

Having examined Mulholland's personal effects, this writer can attest to his strength and dexterity. The weight of some of the special Chinese coins he performed with are significant. One prized coin he kept in a special leather case was from the middle 19th century and celebrated the 17th century dynasty of Xian Feng. The characters on this antique coin mean: "heavy, important, essential and precious." No doubt the magician used the folkloric vestiges surrounding the coin to transcend common magician's coin tricks.

The New Yorker noted his dexterity and showmanship with coins, describing the ease with which Mulholland was able to roll five coins across his fingers when most can barely manage one.

Mulholland's talents proved captivating to children as well as adults, which is not always the case. One Mulholland performance featuring the Chinese Linking Rings, a standard magician's effect, proved so memorable as to remain a topic of conversation at family gatherings forty years later. The children, recalled one of the parents, were more entertained than they had ever been in their lives. One of the children, Diane Gordon, now an adult, remembers, "I tossed the rings to him and he would link them to the others. It was real magic. He was a god to me. I think he was a genius."

Throughout his life Mulholland asserted that the practice of magic was 80% psychology, 10% manipulation, and 10% apparatus. His emphasis on psychology may help to explain why, during the 1930's, he was in demand by police forces throughout the U.S. to help debunk and combat psychic fraud. His lecture brochure of 1945 details six different lectures: *War, Politics Magic; Beware Familiar Spirits; The Science of Soothsaying; The Way You're Fooled; A Magician in Many Lands* (a title he appropriated from Charles Bertram's autobiography); and *Pedagogue and Conjuror* (a reprise of his first published work with Milton Smith).

A brief biography Mulholland submitted to his friend Barrows Mussey's 1949 *Cyclopedia of Magic* shows the attributes of his character and life at age fifty that made him the unusual combination of scholar and showman:

> *Mulholland, John (born 1898). American magician, magic historian, collector and traveler. Mulholland is an outstanding private and close-up performer, who also handles large crowds well; at one time he was booked as a lecturer, merely showing tricks to illustrate an occasional point in his talk. HERRMANN* (his use of capitals) *and others in the late nineteenth century made magic socially respectable; Mulholland, and to a rather smaller extent HOUDINI, have made it intellectually respectable. Mulholland is outstanding for his inexhaustible knowledge of tricks, PRESENTATION, PSYCHOLOGY, PUBLICITY, HISTORY, and LITERATURE of magic; he is editor of The Sphinx, the oldest and solidest magic magazine now being published, served as consultant on conjuring to the Encyclopedia Britannica and the Merriam-Webster Dictionary, and is the only magician listed in Who's Who In America. He has written several books on the history and practice of magic.*

Citing Houdini as a lesser influence on making magic intellectually respectable was likely the magician settling old scores with the man with whom he had a tempestuous relationship. However, this was not simply Mulholland's ego on display, it was the historian striving for accuracy.

MAGIC IN PATRIOTIC SERVICE

In 1941, Mulholland was prominently featured in an article in *The New York World Telegram* describing the situation of fellow magicians in Hitler's Germany. Mulholland lamented the persecutions of fellow wonder workers, such as the comedy card magician Fred Roner who emigrated in 1938, later joining the banquet performance world of New York just prior to the U.S. entering World War II. Discrimination was based on religion, profession, accent and heritage. Humiliations suffered by supper club entertainers to stars of the world-famous Wintergarden Theatre disgusted and saddened Mulholland. Nimble fingered artists were threatened with death if they did not dig trenches. This offended Mulholland on every level. He spoke of shortages from silk handkerchiefs to cigarettes endured by fellow conjurers. He hoped that the cleverness by which magicians produced their stage illusions would ultimately aid the plight of his brother conjurers living under Hitler's tyranny. Letters Mulholland received from "The Man With 1000 Cigarettes" Jose Frakson cemented the facts repeated in the world's dailies.

Mulholland had to have been aware of Erik Jan Hanussen, who became known as "The Prophet of the Third Reich." Hanussen was a typical stage mind reader who uncommonly ascended to heights unknown by his music hall contemporaries who also used spoken codes to transfer information, and gleaned information about the audience by poking around in their lives before they entered the theatre. Hanussen's real name was Hermann Steinschneider. He was eventually murdered by the German SS for being perceived as knowing too much.

The U.S. War Department's strong suspicion that Hitler had conducted serious inquiry into the occult began to spread through the upper levels of command. Allen Dulles – shortly after the OSS closed in 1946 – personally briefed members of Congress, and the White House Chief of Staff under Truman, about activity in this regard. The paranoia that made soldiers believe that the Nazi General Rommel had a sixth sense about battle, and was therefore unbeatable, fed the narrow minded fear bubbling to the surface of Allied Forces prior to the U.S. involvement in WWII. If the Axis powers had a psychic edge, no amount of fire-power could combat this kind of evil. Some believed Hitler was in league with the devil. This was the kind of psychosis Mulholland had met, matched and defeated throughout his career battling psychic fraud.

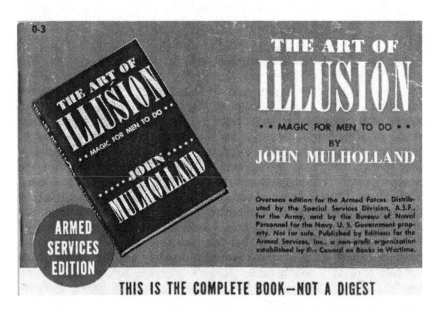

Well connected in police circles, Mulholland aided the fight against fortune tellers and other swindlers. His original assignment with the CIA came about because of the Agency's face-to-face meeting with a supposed psychic. The U.S. government was concerned with "how" the psychic accomplished his miracles. As well, the government was also concerned with developing real psychic capabilities! Psychic phenomenon was accepted as real by some intelligence officers, and while the magician largely disagreed, he knew he could aid the CIA as their best consulting critic in their search for the "unlimited powers of the mind."

In many ways, Mulholland's talents were perfectly suited to the needs of the embryonic CIA. He was well-traveled, having been to forty-two countries and was well known in Washington DC from his eight performances for the Roosevelts.

By 1953 he had authored six books covering all phases of conjuring and, of course, had defined terms for international encyclopedias and dictionaries. His editorship of *The Sphinx* positioned him as a leader in his field. His performance career spanning thirty-eight years gave him the knowledge of human behavior that was unobtainable any other way. The combination of scholar-performer perfectly set his candidacy for intelligence work.

His love of illusion and deceptive techniques was copious. The great variety of deceptive techniques crossed boundaries with the techniques of espionage. Such familiarity made him fit right in with the intellectual crowd assembling in 1947 at the newly born CIA.

He stood alone, unchallenged as quite literally the most knowledgeable magician alive, and had the goods to back it up.

It is reasonable to assume that Mulholland would have been happy to help when the CIA first approached him. Having been sickly as a child after surviving rheumatic fever, he was not a candidate for service during World War I, and he regretted that he had not been able to fight for his country. His last literary collaborator George Gordon said "John was an American and he loved his country, and the fact that he worked for an intelligence agency run by our government made him very proud. He was a patriot. Sounds sort of old fashioned now, but he was."

His patriotism was evident in his lectures. A prominent orange lecture brochure titled "Unmasking Propaganda Through Magic" from the 1940's distinctly put forth the lecturer's objectives. "The public likes to be fooled by a magician, but hates to be fooled by a dictator," was part of the text. Then Mulholland went on to expose audiences to propaganda in newspapers, magazines and motion pictures. He posited that the trickery used by Germany, Japan and Italy was best seen through the eyes of a magician. *The Philadelphia Inquirer* covered his performance of this lecture at Town Hall in New York and wrote, "Mulholland electrified an audience when he declared that the technique of subversive propaganda is identical with the technique of the rabbit-out-of-a-hat."

These credits combined with his affiliations in Germany and throughout Europe, made him a man the United States government wanted on their side during World War II and the ensuing Cold War of the 1950's and 60's.

Mulholland was only too happy to oblige.

(courtesy of William V. Rauscher Collection.)

Sherman C. Grifford

May 5, 1953

Mr. John Mulholland
507 West 113 Street
New York 25, N. Y.

Dear John;

The project outlined in your letter of April 20 has been
approved by us, and you are hereby authorized to spend up to
$3,000 in the next six months in the execution of this work.

Enclosed find a check for $150.00 to cover the last voucher
you submitted to us. Please sign the enclosed receipt and
return it to me.

A very crowded schedule of travel makes it necessary for
us to delay until June 8th our next visit with you. An effective
alternative to this would be for you to come down to Washington
on May 13, 14, or 15 to discuss the current status of the work.
Is this possible?

Very sincerely yours,

SHERMAN C. GRIFFORD

Enclosure

Initial authorization letter from Gottlieb writing as "Grifford."

III. MULHOLLAND & THE CIA

"Nobody stop and scrutinize the plan."

– Paul Simon, *Learn How to Fall*, 1973

"Because of the glamour and mystery, overemphasis is generally placed on what is called secret intelligence, namely, the intelligence is obtained by secret means and by secret agents. During war, this form of intelligence takes on added importance, but in the time of peace, the bulk of intelligence can be obtained through overt channels, through our diplomatic and consular missions and our military, naval, and air attaches in the normal and proper course of their work. It can also be obtained through the world press, the radio and through the many thousands of Americans, business and professional men and American residents of foreign countries, who are naturally and normally brought in touch with what is going on in those countries. A proper analysis of the intelligence obtainable by these overt, normal and aboveboard means would supply us with over 80 per cent, I should estimate, of the information required for the guidance of our national policy..."

– Allen Dulles, second Director of the CIA,
memorandum to Senate Armed Services Committee,
1947.

Beginning in 1953, three-months prior to his 55th birthday, Mulholland was in contact with a man who signed his name: Sherman C. Grifford. "Grifford" was the clandestine name used by Sidney Gottlieb, the head of the Technical Services Staff (TSS), which was an arm of the new CIA. While "spy names" are some of the most sensitive of all information in the world of covert operations, this name was used by Gottlieb until it changed to Samuel Granger about one year into his association with John Mulholland. The initials SG remain the same. That Sherman Grifford and Samuel Granger was, in fact, Sidney Gottlieb was confirmed in 1975 when Gottlieb testified under oath before the Congressional Rockefeller Commission investigating abuses of power in the CIA during the Cold War. John D. Marks also notes Grifford being Gottlieb's clandestine name in a footnote in his book *The Search for the Manchurian Candidate.*

In 1999, while investigating the abuses of power by Sidney Gottlieb and his MK-ULTRA Project, New York Assistant District Attorney

Steven Saracco inspected the documents in this writer's possession concerning the affairs of MK-ULTRA, and sighed, "Gee, I wonder if this fellow Grifford is still around?" When I remarked, "That's Gottlieb" the assistant DA exclaimed "Oh! So you do know what you are talking about."

Dr. Frank Olson

Dr. Sidney Gottlieb

Dr. Robert Lashbrook

Dr. Harold A. Abramson

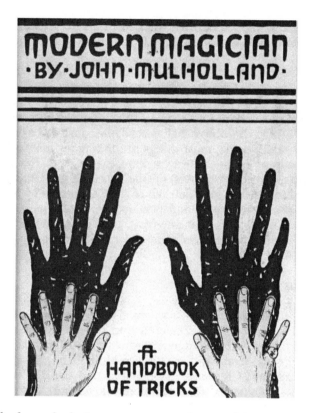

MODERN MAGICIAN
·BY·JOHN·MULHOLLAND·

A
HANDBOOK
OF TRICKS

Grifford worked for a company in Washington D.C. called Chemrophyl Associates, though his job title was never specified. While Grifford's Chemrophyl Associates appeared as an austere research facility, it is likely that this "company" was nothing more than a dummy corporation set up as part of the CIA offices with only a post office box at Southwest station as an address. No phone number adorns either Grifford or Granger's stationary, which was usually used when corresponding with the magician.

It should be noted that the original Washington headquarters of the actual CIA was at 2430 E Street, in the Foggy Bottom section of the city. It sported a sign out front that said "U.S. Printing Office" until even tour guides of Washington routinely pointed this building out as the Agency's new home. The Agency moved to a large tract of nearly 750 acres of privately held land in Langley, Virginia in 1961.

Grifford typed his own letters (though added a secretarial initial of "mk" which was actually the title of the program "MK-ULTRA")—which stood for "mind kontrol (sic) ultra." In his letters to Mulholland, Grifford addressed the magician as "Dear John."

Mulholland replied to his official, though friendly-sounding correspondent, as "Dear Sherman." It is suspected that the company title of:

Chemrophyl Associates

was actually an acronym for the CIA. The stationary bore a script that makes the "l" in Chemrophyl, just as easily be construed as an "I." Just as in the world of magic, most things in the clandestine world are not what they appear to be. However, hard evidence of the magician's relationship to Gottlieb is proven by one "smoking gun" document that ties Grifford to Gottlieb and Gottlieb to the CIA: a note by Mulholland with Grifford's name typed, and penciled below the name is written "Dr. Sidney Gottlieb." There is an arrow, penciled by the magician that suggests all work done by Mulholland for Grifford was to be handed into the "CIA Security offices."

Why was Mulholland contacted?

For the most part, the CIA was created from a pool of intellectual talent drawn largely from Princeton and other Eastern Ivy League universities, along with prominent members of society and industry – all of whom came from similar stock as Mulholland, the professorial magician. Columnist Steward Alsop noted that the CIA was riddled with "Old Grotonians, Establishmentarians and Ivy Leaguers." Mulholland fit right in with this crowd.

While Mulholland may not even have had a high school degree, his career over the past 30 years had brought him into contact with a large body of universities and colleges. His editorship of *The Sphinx* made him not only an authority, but a publisher. He could gather knowledge and dispense it. He understood the mechanism of academia and working with small groups like the one Grifford headed. Having been a schoolteacher, Mulholland's general manner was that of an academic rather than an extroverted stage performer.

It should be noted that the Agency sometimes recruited those that did not fit the mold, such as the famous film clown, Harpo Marx, who was asked by the precursor to the CIA, the OSS (Office of Strategic Services) to smuggle special documents given to him by the Russian ambassador Maxim Litvinov out of Russia in 1933. Another actor-turned-operative, Leonard Rosenberg, who took the stage name Tony Randall, was given the responsibility at the end of his duty in World War II to deliver classified documents to offices in Washington after his "communications unit" commander informed the young actor-soldier "Now you have a most serious role to play." To act with intelligence, one must first have intelligence, and sometimes act without the appearance of possessing intelligence, covert or overt.

H. Keith Melton, author of *The Ultimate Spy Book* and an expert concerning intelligence history, agreed with this writer during a late night interview that the world's greatest spy *would never be known.* Melton sided with this writer that intellectuals made up the majority of those involved in intelligence work. It should also be noted that Mr. Melton defined "intelligence" as the act of taking secrets and "counter intelligence" as the act of "catching those trying to steal secrets."

Melton says that most people's idea of a spy is James Bond but, as he noted in *Smithsonian* magazine, "James Bond was a figment of Ian Fleming's imagination. James Bond in the real world of espionage wouldn't last four minutes. Whether from the Russian SVR, the CIA, or the British MI6, intelligence officers are most often scholarly individuals who are comfortable chatting up unwitting sources at a bar or socializing over dinner, beginning friendships that may lead to acquiring information . . . intelligence ends when you pick up a gun." *Smithsonian* writer Hank Schelsinger noted that the work of spies is really "more cloak than dagger."

Perhaps the most important fact to remember concerning Mulholland's involvement with the CIA is that the Cold War was getting hotter. After rumors of "induced suicides" and political assassins being built through "brain washing" in Korea in the early 1950's – the guts of the story *The Manchurian Candidate* by Richard Condon – the U. S. government sought to explore the potential of various methods of gleaning the truth via drugs, hypnosis, sleep deprivation and electric shock.

A report commissioned during President Truman's administration declared:

> *"It is now clear we are facing an implacable enemy whose avowed objective is world domination by whatever means, at whatever the cost. There are no rules in such a game. We must develop effective espionage, and counter espionage services, and must learn to subvert, sabotage, and destroy our enemies by more clever, more sophisticated, and more effective methods than those used against us."*

The crafting of the covert response was outlined by Deputy Director Richard Helms, as an ultra-sensitive program of research and development in clandestine biological and chemical warfare. Such broad sweeping power, with such adventurous technology, was broken down into the research and goals by Gottlieb's MK-ULTRA team.

During these embryonic years of the Cold War, the United States, Russia and other governments investigated many other avenues of warfare besides dropping bombs on foreign soil. In 1947 the CIA was actively developing biological tools of assassination; using toxic microbes, shellfish toxins, and bacteria. Typical to covert action, it has taken the U. S. Department of Defense nearly fifty years to admit this – and then only in reference to Saddam Hussein's development of biologic warfare, used throughout the Gulf War, producing "Gulf War Syndrome."

Concerning the role of biochemical research during the Cold War, historical biologists Roland F. Line and Clay Griffith write in their authoritative *Stem Rust of Wheat: Ancient Enemy to Modern Foe* on research of the epidemiology of stem rust of wheat during the Cold War:

> *It is a little known aspect of the Cold War that the international tensions that defined global politics in the decades after WWII also sparked sweeping developments in plant pathology. Just as WWI sparked enormous progress in plant pathology, such as the work on barberry plants to control stem rust, military-sponsored research during the Cold War likewise created major advances in science of plant pathology, and the control of plant diseases. Although plant pathology may seem to be a science with little connection to superpower conflict, it was, in fact, deeply enmeshed in the quest for national security. The chronic specter of war between the United States and the Soviet Union during the Cold War included a possibility of large-scale biological warfare, a possibility for which superpowers were compelled to prepare. Because of this "peacetime" war, the US government accelerated its bio-research programs in the late 1940's.*

The MK-ULTRA scientists continued seeking advice and guidance from top experts whether in the military service or at civilian institutions. Research focused on developing the production of, and stockpiling, disease-causing agents as well as creating effective delivery systems. While the general food supply and consumption rate of China and Russia was looked at as population indicators, such food stockpiles were also looked at as avenues of attack. Line and Griffith indicate that the directive to understand the chemical adaptation and acceleration of poisonous mold growth and stem rust could be used in limited quantities for singular offensives, and some "executive action" missions, or assassinations.

John Mulholland was the man the United States government looked to for the creation of surreptitious "delivery systems" for these chemical and biological forms of warfare. He was also familiar with the term "brain washing." The term "brain washing" had been jargon of the psychological community dating back to the 1890's but was replaced by the more clinical "auto suggestion," and "self-hypnosis." Mulholland's own copy of Dr. James R. Cocke's dissertation published as *Hypnotism – How It is Done Its Uses and Dangers* is in the author's possession. The pages on the acceptance of false information clearly have been read many times.

Because of Mulholland's in-depth study of the human mind's acceptance of deception for the sake of illusion, and his work debunking false prophets, he clearly saw how the vulnerable mind was influenced through the repetition of true or false information. The repetition of false information would become part of the methods he would create for the surreptitious delivery of the chemical and biological antigens. His typical point of view concerning the mind's absorption of detail is illustrated in a show he gave at Caleb Mills Hall on February 28, 1930. Reviewed by Eddie McLaughlin, the magician is quoted as saying:

As an illustration of how people imagine things, and in telling about tricks they don't tell what they saw but what the magi told them. For instance, in lecturing before a psychology class I used to do 3 or 4 different tricks, that is, I did two of them, but for the third I told them of an effect that I used to do where I would take three twenty dollar gold pieces and hold them in my right hand, and cause them to vanish and then reappear in my empty left hand. Now, a day or so later I would have them write papers describing the trick I had performed and their actual effects. 82% claimed that I had actually performed the trick with the 20 dollar gold-pieces. I need not give any reasons.

Later Mulholland wrote about his forty-year search for the truth behind the Indian Rope Trick. He concluded, in his foreword to *Sorcar on Magic,* that the mythological trick was due to the effects of a story being repeated through the ages, and writes, "I am convinced now that the process by which people come to believe in the Indian Rope Trick is akin to brain washing."

Clearly, as a result of many years' study, Mulholland was rather familiar with the effect of information repeated to the inquiring mind, no matter how ambitious.

Consequently the magician was a perfect consultant for the bizarre worlds created and encountered by the heavily funded counter intelligence program that became "MK-ULTRA."

MK-ULTRA

Grifford and Mulholland had a lengthy conversation in person at an unknown location, probably in New York City, on April 13, 1953 the same day that MK-ULTRA was approved by CIA Director Allen Dulles.

The aim of MK-ULTRA was to control human behavior, and to understand how the mind worked. The goal was to penetrate the mysteries of the mind, first through the behavioral sciences. The inquiry hoped to isolate what was a "passive" area of the brain, or an area that could be influenced easily. An example of a passive area of the mind would be seeing an oncoming bus, but not noting what color shirt the driver was wearing. This is the passive acceptance of information, without the cognitive processing of that information.

Conversely, an "aggressive area" of the mind would be one where not only curiosity was engaged, but the mind sought solutions to potential problems or deeper information. This aggressive tendency might be illustrated by the simple act of looking at a map. If one needed to turn the page for more direction, the brain was challenged to remember where construction was on roads on the previous map. Using information not in front of a person, but information of which one was aware, was a basic tenet of the "aggressive" aspect of the brain.

An aggressive area of the brain was theorized as being as fluid and impressionable as passive areas. If the information supplied to the brain actively engaged the mind's interest, or more importantly, the creative imagination, it was then assumed that the information going into the brain might unlock previously unused areas or also highlight *more* malleable areas.

The researchers quickly learned that the brain was always processing information, and there was never a dormant time when the mind was not actively engaged. Therefore, directing how the mind was engaged, and isolating what areas of the brain were responsible for functions was just one of the goals of the MK-ULTRA scientists. If the mind could be trained to receive instruction, and to have induced amnesia, then the government men were most interested. Fifty years later, it is quite evident that the notions expressed as fiction in Richard Condon's novel were not entirely fiction. (In fact, this writer has seen a copy of his *Manchurian Candidate* inscribed to one army intelligence officer whom Condon thanks for "help beyond the call of our country, and especially because of our country.")

The Technical Services Staff chief, Sidney Gottlieb, interested in the magician's talents, prompted Mulholland to respond to the Agency's inquiry on April 20th with a long letter that detailed what type of help he could give their experimental practices.

The magician addressed his concise response letter to Sherman C. Grifford and offered to write a manual to teach field agents the art of sleight of hand. He explained that three points would be central to the manual:

1. Supplying physical and psychological background facts for understanding why a "procedure" was suggested. Part of the background would address erroneous views on description such as the hand being quicker than the eye.

2. Detailed descriptions of techniques for use in all operation that would be outlined by the magician. Materials of solid, liquid or gaseous

113

form would be addressed. Manual skills would be outlined for mastery.

3.   A variety of examples would be provided to show in detail how to make use of techniques and methods previously described. The examples would be given with varying situations and accommodate procedures that were physical, verbal or psychological.

The techniques, the magician explained, could be responsible for covertly administering materials of a "solid, liquid or gaseous form" without detection. In typical Mulholland fashion, he addressed the psychological background of deception, explaining that he would have to re-train the minds of the agents, or, as he put it, "the operators."

The contents of this letter, only previously viewed with large amounts redacted by the government, is one full page, and encourages the reader to understand that no muscular technique of years training would be required. In fact, though the subtlety for which Mulholland was renowned was the product of fifty years practice, he knew that he would be addressing ham-fisted novices. Therefore he would have to create, teach and train agents in methods that were not only clever but also easily grasped, so that they could be quickly understood, re-taught, and then put into practice.

He wrote, "No manipulation will be suggested that requires training of muscles not normally used, nor any necessitating long practice." He noted that his work would take eighteen to twenty weeks and he understood that his work would be reviewed every two weeks. While his letter was varying in its degree of specifics the contents obviously made sense to Gottlieb: it got Mulholland the job. In fact it may have been his discretion that helped get him the assignment; Agency procedure was to never mention anything by name, specifically projects and people's names.

One of the interesting documents concerning John Mulholland's involvement with U.S. government and the MK-ULTRA team was the oath of secrecy he was obligated to sign. Called "Restricted Security Information: MEMORANDUM OF UNDERSTANDING" he signed a four-point document that stated:

1.   I acknowledge the fact that because of the confidential relationship between myself and the U.S. Government, I will be recipient of information which, in itself, or by implications to be drawn there from, will be such that its unlawful disclosure or loose handling may adversely affect

the interest and security of the United States. I realize that the methods of collecting and of using this information itself, as well as the identity of persons involved, are as secret as the substantive information itself and, therefore, must be treated by me with an equal degree of secrecy.

2. I shall always recognize that the U.S. Government has the sole interest in all information which I or my organization may possess, compile or acquire pursuant to this understanding. No advantage or gain will be sought by me as a result of the added significance or value of such information may have, due to the Government's interest in it.

3. I solemnly pledge my word that I will never divulge, publish, nor reveal either by word, conduct, or by any other means such information or knowledge, as indicated above, unless specifically authorized to do so.

4. Nothing in this understanding is to be taken as imposing any restriction upon the normal business practices of myself or my organization; i.e. information normally possessed by us or gathered in the regular course of business will continue to be utilized in accordance with our normal guidelines.

Signed,   Countersigned,

John Mulholland   Robert V. Lashbrook
November 14, 1953   Technical Services Staff

Four years into his work for the CIA, on October 3, 1957, Mulholland wrote to Gottlieb:

Dear Sir,

The task you assigned to me is progressing to my satisfaction and will, I believe, please you. However, since I saw you, I have reached the conclusion that further examples should be offered in the work I am doing. These will not, I feel certain, extend the time needed to complete the task and should make my work of more use to you. I shall go ahead on this premise unless I hear from you to the contrary.

I have arranged my schedule so as to work steadily on the assignment until it is completed.

Sincerely yours,

John Mulholland

Surely, Mulholland was adopting the Agency code of silence and also standing by his edict to younger magicians, "Always make the client feel as if they are getting quality at a bargain."

From 1953 to 1958 he combined his expertise as a teacher, writer and performer to create methods of deception for the Cold War that were "physical, verbal and psychological" as stated in his original letter to the Agency from April 1953. Mulholland had every reason to believe that the elements of the magician's craft he brought to the War Department would be helpful. Jasper Maskelyne of Great Britain had already proved how important a magician's contribution could be in World War II by outwitting the Desert Fox in North Africa.

In 1947 the U.S. Army felt they were woefully behind the efforts of Soviet and Chinese psychic research. The uncommon practices included torturous interrogation techniques such as partial drowning and sensory deprivation. Torture was not enacted solely for the sake of beating up an enemy. The exhaustion of the mind well beyond feeling pain created a pathway for information to be "attacked."

Harnessing such "mind power" was of great interest to the MK-ULTRA scientists. The scientists believed that the mind that no longer had fear was a more sensitive mind. They conjectured that a mind that was exhausted would pick up subtler signals of "psychic communication." Declassified materials from 1949 indicate that experiments using sensory deprivation also wrought a state of mind where sensory deprivation also brought on another kind of heightened "sensory awareness."

In 1947 the U.S. Department of War knew that China had a 2000-year history of conditioning the mind. This included such precise dogma as what vitamins obtained from roots and berries aided better memory *and intuition*. Chinese medicine, in 1953, was still grounded in some ancient tenets of Tibetan Buddhism. These medical practices were endorsed by the Tibetan leader in exile, His Holiness the Dalai Lama. The affect of Chinese medicine – including consultation with an "Oracle" who seemed to speak in divine tongues – was mysterious enough to be taken seriously as an area of inquiry by Pentagon officials seeking defense against a complex enemy, already using practices that did not come under what would become the Geneva Convention. The notion that the Americans found intriguing and disturbing was that "developed" minds were capable of spreading Communist propaganda. The U.S. Army felt incapable to train operatives in such "mind control" methods that were practiced behind the Iron and Bamboo curtains.

It is reasonable to assume that the Russian intelligentsia was aware of Dr. J. B. Rhine's worldwide fame as a psychic researcher at Duke University. It was also strongly suspected that the Russian intelligence agencies actively sought verification of extra sensory perception through laboratory testing. Such testing was later verified by a researcher named Leonid Vasiliev, a professor of physiology at the University of Leningrad and founder of the Soviet psychical research movement. Statistical experiments were undertaken that involved correct "hits" or guesses by psychic test subjects at nearly forty different universities across the USSR. It was hoped that these tests would verify the genuine nature of clairvoyance, precognition, and possibly the complicated concept of retro-psychokinesis, which, briefly, is the notion of altering the course of time. The method was to isolate "psychics" and see if their thoughts could be "sent" great distances. The MK-ULTRA scientists in Washington adopted this practice (known in the 1970's as "Project Stargate"). Vasiliev theorized that telepathy could be induced through a "post hypnotic trance" and was used to attempt "seeing" over vast distances. One student group in Moscow (alluded to in declassified papers from this period) hoped that Communist doctrine could be spread by hundreds of "sensitives" psychically projecting their beliefs. It is unknown if the U.S. government knew of Vasiliev at this time, but telepathy during the Cold War years was a hot topic behind closed doors of those infected with so-called "Cold War paranoia."

The House Un-American Activities Committee suggested that a Hollywood party game called "Read My Mind" practiced by actors, dancers and directors was, indicative of Communist sympathies. Given the extroversion of the players, usually one man in drag get-up would adopt the role of a seer, sometimes called "Madame Fifi" and have the audience howl at "her" outlandish and accurate claims. Sometimes whole parties were organized around this game, which drew the attention of undercover watchdogs for Communist practices in Hollywood. Noted TV director Stanley "Stosh" Prager, and dancer Paul Draper were blacklisted because of such scandalous accusations being included in dossiers assembled by the FBI about "agitating miscreants" (J. Edgar Hoover's words describing Charlie Chaplin and other assumed Communist sympathizers). The investigation of "un-American activities" reached the highest echelon of the American film community. For example, director Elia Kazan willfully provided names of his contemporaries as Communist sympathizers. Rumor and fact combined indistinguishably creating a blizzard of paranoia, and helped fuel Senator Joseph McCarthy's "Red Scare."

The world of intelligence, during these embryonic years, was skewed, driven and wrought with indifference to the public it investigated. However, the enemy perceived was real, and Communists had the upper hand in psychological warfare.

Mulholland was a welcome addition to the defense of the United States by the CIA to help quash the spread of propaganda and worse. In the 1960's Mulholland consulted with an un-named source to help not-so-subtle pro American messages intertwined in the broadcasts of Radio Free Europe.

CIA operative Philip Agee described the Agency in his book *Inside the Company* as "a bastion of covert activity that were somewhere between correct, polite diplomacy and outright military invasion."

"World Renowned Magician"
John Mulholland

Mulholland was obviously more suited to the diplomatic world. It was said of the magician during his lifetime that he was "like a diplomat." His command of history was clever and often useful when dealing with the political problems of running a magazine. Therefore, his negotiation of and position in the organized world of illusion provided the talents he needed as an attaché to what government researchers David Wise and Thomas Ross term the "Invisible Government," or the intelligence community at large.

What the magician did not know, however, was just how deep his contributions would be. On the surface he was just a hired hand – a consultant, nothing more. Soon enough, however, the paranoia-driven scientists would seize upon Mulholland's thoughts and writings and become obsessed with controlling the mind – something the magician was rather adept at.

IV. THE CIA & LSD

"There are ways in which it can go wrong.
As that is so of any operation of war.
And certainly in a deception plan."

– The Hon. Ewen H.S. Montagu,
from *The Man Who Never Was*, 1943

LSD (lysergic acid diethylamide-25) was discovered by Dr. Albert Hoffman in 1938. Dr. Hoffman found that the drug had the potential to be a respiratory stimulant and originally intended to market it as an asthma medication. LSD is a white, odorless powder, and is one of the most potent mind-altering chemicals known to man. During the 1960's, LSD was legally prescribed and was trademarked as Delysid. Its effects are highly variable. A typical "trip" lasts anywhere from 8 to 12 hours, gradually tapering off in intensity. The "journey" the mind takes under the influence of LSD can include anxiety, heightened awareness (noticing cracks in paint), hallucinations of a visual and audio nature, and radical temperature change. The popular culture representation of the psychedelic aspects of an LSD trip are not universal. The LSD "flashback" is a reality – the repeating of experiences weeks and even months after the drug has, seemingly, worn off.

Sidney Gottlieb's nickname was "Merlin the Great Wizard." Known as the "chief poisoner" for the Agency, he began his service in 1951, after obtaining a degree in chemistry at California Institute of Technology. He retired in 1973 amidst front-page controversy for Agency tests on "victims of surreptitious drugging" between 1953 and 1966. He was also given the CIA's greatest medal for achievement upon his retirement. It was Gottlieb who brought LSD to the CIA. He said, in 1999, that he had experimented with the drug 177 times and enjoyed the drug that Bob Dylan said, "gave people the right idea." Drugging the staff was nothing new.

The OSS was the precursor to the CIA, and had been developing a truth drug, derivative of marijuana, as early as 1943. Marijuana too was disseminated without the public's knowledge, on "unwitting subjects." This phrase is the cornerstone of the MK-ULTRA project and is perhaps the most important detail concerning John Mulholland's involvement with this massive war plan. LSD was code-named "stormy."

Another element added to the use of LSD was hypnotism, as detailed in warfare by G. H. Estabrooks as early as 1943. The plan for induced amnesia was fully detailed and was argued as "not theoretical" by several well known psychologists. It gave the government men pause to consider that such "technology" could be used against their forces, who were ill-equipped to deal with such "programming."

On June 9, 1953 Dr. Gottlieb wrote a "memorandum for the record" concerning LSD. He stated that the work on the drug had been approved as TOP SECRET and that the budget was $40,290 to be spent until September 11, 1954. The money was specified as a "philanthropic grant." The Agency has kept secret where this money initially came from.

A source of this money may have been Nelson Rockefeller personally. During the course of this research, this writer met one insider who said of Rockefeller's involvement in covert activities, "Oh, Nelson was strictly State Department." Nelson Rockefeller was heavily involved in the creation of intelligence agencies before, during, and after World War II. It is also possible that these funds were funneled through the Geschickter Fund named after Dr. Charles Geschickter who was a researcher and founder of MK-ULTRA. Others have suggested that The Rockefeller Foundation or Rockefellers Brothers Fund channeled money to this operation, but no evidence has been found to support this hypothesis. From roughly 1947 to 1963, the Agency spent nearly eight million dollars on clandestine practices involving drugs and hypnosis. However, the Agency has only admitted (in 1995) to spending 10 million over 20 years. The yearly budget for MK-ULTRA was between $400,000 and $650,000.

One thing was for sure. Every penny during the beginning years of clandestine intelligence operations was scrupulously looked after, as further funding came because of "results."

Gottlieb specifically stated that LSD was to be used in conjunction with hypnosis—to render subjects more susceptible to the process—and that the team would study the "biochemical, neuropsychological, sociological, clinical and psychological" effects of the drug. Another aspect of the Agency's use was to induce anxiety in subjects and investigate other reactions in the name of science.

The first person known to take LSD in the U.S. was Dr. Robert Hyde at the Boston Psychopathic Hospital in 1943. It seemed no one made the obvious connection to Robert Louis Stevenson's character of Dr. Jeykll's drug-altered ego Mr. Hyde and the transformative nature of the drug LSD. Hyde was a consultant to the Agency. Gottlieb and his staff all took the drug. The work with LSD for covert practices was carried out over a 20-year period under the project names: BLUEBIRD, ARTICHOKE, MK-ULTRA, MK-SEARCH, MK-DELTA and finally as a project of the Office of Research and Development (ORD).

Though illegal in the U.S. today, LSD is still being used by psychiatrists in Switzerland. It is used in the treatment of paranoia and schizophrenia. Sometimes dramatic, unpleasant psychological reactions occur. These include panic, confusion, and anxiety. The building of anxiety was one definite goal of the MK-ULTRA scientists. The hazards of this drug are purely psychological. The common problem is that the drug can release a latent psychosis or exacerbate depression. There is also the danger of incautious behavior such as misjudging distances or, "thinking one can fly." In one detailed 18-hour trip, one LSD user kept sane by recording his thoughts in a journal during the experience. Time dated intervals give a detailed picture of the free associating mind calming down over the period during which the drug took hold. In a scrawling hand, he records, "my eyelashes are rainbows that drip like slow molasses. Taking off like rockets, a sea of unending dots were the exhaust. Christ was walking around my closet in miniature looking for water while carrying a hoe. A German shepherd sat speaking English to me on my bed while I wondered why my genitals ached so." The most tell tale aspect of this unique record is the handwriting. Two words per page indicate the speed at which he wrote, and as the tripper "comes down" his handwriting slowly begins to conform to the page.

Purportedly, the best remedy for someone feeling bad effects is calm talking, and the reassurance that the "trip" will soon end. A safe, comforting environment is key to any remedy.

Mulholland's papers concerning his work for the Agency during this LSD experimentation period tell the dramatic story of magician Mulholland acting with patriotism.

In April 1953 there is indication in Mulholland's handwriting of contact with people with the last names deFlores (actually Admiral Luis deFlorenz who was the Agency's research Chairman and who opposed prosecution of Gottlieb for his LSD experiments), Lashbrook, Cornelius, Roosevelt, and the notorious Dr. Gottlieb. Along with the handwritten names by Mulholland and Wolf are the government men's phone numbers. The notations reflect meetings prior to March 1953. It is conjectured by some that Mulholland may have actually been involved with the OSS when it was in formation and simply came along with the staff that formed consultants to the CIA of 1947.

Perhaps the most notable aspect of the correspondence Mulholland kept is the expense record all parties kept very careful tabs on. After Mulholland's first letter of April 20, 1953, "Sherman Grifford" responded on May 5, 1953:

The project outlined in your letter of April 20 has been approved by us, and you are hereby authorized to spend up to $3,000.00 in the next six months in the execution of this work.

At a median of $500 per month for six months, the magician had a nice added income amidst show and lecture fees. This was considerable earning in 1953. $3,000 in 1950's currency is the equivalent of $15,500 in the early 21st century. One notable point about the money and the timetable is that the government men wanted Mulholland's manual on deception for field operatives as soon as possible. There is urgency written into the timetable for payments to the magician and the due date of the material he was writing.

That "Sherman C. Grifford" was, in fact, actually Sidney Gottlieb is reinforced by the fact that Mulholland's handwritten notes (which usually preceded typewritten copy) depict visits from Gottlieb at the magician's New York office and home. On one sheet, Mulholland scratches out the typewritten contact with Grifford, as if to remind himself that Grifford was only the pen name of the man he was meeting[8].

Yet, it is Sherman C. Grifford who approves Mulholland's contract to "execute" this written work. The CIA men were looking for a powerful truth drug because they feared a "Manchurian Candidate" brainwashed assassin hidden within the folds of government power. What had been tried in 1943 with marijuana by the OSS was now used by the CIA in 1953 with LSD. "Truth" is important to define here. The words "truth drug" do not refer to the notion popularized in motion pictures as a "tell-all" drug. The truth behind the truth drug is, rather, a simulacrum to a prosthesis that would extend the human perceptual apparatus into "hidden realms" or information previously kept secret, according to psychedelic writer and researcher, Terence McKenna.

Richard Condon's 1959 novel, probably written while some of these events were actually occurring in Washington labs, was drawn from discussions he had with military intelligence officers who alerted him to events in Korea in the 1950's. "Conditioning was intensified repetition," one character remarks in the opening pages of *The Manchurian Candidate*. What the public was yet to learn was that these words were written with the truth in mind. While dramatized, history has borne out the unfortunate revelation that this story was in fact based on genuine experimentation in mind control by the U. S. and Communist powers since the 1940's.

John Mulholland officially signed his oath of allegiance to the CIA in November of 1953, shortly after his first assignment began. The oddity of his signed pledge was that it is the first and probably only official document corroborating his allegiance to the Agency.

He probably spent the rest of his life associating with those involved in the cult of intelligence. As an intellectual, he had finally jumped the greatest hurdle of his career: his intelligence and passion for deception had now grown into a paid consultancy to the most elaborate intelligence agency ever created.

In 1975 ex-CIA operative Philip Agee wrote that the CIA:

> "Is the biggest and most powerful secret service that has ever existed. The CIA has 16,500 employees and an annual budget of 750 million dollars. That doesn't include its mercenary armies or its commercial subsidiaries. Add them all together, the Agency employs or subsidizes hundreds of thousands of people and spends billions every year. Its official budget is secret; it's concealed in those of other Federal agencies. By law, the CIA is not accountable to Congress."

To this, only Kurt Singer's pithy remark can be added, "The history of warfare is the history of espionage."

In 1925, John Mulholland had spent a considerable amount of time together with Jasper Maskelyne and another Maskelyne theatre performer named Oswald Williams. Seen with interlocked arms at the stage entrance, Maskelyne and Mulholland who became the two most famous war magicians of the 20th century, little realized during their backstage "magic jams" that their expertise for deception would be called upon by their governments for extended periods of time. However, learning of Maskelyne's aid to the British military against Rommel during World War II left no doubt for Mulholland that he could do the same for his country.

After a life of regret not being able to help the country that provided him with a first class education and travel to foreign lands; the country that gave him opportunity to pursue his passion for an old, but newly recognized art form (largely due to his contributions), John Mulholland, age 55, became an intellectual patriot – a role perfectly suited to his interests.

Eight months prior to his first recorded involvement with Gottlieb and the MK-ULTRA world, Mulholland published a penetrating review of the flying saucer phenomenon in September 1952. While he brought his considerable eloquence to bear on modern phenomenon, he also ventured into interpreting hallucinations. Like his debunking of the

Indian rope trick throughout his career, he wrote that "hallucinations were commoner than you may think" and went on to substantiate that ten percent of all people considered well-balanced experienced hallucinations. He also concluded that because of the atomic bomb detonated in Hiroshima, people were jittery about the Atomic Age and this led directly to the hallucination and fear of flying saucers. Though, he did offer tongue-in-cheek that:

> "I could be wrong 100 per cent. Maybe next week a saucer will land on the earth and be put on exhibition where we can see it, touch it, examine it. Until then I shall go right ahead thinking that flying saucers are a state of mind for four decades of magic have taught me that honest, intelligent, alert men and women can, by suggestion, quite easily be made to see things which aren't."

Aspects of the science fiction alluded to by the magician became very Earthly realities during wartime. Mulholland's illusions taught him about hallucinations and faulty perception. In fact, he'd had forty years practice as an illusionist. He, perhaps, had more "field work" than anybody really knew.

On the right, Oswald Williams, John Mulholland, Jasper Maskelyne outside St. George's Hall, 1925, England.

John Mulholland shown wearing tag and badge of 1939 convention, shown below. He truly never threw anything away! His familiarity with such articles gave him the tools with which to create "tricks" with common objects for intelligence work. Photo: Everett Duncan.

14TH ANNUAL International Brotherhood of Magicians CONVENTION BATTLE CREEK MICHIGAN 1939

JOHN MULHOLLAND

"He never threw anything away."

1. Background Discussion of Deception.

2. Pills
   a. About 1/4 size of aspirin tablet.) (1) Standard shapes.
   b. Aspirin Tablet.   ) (2) Unusual shapes.
   c. Alka Seltzer tablet.   )

3. Liquids
   a. One drop.
   b. 1 cc (20 drops, about 1/5 teaspoonful)
   c. 5 cc (about 1 teaspoonful)

4. Solid material in loose form (like salt)
   xx one speck up to about 1/5 teaspoonful

5. The Theory and Practice of Free Choice.

6. The Theory and Practice of Picking up Things.

7. Concealment.

8. The Proper Time and Place.

Dr. Sidney Gottlieb
Robert Lashbrook
District 7 - 1334

126

V. SOME OPERATIONAL APPLICATIONS OF THE ART OF DECEPTION

"It was Herrmann's contention that a magician is born and not made. Probably he was right, for a performer has to be naturally adapted to magic. He also has to be trained, even as training is necessary for a singer possessed of an exceptional voice; but he must be born with an aptitude for mystifying."

– John Mulholland
The New York Times Magazine, 1933

After three weeks of discussion, on May 5, 1953, Mulholland was officially on the payroll at a median of five hundred dollars a week to write a manual that would cover as he detailed in a handwritten outline:

I.   Methods of trickery contrary to popular opinion
II.   Examples of wrong thinking about methods of magicians, gamblers, pickpockets etc. and confidence men. Note why each is wrong.
III.   Cite differences between magicians and all other tricksters.
IV.   No single or right way to perform any trick.
V.   What is time! Be not observed (How to remove salt from table and put in pocket)
VI.   Timing – Naturalness of manner
VII.   Planning a trick
VIII.   Suggestion by pantomime
IX.   What is not noticed; manner, attention, posture, actions. Descriptions (false) of supposed aid or enemy
X.   Thinking behind trickery and knowledge of those for whom trick is done
XI.   Attributes of successful performance

Mulholland titled his manual *Some Operational Applications of the Art of Deception.*

Mulholland's outline was quickly condensed during the next two months. After further discussion with Washington he reduced the manual and submitted five sections, as of November 11, 1953, covering:

I.   Underlying bases for successful performance

II.   Tricks with pills
III.   Tricks with loose solids (such as salt)
IV.   Tricks with liquids
V.   Tricks whereby small objects may be obtained secretly

Continuing in the cloak of magicians' and spy secrecy, at no time was John Mulholland ever to represent the methods he detailed in direct terms. "Tricks" was the applicable word for operative missions, as the Agency had to have been watching for what he was doing before his tome was complete.

When it is seen what the magician offered and what the government requested and received in six months, a definite target is seen: a manual for the covert deployment of substances, most likely pernicious drugs. Whether the drugs were administered to kill or to alter behavior under observation is a matter of conjecture.

It is probable that both were goals of the Agency at this time.

Chapter Five (Tricks Whereby Small Objects May Be Obtained Secretly) is particularly interesting in that it typifies the first assignment of the magician's work for the Agency. Chapter Five also has the most deletions of any chapters released to the public by the CIA. It reveals the directions of why certain things are noticed and other actions are not – the guts of covert work.

The reader not familiar with deceptive ways might gloss over the words "small objects." However what these small objects were is paramount to understanding the entire MK-ULTRA program. Especially when it is added that whatever these things were, they had to be small and it had to be a secret that you had it (or had obtained it).

What is small and "to be obtained" secretly?

The manual details paper matches, paper money, a coin or two, a pencil, and perhaps a woman's compact – all articles used to deliver unspecified powders and liquids, and the most exotic of drugs and chemical and biological agents such as a hit of LSD or a "fast acting" (dissolving) pill secreted on a concealed needle.

He detailed how to remove the rubber eraser end of a pencil, hollow out the pencil a little, shave down the rubber eraser and then create a hiding place for powders, of one to fifteen grains, to be disseminated when the rubber stopper was removed just like uncorking a small vial. He later gave more elaborate instruction for a pencil that would deliver greater quantities of loose solids, and the directions on how to switch in a "loaded" pencil for one that had been making sketches on a beer matt. Later, when discussing liquids covertly deployed, polyethylene tubing replaced the pencil to discharge 2cc's of liquid in an almost invisible stream. One can see Mulholland's technical training from his school days in this area of *Some Operational Applications of the Art of Deception*. At one point in the opening chapter he even acknowledges his verbosity but claims that, "The writer is quite willing to acknowledge being both wordy and obvious provided the reader, thereby, invariably has success in his work." He grilled his students because he wanted them to do well.

Small objects could be concealed easily and would avoid any particular notice if the object were common enough. The magician writes about the differences between old money and new money, "You will arouse no suspicion if you take some loose old bills out of your pocket and they are slightly crumpled. Were you to present five crisp new bills, the mind is stirred to examine what it does not frequently see. Old money goes unseen because it is so common. New money gets a second glance. It draws attention."

Above all he stated over and over again in the final manual: DO THINGS WHICH ARE NOT UNUSUAL TO MAN OR WOMAN. Or, he put it a little more elegantly, "Tricksters should never do anything to attract notice." He also counseled the agents with a slight variation of advice he received from his teacher John William Sargent who taught him to perform in his own manner, not as an imitator of others. He writes in Chapter One of his manual:

> *"There is never a single secret for any trick. Neither is there a correct or an incorrect way to perform a trick. The sole criterion is that the method to be used is the one to insure the trick's success. There are two chief reasons for picking a particular method. One is that it fits the physique, mannerisms, and personality of the performer better than any other method. The other is that the conditions at the time of performance favor a particular method."*

He goes on to discuss timing and writes: "The other point in timing is the cadence in a series of actions. The accent is given to what is to be noticed. There will be little attention to those actions which are not stressed."

In fact, Mulholland went so far as to train the agents only how to do things that they already did. He discusses reasonable action combined with timing. He notes that spectators – a term used by magicians frequently when discussing audiences – are often given something reasonable to think about by a magician, or in this case, trickster. He notes, "Apart from the required actions, the extra actions (covert operations) will not be noticed". Primarily, he concedes, trickery is "an acted lie."

He notes that it is hard to perform a trick when the agent is nervous. He writes "It is hard to act at ease when you are up to trickery...there is more thought and care needed to act out a lie than tell one." He notes that false actions must remain natural, which brings to mind the assassination of a Mafia informer, named Pauly, in the film *The Godfather*. The driver of the car, Pauly, is put at ease as one man leaves the car to relieve himself. In a moment of pause the assassin strikes, much as Mulholland dictates, though in less direct terms.

Mulholland notes the crucial context in which trickery is performed successfully. He cites the importance of posture when executing trickery and warns agents, "Confidence is a direct result of preparation. The easier a deception is to do, warrants that you have every detail firmly in mind." And he counsels that natural actions are the height of deceptive practices and that "a person who seems to be interested in what it is that he is doing will not be noticed. But, one whose interest is directed toward what others are doing will attract attention." Later he points out that a certain "cadence of actions" is inherent to a trickster's success, and quotes Alphonse Bortillon's statement germane to the psychological precepts of performing trickery: "Only can one see what one observes, and one observes only things which are already in the mind."

Cardini working in close for John Mulholland &
Dorothy Wolf at the magician's home.
The closer you look, the less you see.

Prior to his expertise being put to use by the CIA, John Mulholland was a veteran at selling and publishing articles on how magicians do their work in popular magazines and newspapers. In *Stage* magazine in the middle of the Great Depression, he wrote a full two-page essay about how the audience fools itself. With a portrait of his hands by Alfredo Valento – who also made a photographic portrait of Helen Hay's hands in the same issue – Mulholland no doubt intrigued the reader with such truisms of the magician's craft as: *The magicians can largely discount the factor of memory in the observer.* And then as if he were a school teacher, when discussing the vanishing of a coin, he writes:

> *"Let me illustrate. Making the coin disappear (one of the simplest, and therefore one of the most difficult, of tricks) involves at least fifty separate operations on the part of the magician ... Now the alert observer knows in his subconscious, as well as in his conscious*

mind, what is the normal and to-be expected sequence of events – especially in his subconscious mind, which rules him to a greater extent than he is aware...Just because the observer is alert, his imagination jumps ahead of the magician's operations. While he is ahead with the expected, the unexpected quietly takes place. If the observer is exceptionally keen and attentive, he is only the more completely in the magician's power."

Discussing the field of vision, the magician shows the difference between a performer on the stage and close up actions. For example, when standing next to a person, the ability to view a hand entering a pocket is nearly invisible. Mulholland was familiar with practically every magician in North America from the turn of the century on, and his wisdom on deception imparted to operatives is actually drawn, in this case, from one "Professor" Louis (nicknamed "Pop") Krieger, the first in a line of a dynasty of magicians that included his son-in-law, Al Flosso and his grandson, the late Jackie Flosso.

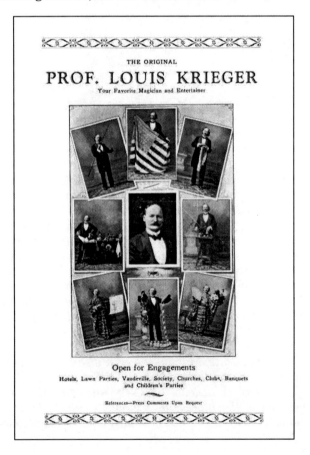

THE ORIGINAL

PROF. LOUIS KRIEGER

Your Favorite Magician and Entertainer

Open for Engagements

Hotels, Lawn Parties, Vaudeville, Society, Churches, Clubs, Banquets
and Children's Parties

References—Press Comments Upon Request

*Krieger's methods influenced Mulholland's
technical writing for the CIA.*

Krieger was known as a friend of the outcast, one to hobnob with the poor and downtrodden and to bring smiles and laughter to the melting pot of New York between the late 1880's and his death in the 1930's. What was so unusual about Pop Krieger was that he liked to work with his audience so close at hand that he could feel their shoulders touching his own. Having been booked by an agent known to Houdini, named Fred Melville, Krieger went to Europe to entertain at Maskelyne's Theatre of Magic called the Egyptian Hall (and later St. George's Hall) and wound up with a Command Performance for King Edward VII.

However, because of differences between Krieger and the Maskelyne theatre proprietor, David Devant, Krieger abandoned the engagement and had to be found in time to fill the Command Performance for the king. The king was astounded by Krieger drawing from the king's pockets a string of dainty ladies lingerie, and the stunt sent the king howling. Edward the VII was so close at hand, he did not see Krieger "load" the king's pockets; a doubly astounding feat because the royal guard had distinctly informed the German–accented magician that he was not to get more than twenty feet near the king. Mulholland notes in his manual "It is more than twice as hard for the spectator to observe the simultaneous, though varied, actions of two hands as it is to follow the movements of one hand."

A commoner by nature, but devious and clever as a fox, Krieger was the model for Mulholland's statement that, "However, to be able to appear stupid purposely in order to enhance one's work shows a considerable degree of intelligence as well as an appreciation of the art of acting." Like many actors' preparation, the planning of a trick by a magician, trickster, or government operative was the result of great planning provoking Mulholland to write: "He (the trickster) must know, as well, when conditions of the moment demand a change in the prepared procedure and how to make a such a change without being disturbed. Actors call this "ad-libbing," magicians call it "improvising," athletes call it "working the time."

Some of Krieger's methods became integral to Mulholland's dictum to agents for the CIA during the Cold War!

Later in Mulholland's manual, he entertains himself at the agent's expense (perhaps without the agents knowing it).

The magician counsels the agents to affect a stupid gaze and demeanor.

Mulholland even drew two self portraits (though the agents reading this were not aware that the portraits were of the author) concerning this use of facial muscles. Relaxed for happy and stupid; wild and flaring to signal alertness and attention getting.

Of asking the agents to affect a stupid demeanor, he writes "This writer suggested earlier in this manual that I would only ask you to perform tasks common to your every day duties. At this time I might ask the exception that in the course of performing trickery you act with the appearance of stupidity. Surely this is something not regular to your routine and I offer my apologies for this exception."

Mulholland suggests that agents observe a necessity in assigning blame to a "fictional party" were an "operation" fouled up. He counsels to keep the description average, describing a person of average height and weight. Normal coloring, but with the exception of perhaps, a missing digit! He offers to the "readers" of this manual (Gottlieb among them):

134

1. *Tricksters have reason to credit or accuse some imaginary person with what has been done. The correct and incorrect use of details in telling an unfactual story is somewhat confusing. Given that these methods are easy, there should be no difficulty with words.*

2. *With your mind and my methods there should be no real difficulty.*

3. *A natural mistake is to describe someone of form and actions, which are universal and striking. Have some remarkable footage such as a missing joint. But otherwise of a natural countenance. Note a large mole on the face. Make your story acceptable to listeners, but hard to track.*

The note of a missing digit and the curious use of the word "footage" may have been directed at Sidney Gottlieb. Gottlieb was known as "The Gimp." He was born with a clubfoot although he later mastered folk dancing. Gottlieb also stuttered.

Mulholland seems to be directing agents to pick an imaginary character who resembled the head agent who employed him. As his friend George Gordon often said, Mulholland had an unusual sense of humor. One person noted that he was similar to a fox, clever and resourceful.

Later in the final manual, when discussing the practice of sending information through physical cues (to be explored later) he instructs the agent in a process of counting. With two agents working in collusion, each would begin counting to themselves via the repetition of the phrase "One great big chimpanzee. Two great big chimpanzees..." and so on.

Basically he was instructing the agents to:

First, appear stupid.

Next, silently count to themselves using a ridiculous phrase concerning monkeys.

Third, if there was need for assigning blame to an imaginary person, the description should suggest a person with a deformity, perhaps a missing digit.

A look at the final manual Mulholland submitted shows the magician writing with precision. He shows a level of human understanding and observation that would dazzle most psychologists.

He viewed his instructions to agents as virtual minuets of deception that became unstoppable plans of attack.

He was the perfect man for the job, with a clean record of group affiliation. And, to use the CIA's own words, he was also available to be "exploited." Further definition of "exploitation" via CIA inner dictum is unavailable. Most likely when someone joined the Agency, *the work came first*. This was clearly demonstrated by Sidney Gottlieb experimenting on himself. The work came *first*. An insight into the Clandestine Services oath can be seen in the "outing" of Valerie Plame, the CIA operative wife of Ambassador Joseph Wilson. Plame said, "If I did not talk about what I do when I was under cover, then I will certainly not talk about it now."

His role and how the CIA scientists viewed him can be glimpsed in Mulholland's opening page in his 1963 *Book of Magic*. He writes in the second paragraph: *"Realizing magic deals only with what to other people is impossible, modern magicians have to keep ahead of scientists who daily open doors through which just yesterday only magicians could enter. "* Hiring a magician also fulfills Agency dictum that the embryonic CIA was made up of unusual consultants.

In addition to showing how to dope up someone's drink, the methods he dictates are brilliant and simple. Mulholland wrote in his *Book of Magic*, "The simplicity of the plot adds to the effectiveness of the magic." Had he been discussing his role as a CIA training operative, he would have replaced the word "magic" with the word "mission." In both texts he added "What people recall seeing is often the case of remembering details which assume primary importance. Actually all details are important. As the reader is well aware, in magic all details are important and particularly those which appear to be inconsequential."

Somewhat oddly, he adds to this 1963 text: "The successful performance of magic is not the result of hypnosis or mind control." Later, after meeting George N. Gordon, he became enamored of the work of Dr. Theodore X. Barber, an MIT University author on LSD and hypnosis. Though he still felt "lukewarm," (according to Gordon) that largely the reactions by people to hypnotists were "a bunch of bunk" he did tell his friend Gordon that he had "re-evaluated his position on hypnosis in light of what Dr. Barber says." Gordon also noted that Mulholland was influenced by the thoughts of Solomon Ash at Queens College.

Given the mind of the magician, it is clear Mulholland was able to make suggestions to the MK-ULTRA scientists and to open their minds to further areas of inquiry – the primary job of the magician.

VI. THANKSGIVING 1953:
DR. FRANK OLSON'S DEATH

"I am sure that all of you have learned that old wives tale," Yen stated, "which is concerned with the belief that no hypnotized subject may be forced to do that which is repellent to his moral nature, whatever that is, or to his own best interests. That is nonsense, of course."

— Richard Condon, *The Manchurian Candidate*

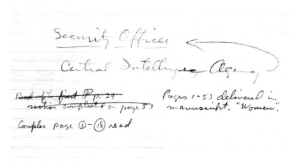

John Mulholland's note on delivery of materials.

Mulholland originally suggested a six-month timetable to write his manual. On November 11, 1953, Mulholland requested an extension until May of 1954. Sidney Gottlieb wrote a memorandum dated 29 April 1954, which stated:

Subject: Extension of Time for MK-ULTRA, Subproject 19:

1. Subproject 19 is an extension of Subproject 4. The original description of subproject 19 is attached to this memorandum.

2. An extension of time is needed in order to grant Mr. Mulholland more time to complete this task. The original estimated completion date was May 1, 1954. It is noted that the completion date estimate is now extended to November 1, 1954.

"Grifford" approved this request for an extension, and as of December 31, 1953, Mulholland provided a statement to the government showing receipt of $3,703.26 for the previous year's work.

During Mulholland's involvement with the MK-ULTRA scientists, Dr. Frank Olson, a military biochemist and the acting temporary head of the CIA Special Operations Division (SOD), was given a dose of LSD on November 19, 1953 without his knowledge by Dr. Sidney Gottlieb. Dr. Frank Olson ingested the LSD unwittingly.

Eight days later, the day after Thanksgiving, on Friday, November 28, Olson, age 43, the father of three young children, apparently committed suicide by hurling himself out of a tenth story (sometimes mistaken as 13th story) window across from Penn Station in New York City.

In the aftermath of this debacle of Cold War efforts, the conclusive report stated that Dr. Frank Olson suffered from manic depression. Poor Dr. Olson did not have the benefit of writing his thoughts as they came – it might have calmed him down.

There is no record in Mulholland's very detailed files that there was trouble brewing with the men he was involved with on November 25, 1953. That was the day that Mulholland met Frank Olson[§].

The government's intention for the meeting was that the magician might cheer up the unsettled scientist, who clearly stated that he wanted "out" of the newly born CIA. Olson realized that his synthesizing deadly microbes into modern aerosol sprays, which were tested on humans in prisons in Europe and on university campuses, was inhumane.

Seven days earlier, a group of scientists from the Army Chemical Corps met at the Deep Creek Lodge in the woods of western Maryland. Dr. Frank Olson attended.

On the second day of this retreat, November 19, 1953, against the Clandestine Services order, Dr. Sidney Gottlieb spiked the after dinner liqueur, Cointreau, with LSD--even though in later testimony during the Rockefeller Commission hearing, Robert Lashbrook claimed *he* dropped LSD into the Cointreau. All of the attendees were subjected to the drug without their knowledge. However, on this occasion, Gottlieb did not take the drug. Olson, an alleged manic-depressive with ulcer problems, exhibited a psychotic reaction to the drug and became deeply depressed. This behavior grew much worse the following Thanksgiving week. It is unknown if Olson ever knew he had been given a dose of the mind-altering LSD.

[§] Hank Albarelli, a writer on the Olson death, claims that John Marks' recanted his "surmising" Olson was taken to see Mulholland. Fact is, no one but the principle players were there in November 1953. Modern researchers are left to conjecture.

Following a weekend with his wife that brought a downward spiral of severe depression, Dr. Olson admitted to his wife that he had made a "terrible mistake" and exhibited signs of clinical paranoia. Olson approached his superior, Lt. Colonel Ruwet, on the mornings of November 23rd and 24th. Olson did not sleep more than a few hours from the time he took LSD to the time he approached his commander. Ruwet found Olson waiting outside his office at 7:30am, Monday morning, November 23rd. Olson repeatedly claimed that he was "mixed up" and wanted to quit the Special Operations Division, or be fired from his longstanding position. Ruwet ordered him to go to New York the following day with Gottlieb's deputy, Dr. Robert V. Lashbrook. At the last minute, Ruwet decided to go to New York with them. A situation meriting this kind of attention and travel was unique to this group of experimental scientists.

They sought counsel from, Dr. Harold Abramson, an allergist, who worked at Mt. Sinai hospital in New York City, and had CIA Top Secret clearance to treat Olson. (Olson had been part of a team experimenting with biological warfare since 1947, and was "classified" to have come in contact with secretly experimental diseases on a regular basis.) Abramson had interest in neurological disorders, but no qualifications to treat manic depression or the problems attendant to ingesting LSD, which had been manufactured by the Sandoz Company of Switzerland. He was selected because he could keep Olson's treatment quiet, and be relied upon to play ball with "The Company." Limiting the participants' knowledge concerning actual circumstances was standard CIA procedure. In this case, a need-to-know basis was crucial, but it is likely the offending drug was not explained to Abramson.

In fact, on his second visit with the troubled Olson (in one 24-hour period), Abramson brought Olson a bottle of bourbon and the sedative Nembutal to quiet his nerves. It may not have been a bad idea for a general remedy, but combined with the after effects of a dosage of LSD, it was a radical position to take. It has never been disclosed to how many microns of LSD Olson was subjected. Before the third meeting with Abramson, the morning of Wednesday, November 25, Lashbrook, Ruwet and Olson visited Mulholland at the magician's office on West 42nd Street in the center of Manhattan.

Mulholland's secretary Dorothy Wolf was not present, having been away on Thanksgiving holiday. Mulholland's correspondence shortly before and during Ms. Wolf's departure indicates how much the magician missed her company and expertise. She organized all his lecture and show bookings, and answered his phone so he could write and have meetings. The perfect secretary, she expedited his business, bought his materials and traveled with him. As noted previously, Ms. Wolf was also the magician's well-known mistress.

Lashbrook suggested that the magician would be able to cheer up the depressed biochemist. The visit was predetermined during the Washington military men's New York stay, as confirmed by a letter to Mulholland shortly before their visit. Olson was not mentioned by name. Names were often omitted. However, Olson found Mulholland suspicious, especially because of the memorandum that Mulholland was employed to write a manual concerning "the delivery of various materials to unwitting subjects." However, Mulholland performed a few tricks such as the disappearance of a coin and its reappearance in a sealed box of matches inside a ball of wool. Olson ran to the other side of the room, terribly frightened. While Olson did not read Mulholland's manual of deception at this point, he knew what it concerned. The visit was cut short and the magician never saw Olson again. Neither did Olson's family.

That night, November 25, the three Defense Department employees (Ruwet, Olson and Lashbrook) went to the Rodgers and Hammerstein Broadway musical *Me & Juliet*. Curiously, while this musical was generally regarded as not one of the duo's best, the 2nd Act did begin with a notable lighting design, with dazzling spectacle, that may have affected Olson.

Olson left after intermission with paranoiac thoughts that agents outside the theater would arrest him. Olson had enjoyed practical jokes in his life and at the office, often being suspicious of his fellow workers and accusing them as being "a bunch of thespians" when he suspected a prank afoot.

Before their return flight to Washington, Thanksgiving morning, Olson shredded all his money, threw his wallet down a chute, and went missing for hours until he turned up in the Statler Hotel lobby, rocking like a baby in a hotel lobby overstuffed chair. He believed that the cash he carried might be tainted with pernicious chemicals and that his associates were trying to kill him. The biochemist's fears were well founded. Mulholland had been consulting on the transmission of chemicals through common, everyday objects such as coins and currency.

Thanksgiving morning, Thursday, November 27, 1953, the three government men flew to Washington. Upon their arrival, a Special Operations Division driver met them, and Olson lost control, forcing the driver to pull into a Howard Johnson's parking lot, where Lashbrook called Gottlieb, pulling the head CIA scientist from his Thanksgiving dinner.

Gottlieb ordered Lashbrook to take Olson immediately back to New York that afternoon to revisit Abramson. Ruwet stayed in

Washington D.C. while Lashbrook and Olson flew back to New York to meet Abramson at his Long Island office.

Later that night, November 27, Abramson drove Olson and Lashbrook into Manhattan, where they had been earlier that morning departing for Washington. Olson agreed that he was exhibiting psychotic behavior rooted in paranoia.

Twelve hours later, at about 3am, the morning of November 28, Lashbrook stated that he woke at the Statler Hotel to see Olson make a dead headed run and crash through the drawn curtains and window of their hotel room and fall to his death moments later. Amazingly, Olson did not die immediately upon impact and uttered indecipherable words to those that found him on the ground.

Hours before Dr. Olson's fatal plunge, he called his wife from New York and sounded reasonable and sane. The *in house* official verdict of the Agency was that LSD agitated his depression and gave him delusional thoughts of persecution. This is what military men, who met the New York City police said at the discovery of the death afterwards.

John Mulholland's initials and phone number were found in Lashbrook's wallet, when he was asked for identification by the New York City police. The work was routine since Lashbrook was the only person on site at Olson's death. (Conversely, amidst John Mulholland's most private papers was a small pencil written phone message — he genuinely threw nothing away — and on it was the number MU6-5730. The number for the local office of the CIA in New York at this time was MU6-5517.) It seems that no one in intelligence work is regularly addressed by his or her proper name.

Before Lashbrook called the New York police to report the suicide, he called Sidney Gottlieb in Washington. According to the Statler Hotel concierge, who claimed to listen in on the call, Lashbrook told Gottlieb, "Olson's gone." Gottlieb's alleged response was "That's too bad." Why the concierge seems to have listened in on a single hotel call from one of over one hundred rooms seems unlikely and remains unexplained.

Were the CIA men expecting Olson's death?

Later, Lashbrook told the New York City police that he worked for the Department of Defense and invoked high government affiliations. Other than that Lashbrook remained quiet on the matter; and did not offer any explanations for Olson's fall from the hotel window. One New York City detective reported that getting information out of Lashbrook was "like pulling teeth." It still is.

As of 2003, Lashbrook lives on a farm in California under immunity from prosecution and doesn't speak to anyone concerning these matters. It has been the opinion of law enforcement for fifty years that Lashbrook, largely an intellectual, was never in the "muscle" end of the CIA.

Sometime between November 1953 and the final submission of Mulholland's manual in May of 1954, the sentence "Trickery is not practiced on husbands" was put in the manuscript. Was this a refutation that the CIA did not kill men with families? Could this have been a casual denial referring to the doomed Dr. Olson?

The CIA carefully buried the secret behind and circumstances surrounding Olson's death for 22 years. In fact, after Olson died less than three months passed before there was official paperwork discussing the "cover" of the dead biochemist who had a military position. "Covering" Olson's involvement would keep insurance companies from unearthing causes behind the death. Such investigators would also be barred from discovering the true nature of Dr. Olson's work. Disclosing Olson's involvement in various sub-projects and the depth of research was what concerned the MK-ULTRA team.

MK-ULTRA was the program that the U.S. Government was banking on to combat the advent of a "Manchurian Candidate" (real or imagined). Exposing Olson's role in the MK-ULTRA program would have been more disastrous for the clandestine program if discovered at the time of his death. While the death was carefully swept away as a dire consequence of the scientist's clinical depression, the investigators wrote in their reports that "there were many unexplained details." There still are.

The autopsy revealed no cuts due to glass shards. There also was no blood on the broken window Olson apparently jumped through. In addition, there is suspicion that a man could not exert enough force to crash through the window at such a short distance.

Dr. Gottlieb admitted to destroying evidence just prior to the formal Rockefeller Commission investigatory hearings into the matter. This was described by one writer as "to limit the damage."

Perhaps this was a euphonious way of saying that the "fix was in." The Rockefeller Commission's investigation into these matters, some twenty years after the fact, sounds very official, but brought very little change, and did not construe the facts of the case, nor mention all the key players. It is very possible that because of the clandestine nature of the operations that little was ever meant to be exposed even though the hearing had the most official name possible.

Former operative Victor Marchetti put it succinctly, "The CIA is powerful, arrogant, and elitist." It is well to remember Lord Acton's statement, "Absolute power corrupts absolutely." In light of the tragic strains of this story, it is likely that the quest for defensive power was overtaken as the group that became bent on discovering *true* power. After all, the title of the expensive clandestine operation was "mind-kontrol-ultra."

Every person who had been with Olson up to one week prior to his death was asked to file a report concerning the mental state and actions of Dr. Olson. John Mulholland would have had to file such a report. No report by Mulholland has been discovered.

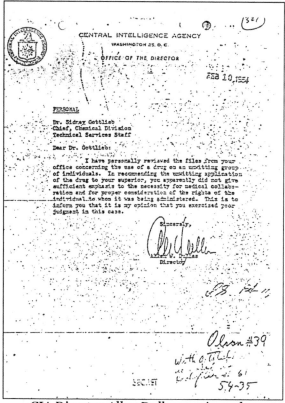

*CIA Director Allen Dulles reprimand to
Gottlieb over Olson's death.*

John Mulholland was friendly with Nelson Rockefeller, former Governor of New York, who presided over this Commission. Mulholland's role as an MK-ULTRA consultant may have been suppressed by the Rockefeller Commission, headed by Senator Ted

143

Kennedy and Nelson Rockefeller, who knew and cited the magician in a state proclamation in 1966 and 1967. John Mulholland's publicity sheets mention his entertaining members of the Rockefeller family at their home called "Kykuit" in Pocantico Hills, forty-five minutes north of New York City. While it may be an exaggeration of showman's press, it was noted that Mulholland, Al Flosso, and Al Flosso's father in law, Louis Krieger, traded off entertaining the Rockefeller family at social affairs over twenty five years.

The point is that Nelson Rockefeller knew and lauded the magician publicly in the later sixties. Further, it was under President Gerald Ford, who replaced Richard Nixon (from 1974-1976 after the President's resignation) that Nelson Rockefeller became Ford's Vice President. Whether he was a shadow figure in the world of MK-ULTRA, is not known, however, Rockefeller co-headed the investigation and was also was present in the 1976 administration that paid the Olson family compensation for Dr. Olson's death.

In 1975, just six months after Nixon's resignation, President Gerald Ford personally apologized to the Olson family in the Oval Office on behalf of the U.S. Government. Congress then passed a bill in 1976 to pay Mrs. Alice Olson (and children) $750,000. Obviously, if the government had done nothing wrong, no payment would ever have been made. The government position was that Olson had regularly come into contact with deadly microbes and that this was the cause of his chaotic state of mind, and there was no foul play. Rather, it was "an unfortunate set of circumstances." With the payment of $750,000 the family also signed away any further claims against the government. One former CIA communications officer told this writer, "So they got into trouble with that scientist, but John (Mulholland) was never involved in any wet work." "Wet work" is Agency jargon for the purposeful spilling of blood or assassination.

Until Alice Olson's death in 1993, her husband's superior, Lt. Col. Vincent Ruwet, regularly visited Frank Olson's widow. Apparently the government kept tabs on Mrs. Olson because of information her husband possibly gave to her and the security leaks they feared.

The payment was also contingent upon the agreement that the family would not seek further injunction against the U.S. government for wrongful death. Mrs. Olson signed on to that agreement. Her son Eric claims that he did not and is therefore not bound by the constraints imposed on his mother. He has since been an antagonist to the CIA concerning his father's death.

After President Richard Nixon outlawed the United States' use of biological warfare in 1969, public inquiry brought the Rockefeller Commission investigations from 1973 to 1975 into the work done by

144

Gottlieb, Lashbrook and Olson from 1953 to the 1960's. (As well, this review also came during the height of Watergate, and this larger story overshadowed the investigation and press surrounding the events from 1953.) From 1973 to 1977 hundreds of articles appeared on the front pages of U.S. newspapers, most prominently *The New York Times* and *The Washington Post*. Olson's wife never believed that her husband would simply desert her and their three children. Their son, Eric, a Harvard-trained psychologist, has been trying since his father's death to bring the government to justice for what he feels is a clear case of murder.

Professor of Law and Forensic Science of George Washington University, James Starrs inconclusively deduced a hematoma on the forehead skull section of Frank Olson when the body was exhumed in the late 1990's. The hematoma is possible evidence that Dr. Olson had been hit in the head prior to his fall from the hotel window. It is also possible that he hit something on his way down to the sidewalk from the window of room 1018A at the Statler Hotel.

Upon Olson's initial loss of sanity, the people responsible for his condition counseled him to: travel back and forth between Washington D.C. and New York three times in thirty-six hours, see a magician, a psychiatrist, drink alcohol, take sedatives, and see a Broadway show. What else happened during this bizarre scenario that we will never know?

Is it conceivable that the "remedy" actually created a haphazard obstacle course for Olson's free-associating mind to wander?

Gottlieb and Lashbrook were never prosecuted for any criminal activity concerning the death of Dr. Frank Olson.

New York Assistant District Attorney Steven Saracco convinced a grand jury in New York City in 1999 to re-open the Olson death as a homicide investigation. There is no statute of limitations on homicide in New York, and Sarraco's office is known for the long haul with several twenty-plus year investigations finally solved.

The CIA has maintained that it has never killed a U.S. citizen on U.S. soil. If Olson's death is proven to be a homicide, there might be a rather stringent review of the CIA policies. Though, such "reviews" seem to affect this Agency very little, as the "cult of intelligence" forms what many refer to as "the way things really are, but are not seen to be." The budget of the CIA is not accountable to Congress, after all.

In 1999, another man named Glickman, allegedly "wronged" by Gottlieb's LSD experiments in Paris, during the 1960's, was pursuing his claim against the scientist in the courts of New York City. After several postponements, the trial was slated to begin in late March of 1999. The trial never happened. The reason?

Sidney Gottlieb apparently died at age 80 of an undisclosed cause on Sunday, March 7, 1999 at his home in Washington, Virginia. Or did he?

Those in the clandestine world have said that Gottlieb's death may indeed be fabricated and that the old winner of the Distinguished Intelligence Medal may have gone into "deep cover" for reasons undisclosed. One investigator was informed of Gottlieb's death within 24 hours of the press announcement. In his phone message response he said, "This case keeps getting stranger and stranger." Members of the Gottlieb family declined to be interviewed further about their father.

This writer had one personal encounter with Dr. Gottlieb. On one afternoon in February 1999 I had an appointment to meet with Steven Sarraco. When approaching his office in downtown Manhattan, a man got out of a waiting sedan not far from the entrance of Sarraco's building. The man was tall, lean, bald and stared very hard at me. He seemed to be saying something with his dedicated silence. When I walked toward his car, he stepped in front of me as if to block my passage. I returned his gaze and he cocked his head with a gesture that acknowledged my silent recognition of him.

It was Dr. Gottlieb who was showing his face, perhaps letting me know that he was aware of my holding letters he had missed in his destruction of documents 50 years earlier. Most likely the Agency had tapped the phone of the District Attorney. Only two people knew that I was meeting with Sarraco, my wife and the Assistant DA Sarracco. I am pretty sure that my wife did not call Sidney Gottlieb. A possibility exists that Sarraco mentioned the meeting to Frank Olson's son Eric of our meeting. Given Eric's constant agitation to the Agency, it is very likely he will be watched until his death, as was his mother by Olson's superior Colonel Ruwet.

Gottlieb, would be angered that the cleansing of the trail in MK-ULTRA had missed the documents from Gottlieb's hand that Mulholland kept. Gottlieb also knew that magicians were hard to deal with and were secretive and crafty when they had to be. After all, it was Gottlieb who brought "the world's master magician" Mulholland into the espionage fold. Gottlieb had also been very specific with Mulholland not to keep copies of any correspondence. Mulholland technically complied with this request – after it had been made. Papers in Mulholland's private CIA file pre-date Gottlieb's request.

Had the authorities at the time known of Mulholland's deeper relationship with Lashbrook and a coterie of other agents perhaps the truth behind Olson's death would have surfaced a quarter century earlier. Most of the nasty facts of espionage are carefully buried or surrounded in dis-information near the incidents.

There is no mention of Frank Olson's death in any of the newly discovered papers of John Mulholland. In fact when discussing his work for the Agency to another communications operative, Mulholland never mentioned the death; it being suggested that he put the fatality out of his memory. "John was a positive person, even when his arthritis was killing him. Never knew him to speak about the sullen or misbegotten" said the clandestine operative.

As Gottlieb and Lashbrook removed themselves from the awful (apparent) suicide, the cover-up of the details of the scientist's death began, and the Agency's work continued with "the World's Master Magician."

Mr.Sherman C.Grifford,
Chemrophyl Associates,
Washington, D.C.

Dear Sherman,

This is a memo in regard to expansion of the manual on
trickery.

The manual as it now stands consists of the following
five sections:

1. Underlying bases for the successful performance of
tricks and the background of the psychological principles
by which they operate.

2. Tricks with pills.

3. Tricks with loose solids.

4. Tricks with liquids.

5. Tricks by which small objects may be obtained secretly.
        This section was not considered in my original
        outline and was suggested subsequently to me.
        I was, however, able to add it without necessi-
        tating extension of the number of weeks request-
        ed for the writing. Another completed task not
        noted in the outline was making models of such
        equipment as has been described in the manual.

As sections 2,3,4 and 5 were written solely for use by men
working alone the manual needs two furthur sections. One section
would give modified, or different, tricks and techniques of performance so that the tricks could be performed by women. The other
section would describe tricks suitable for two or more people working in collaboration. In both these proposed sections the tricks
would differ considerably from those which have been described.

I believe that properly to devise the required techniques and
devices and to describe them in writing would require 12 working
weeks to complete the two sections. However, I cannot now work on
this project every week and would hesitate to promise completion
prior to the first of May, 1954.

I shall await your instructions in the matter.

                        Sincerely yours

                        John Mulholland

November 11, 1953

Mr Sherman C. Grifford,
Chemrophyl Associates,
Washington, D.C.

Dear Sherman,

Enclosed is my report on the Parapsychology study. The book is being sent to you under separate cover.

Also enclosed is a very short outline on what I propose futhur to do on the work connected with the manual. In connection with the typing of my manuscript pages please be so kind as to give your Secretary my deepest sympathy. Also please tell her that while I probably did not spell it correctly if I wrote "canoe" that was the word I had in mind. I shall appreciate all spelling corrections but would like to have all the words left.

Also enclosed is my current bill for services rendered.

I shall appreciate receiving the check now in the works as soon as it comes from the mill. I also will appreciate getting the carbon of the text you have so that I can begin making plans on what is to be told the "girls." If there are any parts of my writing which cannot be followed I suggest that those sections be sent back to me for clarification at the same time the carbon is sent.

Regards

VII. THE WOMEN

"Strange things occur between spies, especially spies who, unknown to each other, have been given the same job."

– Nicholas Dawidoff, *The Catcher Was A Spy*, p. 175.

"It is a matter of merely timing and confidence."

– JM, *The Art of Illusion*, p. 65.

The first manual that John Mulholland produced for the CIA was written over the period of twelve months from May 1953 to May 1954. As of March 22, 1954 Mulholland showed receipt for another $750 which covered work completed on January 11, 18, February 12, 19 and March 1, 1954. A twenty-week contract was extended to fifty-two weeks and then to five years. In fact, there were actually two or three manuals, or, one manual that was revised in response due to the CIA's field research and practice of the magician's methods. Three different versions have surfaced. The first draft is nine chapters long; the next submitted to the government is five chapters and the final seems to be eight chapters long.

The following time line concerning the development of events is important:

November 11, 1953: Mulholland writes three letters to Gottlieb all on the same day. There is a possible coded message embedded into all three documents: "team work is needed."

November 17, 1953: Gottlieb writes a Memorandum for the Record concerning Subproject 19 in regard to Mulholland's manual on deceptions and states:

1. Under a previous subproject (Subproject 4) a manual was prepared by Mr. Mulholland dealing with the application of the magician's art to covert activities such as the delivery of various materials to unwilling subjects. The basic assumption in the preparation of the manual was that the "performer" or agent was a man working alone.

2. Subproject 19 will involve the preparation of two additional sections to the manual. These are (1) Modified or different methods and techniques for use if the performer is a woman, and (2) Methods and techniques

that can be used where two or more people can work in collaboration."

3. The work will be done by Mr. Mulholland. It is estimated the job can be completed in twelve working weeks (not necessarily consecutive). It is estimated the job will be completed by May 1954. The estimated cost is $1,800.00.

This memorandum was approved the following day, November 18, 1953.

November 19, 1953: Dr. Frank Olson is given LSD covertly by Dr. Sidney Gottlieb.

November 25, 1953: Frank Olson, having ingested LSD, meets Mulholland in New York City. Olson was afraid of Mulholland because he knew of (but did not read) Mulholland's manual that had been submitted prior to November 11, 1953.

November 28, 1953: Frank Olson dies. Gottlieb's assistant Dr. Robert V. Lashbrook is with Olson at the time of the death.

December 2, 1953: Sidney Gottlieb approves (as an "excellent idea") another $3000 for the manual to have the addition of teams and use of women agents to deploy drugs.

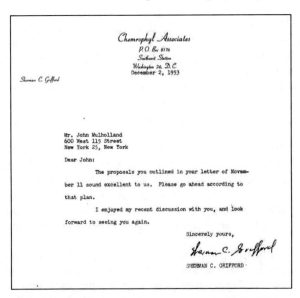

To examine these events in greater detail, from May 5, 1953 to November 11, 1953 John Mulholland wrote a manual for CIA that had five chapters. On November 11, 1953 John Mulholland wrote three letters to Sidney Gottlieb. The message or picture drawn by the date being repeated three times is 11:11. That three letters were written on 11:11 possibly indicates three items or people. That the magician's code is to hide in the obvious is important to understand here.

What changes is the content of the letters. What remains the same is the date or the picture of two people standing next to two people.

The combination of numbers 11:11 are notorious in parapsychological circles. In fact the dubious doctor H.K. Puharich (with whom the Agency was working at this time, and whom Mulholland would meet in less than a month) was literally obsessed with this combination of numbers. Doctor Puharich suggested (in later writing) that these numbers were a "contact point" between humans and a higher intelligence that expressed itself mathematically for communication.

Eleven-eleven is an astrological sign of twins or partnership. Given that Mulholland was suggesting to add this topic to the pre-existing document, it is possible that the date to these letters also included a message about certain upcoming events. Or, that he realized the significance of these numbers to this doctor, and therefore used this to his own advantage.

It is likely that written (in code) among the three letters is his opinion of "team work."

A friend of Mulholland's commented on this numerology stating, "Let me tell you as John would have. Numbers are just numbers. Period. The End. Nothing more." Assumption of hidden writing in Mulholland's manual results from familiarity with the cleverness of the magician as a writer and familiarity with the goals and intricacies of the officers heading up MK-ULTRA. Mind control was for "inter-Agency" work as well. In addition to controlling an unwitting subject, the government needed to control their own agents. Consequently we can see a "secrecy-laden environment," one that Mulholland was familiar with through his own experiences as a magician.

During the UFO craze of 1952 Mulholland wrote for *Popular Mechanics* magazine, claiming that all photographed UFO's were pie tins held on badly concealed strings. Given Mulholland's low tolerance for such abstractions, when it came to the search for "real magic" by the MK-ULTRA scientists, it is likely Mulholland was making use of their obsessions and "hiding in the obvious" by dating a lot of his material with the notorious date of eleven-eleven. This would be especially true if the number had significance for his employers. It did for some.

The final document he assembled for the CIA entitled *Some Operational Applications of the Art of Deception* was submitted in May 1954. The contents are revealing, especially because of what deletions the CIA has kept from public inspection.

The title chapters of the final manual, completed in 1954, are:

I.   Introduction and General Comments on the Art of Deception
II.   Underlying Bases for Successful Performance
III.   Tricks With Pills
IV.   Tricks with Loose Solids
V.   Tricks with Liquids
VI.   Tricks Whereby Small Objects Can be Obtained Secretly**
VII.   Special Aspects of Deception for Women
VIII.   Working as a Team

Of a one-hundred and twenty-one-page manual comprised of eight chapters, the government has only allowed fifty-six pages to be made public. Of the fifty-six pages seen, roughly two-thirds of the pages are visible; the remaining third is redacted (blacked out).

Only 46% of the final manual Mulholland wrote has been made public. However, because of Mulholland's handwritten notes and a rough draft of the manual in the Milbourne Christopher Collection, we can piece together what information the government has withheld from public inspection.

The greatest number of deletions are, sections 3, 4, 5, and 6 (including the chapter titles on the contents page). This is the area that dealt with how to deploy a drug, and of equal importance, what kind of drug would be deployed.

If a liquid, chapter five would explain that. For loose solids, that would be chapter four.

Mulholland describes two simple operations by which a "victim" could be injected with a needle, never feeling or suspecting the injection. It might be thought that when stuck with a needle, one would know, but the ancient practice of acupuncture belies this assumption. Other uses of a needle were to retain a drug in pill form prior to it being released, from the needle tip. Also, a slight scratch from an anointed needle – or sharp tip – is almost Shakespearean in

---

** Mulholland revisits this concept in his last book *The Magical Mind* on page 77 concerning hypnosis as "choice."

root. One need only remember that Hamlet dies as a result being touched by the poisoned tip of Laertes' sword. In *Hamlet* Shakespeare drew upon the ancient art of poisoning just as the MK-ULTRA scientists did when they experimented with deadly shellfish toxins. The fish used the poison emitted through their scales against predators simply brushing against them. Used by the government, the toxin killed after invading the blood stream through a simple scratch.

The first method of deploying drugs was described for use exclusively by men. It should be noted at this point that deceptive practices were very much curtailed by social customs of the day. In 1953 it was directed by how women were seen by men and vice versa.

The gender of an agent was extremely important to the proper "execution" of the mission. Henceforth, the following operation was designed for men, and women used the succeeding operation. Then there was instruction for teams where men and women would work with each other. More on that in a moment.

Mulholland detailed the psychological dynamics of people meeting and having one person poison another person. This was defined as "introducing a foreign chemical agent into the body without the knowledge of this happening."

The operation of the agent was relatively simple. All the agent had to do was to light a "victim's" cigarette in the most nonchalant manner possible.

Basically, without getting as technical as Mulholland's description, there was an exposed needle protruding from the back of the match packet. On the tip of the needle was a chemical agent to be deployed. The type of matches used were the flat, paper kind. When the victim (most likely a woman, though this procedure could also be used against a male victim) leaned in for the match to light the cigarette that was held close to the mouth by the victim's hand, the match would be extended by the "trickster's" (agent) right hand. The matches would be in the trickster's left hand, and by the time the match was lighted, the left hand with the remaining pack of matches would fall to the trickster's left side.

Once the victim's cigarette was lighted by the trickster's right hand holding the match, the trickster's left hand would casually rub against the victim's hand that was not holding the cigarette. Or, a pill secreted on a needle tip would be "dispensed" into a drink – most usually coffee because of the opaque color.

Mulholland taught the agents the old magician's axiom that: "The larger action would hide the smaller action." This is a standard for any sleight of hand procedure. The right hand with a fiery match would receive all the attention because it would respond to the victim's need. The trickster's left hand would be completely unnoticed in the deployment of whatever anointed the needle. In 1963 he revisited these concepts in his *Book of Magic* in writing that a magician in Peiping had fooled him by lighting a match by rubbing the back of his thumbnail against the match, a knack Mulholland conceded he developed as a boy. He noted that he was amazed because the magician had moved his arms in the air and called upon the match to light. He then states, as he did for the CIA: *The big motion completely hid the action of the thumb and because the command instantly was obeyed it seemed magical.*

Mulholland realized that he was instructing agents to give injections or drop a tablet that would dissolve in about a minute (these things were not left to chance and were called "fast acting tablets," "minute-long pills" and "slow agent drugs"). Once the drug was deployed, Mulholland gave lessons in assigning blame to fictional characters. He wrote that there would be a need for this, since the agent wanted to remain unseen at the time of an unexpected reaction.

The section for women was slightly different; it included the same set of movements, just with different, common articles of the day in the pockets of women's clothing from men's. He noted that there was a significant difference. Most women's pockets are tailored for fashion and are not really usable for deceptive practices. Women carried compacts with mirrors that were detachable from their cases. The situation where a woman would act the role of the trickster would usually be in engaging another woman as the victim.

The procedure would unfold in the following manner:

One woman (the trickster) would be speaking with another woman (the victim). The trickster agent would say that the victim had a smudge near her left eye. The trickster would then offer the mirror of the compact with the right hand. Like the matches the man was instructed to use, the compact would be loaded with a needle to inject or otherwise deploy a drug. Upon the victim not finding a smudge, the trickster would retrieve the mirror and casually touch the victim's hand with the needle of the compact as she drew back from retrieving the borrowed mirror.

In fencing terms, the touch was made upon the retreat, not in the attack — and would not be suspected by any wary agent.

Mulholland addresses the point of who had the greatest likelihood of fooling whom. He counseled that men could easily fool a woman by lighting her cigarette because that was a customary action in 1953. It

156

would be an action that would be overlooked because it was so common. One woman offering a make-up appearance note to another woman would not be out of the ordinary . . . yet in this case, the advice might have led to the unwitting ingestion of a potentially lethal, or mind altering drug, such as LSD.

The magician is careful to enlist the magician's credo when administering instructions to the field agents. Mulholland dryly observes that the successful execution of missions is based on preparedness, practice and patience.

Reflecting on his instructions, he cautions the agents that the two characteristics that will get them through operations undetected are: 1) being as prepared as can be, and 2) being confident that the mission can be accomplished.

He quotes Dr. Roy Chapman Andrews upon his return from spending a year in Mongolia. When asked by a reporter what kind of adventures he had, Dr. Andrews remarked, "My dear man, adventures come when you lack preparation. We were on a scientific expedition, and we were all very well prepared." This is standard procedure of magicians as well.

So prepared was the Agency that it employed some whores to dose other whores without their knowledge. This writer met one of the "girls" in Seattle, WA, who confessed the methods employed in a brothel on the Canadian border. Known by the false name "Sweet Sally," she said of the Agency-funded work "The money was good. We got paid whether there was sex or not. That's unusual for working girls. We sort of had fun. I never much liked alcohol, but it got tiresome because you'd want to 'come down' and these guys in ties kept you going, days it seemed. I don't know what they were after. A whorehouse is a whorehouse and they thought it was some sort of shrink lab. Fat chance. One time a guy died they pumped him so many times."

The magician further instructed the agents to begin their rehearsals slowly, to conduct themselves in rehearsal as if they were in a "slowed down moving picture." Mulholland wanted the agents to fully understand their actions before going into the field and bringing the operation up to full conversational tempo.

As to what would not be noticed, he identified old bills and a partially crumpled package of cigarettes as tools of the trade.

In the section specifically about women, he observes that women extend their hands to receive something given to them palm up, while men extend their hand palm down. Mulholland knew this through thousands of performances of close-up magic at which he was an undisputed master.

For a person to be injected with a drug from an assassin's compact or pack of paper matches, the victim's hand would have to be injected with the victim's palm facing down. Such subtleties of human behavior were the magician's specialty. He synthesized such information not only to deploy chemical materials—but more importantly, via these methods the victims never knew they had been injected with, or ingested, anything at anytime. Mulholland counsels the agents, another standard edict of the conjurer's trade "Deception depends largely upon psychology and in order to make use of that subject, the first thing to remember is to be natural or be yourself."

Another feature of human behavior is called "body language." While most apply this term to crossed arms or posture, Mulholland went further. He realized that the magician's tool of psychological "misdirection" was crucial for the covert action of dispersing drugs.

"Misdirection" is best defined as a form of direction or, getting the audience-victim to look in the wrong place at the right time. He taught the government agents how to use their facial muscles to attract or distract attention. Essentially, a relaxed face bearing a pleasant countenance would be far less threatening than a red-faced, angry-looking would be assassin. He drew two self-portraits to illustrate his point. Mulholland knew that the least suspicious moves were the ones that everyone performed without extensive thinking. Magic was devised, he asserted, to fool the mind rather than the eyes, because the hand is not quicker than the eye.

Though, he counseled, "the eyes see a great many things of which the mind takes no notice...those things that we have no reason to notice remain unseen."

The eye has the ability to recollect a situation with some rebuilding of detail. Alternatively, he offers, the mind cannot move backwards to reconstruct a situation in order to obtain a solution in deception. He notes that confusion affects the mind, not the eye. In criminology, these concepts would be applied to "reconstructing the crime." Trouble is, in this type of work, often no crime is thought to have been committed, so there is nothing for the mind to reconstruct. This is why the MK-ULTRA scientists sought to induce amnesia. It would be near impossible to recollect specific incidents.

Mulholland writes in his manual:

Now concentrate on the word you see before you. Stop reading for a moment after you see the following words and think about what they mean:

AIVA NID NACS

Now you didn't realize that what you were looking at was the word Scandinavia written backwards, and broken up, did you? And why would you know this? This just shows that you can see something before your eyes that appears peculiar; when in actuality it is very simple.

The reverse is also true. We "see" something where we believe it to be.

A fountain pen that elicits little attention sitting on a table may actually be the tool of the agent in his mission. This will go undetected. Just remember that what looks alright to the "audience" must be alright. The spectators can only see what they observe and they observe only what they know about. As they do not know of any previous preparation there has been no such preparation as far as they are concerned. If you will accept this fact—and it is a fact—you will never be self-conscious (and have a fully confident manner in all your work).

This passage is practically out of Mulholland's 1944 book *The Art of Illusion*. In that book he used the backwards version of the city Constantinople. Henry Miller wrote that most writers only really had one good book in them. John Mulholland wrote ten different titles in his life, though he was quick to capitalize on Miller's statement by reprinting his *Art of Illusion* book three times. Much of the same writing was synthesized a fourth time in an expanded version in his 1963 *Book of Magic*. The changes are minor, but show his maturity nineteen years later. The repeating of this information over twenty years also shows the integrity of the subject matter.

He gave another example of a word that may have been more telling than one might imagine. After having alerted the reader to the idea that something could be right in front of them, and still not see it (such as in the "Scandinavia" example) he gives the reader the following optical puzzle:

ULNAISVREERVSIANLU

Mulholland points out that even though the mind has been "twice cued" to the nature of letters bearing no apparent form, the reader still does not see that not only is the problem a word of some sort, it is actually the same word spelled backwards and forwards.

The word is "universal" as shown in the following rendering of the puzzle word with highlighting to show the pattern. Mulholland writes of this psychological lesson, "Even though you have been cued twice, you still do not see until told. Once shown, *then* you can only see the patterns and the codes (italics added.)"

U L N A I S V R E E R V S I A N L U

It is entirely possible that the word "universal" was used to trigger agents responses. In other words, when they heard the word "universal," a mission might have been put into play.

Mulholland was good at solving codes, being very familiar with the great mind reading acts of vaudeville where one sitter reads the thoughts or describes details unknowable as projected to him by his partner moving amidst the audience. On one occasion where a friend of his described the interior of Mulholland's pocket watch, the magician played along. The mind reader mentions in his autobiography a year or so later that he was somewhat taken aback when he "saw the Mulholland Cheshire Cat grin" and when Mulholland cracked the reader's code from the audience by signaling the reader the next number to be correctly called![††]

The MK-ULTRA team was experimenting with the use of words to trigger actions. Given the drama of the book by Richard Condon (and movie) *The Manchurian Candidate,* it is believable that the Mulholland manual contains instructions, that are hidden between the lines, or in magician's terms, "hidden in the obvious."

Though it has been suggested that Mulholland may have attempted a post hypnotic suggestion with Frank Olson to jettison his mind from depression and thoughts of leaving the Agency (once Olson learned of testing of deadly microbes on human subjects), this notion has been equally criticized by friends close to the magician who said, "John could not have hypnotized a rabbit with a night stick."

It should be noted that until the early 1960's Mulholland believed that hypnosis was "a lot of bunk." In 1930 Mulholland was quoted as saying during a performance, "Hypnotism is nothing but suggestion and in order to have any affect upon the subject he must be in a receptive mood, conditions must be just right."

[††] See Bamberg, *Illusion Show,* p. 51.

However, it did not matter what he initially thought. There were people at the CIA, the TSS, the DOD and other departments of national security that were investing millions of dollars in the combination of hypnosis and drugs as tools of warfare. One such note from the MK-ULTRA years has survived. As a handwritten testament to the experiments, it is very revealing. The unknown writer states:

> *I have developed a technic (sic) which is safe an (sic) secure (free from international censorship). It has to do with the conditioning of our own people. I can accomplish this as a one-man job.*

> *The method is the production of hypnosis by means of simple oral medication. Then (with no further medication) the hypnosis is re-inforced daily during the following three or four days. Each individual is conditioned against revealing any information to an enemy, even though subjected to hypnosis or drugging. If preferable, he may be conditioned to give false information rather than no information.*

> *This method should be treated every six months in each case in order to be sure that the suggestions established have not "worn off." I would be glad to go anywhere in the world (including Korea) to accomplish this for you. I think the greatest security would be in my traveling as a naval flight surgeon doing research in motion medicine, especially with the project of "motion sickness" in mind. Of course I would be willing to undertake more hazardous investigative methods if you should deem them advisable.*

Mulholland changed his opinion of the phenomenon of the mind and hypnotic influences after extemporaneous reading. One book from his collection was among of the earliest on the subject. *Hypnotism (How It Is Done–Its Uses and Dangers)* by James R. Cocke, M.D., dated 1894. It is a scientific book dealing with the use of hypnotism in surgery, "neurasthenia" and has a long chapter on a subject that fascinated the magician and his co-workers at the Agency. Chapter 16 dealt with: *Telepathy—Thought Transference—Mind reading.*

Given this is one of the very first books on the subject, written by a medical doctor, it held sway on that value alone, even if the magician did not agree with all of the doctor's findings. However, supporting his role as a consultant, Mulholland lent this book with outlined pages to the MK-ULTRA team along with his own 1938 opus *Beware Familiar*

Spirits. He inscribed to Gottlieb on the title page that the sections on thought reading would be advantageous to the scientists.

Mulholland was particularly taken with Dr. Cocke's dissection of telepathy as "experimental and spontaneous." He outlined the passage which states: "Spontaneous telepathic experiences may be received either as simple ideas, or as hallucinations of sight, hearing, touch, or as all three combined." What is essential here is the relation to work being done in the field of hallucination by the MK-ULTRA team. The question is: can purposely induced hallucinations unlock different states of reality, as in a precognitive awareness of events, or are hallucinations merely dreams affected in the waking state? Consequently, we see a bridge between hallucinations induced to discredit people, but also investigated as a gateway to open greater consciousness.

When Alexander Woollcott chose several well appointed words in his autobiography *Long Long Ago*, he chose the word "tricker" (which Mulholland rewrote as "trickster" in his promotional literature) to describe the Mulholland mystique. In his autobiography, Woollcott describes a situation where Mulholland's magic met with difficult circumstances and then a coincidental miracle saved his prestige. Woollcott clearly admired Mulholland as a peer intellectual.

He wrote about methods of deception for the CIA with great authority, with experience from thousands of performances. This was decidedly different from the arm chair scholarship practiced by most amateurs who wrote books about tricks.

As a master of close-up magic he made the disappearance of a coin look like something actually vaporized between his fingers. Simply put: Mulholland made miracles. He was a man who could enjoy a smoke with you and then casually drop into conversation your presumed inner thoughts!

One of his miracles was created with something that is known as "the hooked coin." This is a coin with a small hook less than one eighth of an inch long embedded into the coin. Used in conjunction with sleight of hand, this is a "devastating" prop for the modern magician. Mulholland was given his first hooked coin by his vaudeville pal, T. Nelson Downs, the "King of Koins" in 1923.

Could pills and needles attached in matches and applied on the back of coins been the result of Mulholland's familiarity with the "hooked coin?" Mulholland's own hooked coin is in the author's collection given to him by Mulholland intimate, the great "Coney Island Fakir" Al Flosso.

Mulholland always maintained that the execution of magic, or "trickery" as stated in the manual, is the result of 80% psychology. The balance of the conjurer's craft being equally divided between skill and apparatus.

Largely, Mulholland's showmanship was his scholarship; his demeanor deceptive. In fact, it was John Mulholland who provided the second edition of the *Merriam Webster* dictionary with the definition for the word "showmanship."

Mulholland tried to get the agents to use their personal talents to their advantage in their clandestine practices, just as John William Sargent had ordered him as a young magician to adopt what was singular to his countenance for successful performance.

One gets the feeling reading Mulholland's manual that he was making fun of his employers without their knowing it. Typical to the puzzle within a puzzle, as his manual is so rife, he teaches people to see coded words, but still offers that agents appear stupid, count monkeys and say the guy with the missing digit, "did it." Friends of the magician told this writer repeatedly "John Mulholland was a complete man, erudite, with a wry sense of humor."

In Chapter Five of his manual he addresses story telling, and notes that rational stories are the most believable. By rational, he pointed out, he meant making the details of the story agree. A lion cannot be caught by a mousetrap. He does note that "super imagination" stories can hold up. "A spaceship shot a light at me and I was abducted by a UFO" thousands have been known to say. Again, a giant tale, but essentially, uncomplicated and straight forward. All the details are there and readily understood. Once understood, they can be believed more easily. Every good magician knows a whopper of a tale is easier to "sell" than a small inconsequential story because uncomplicated details are readily accepted, no matter how bizarre.

He applied his thoughts on the reverse of delivering unseen materials. Chapter Five dealt with removing objects from sight without being seen. Again, a magician's knowledge of the psychology of sleight of hand, his training under Sargent and his familiarity with Krieger, comes into play. It is interesting to see how the mind of John Mulholland synthesized the practices of stage illusion to the world of espionage. One wonders how effective his methods really were. Unlike the details of the British war plan detailed by Ewen Montagu called *The Man Who Never Was,* the agents' practices of Mulholland techniques may never be known. In fact, the details of Mulholland's involvement actually should never have seen print, as the nature of clandestine work is hidden.

When the chapters turn to trickery by women, the whole tone of the manual changes and the early 21st century reader gets a chance to peer in on 1950's social customs and attendant phrases from water cooler chit chat at the Pentagon.

He leads off with the admission that a woman in a man's company, while on a mission, must adhere to social customs of letting the man choose her seat and also allowing the man to pull her chair out when she is seated. A woman smoker as many were at this time, would also not find it unusual to have a man light her cigarette. Dynamics of any small party of two women and one man, three women, and three men are all examined for the common strains, and where agent deception can be made to work most effectively.

He discusses certain aspects of women such as fidgeting. When one is nervous, one fidgets. He comments that women fidget more than men when nervous. Mulholland assumes the role of CIA Training Counselor when he barks, "No fidgeting, ladies" in the text. Later, he writes:

> Now ladies, in the company of a man do not try to act masculine. Of course this should not be interpreted as suggesting being girly-girly, but merely not being masculine in actions or manner.

The modern reader will be saddened to read that Mulholland also addresses the women with the frank opinion that a blank look on a woman will not astonish a man. He writes, "Ladies, we might as well face it, men are never astonished when a woman doesn't know something." Such a stance was not new for Mulholland. In September of 1932, he was taken to task in a French magazine for his views on women magicians. While being called one of the "cleverest magicians" the female author contends, that Mulholland revealed in an interview that "men were trickier than women."

Later in his manual, he reasons the circumstances of a woman agent acting dumb in the company of another woman, and advises against this ruse. He notes that women can tell when another woman is acting dumb, and they resent it. To the woman's credit he does state that a woman will think ahead, and might therefore be more suspicious than a man who "generally has a routine step by step mentality...can be led down the garden path anytime. A woman will suspect what is ahead. This may be used against her as well. By performing short, direct tricks to women, they will follow and be deceived more easily."

However, as old world as some of the directives may sound today, they were no doubt true to the social customs of the cosmopolitan world Mulholland lived in.

When he got around to his final chapter, "Working as a Team" Mulholland was at his best. All the knowledge he imparted from page one to this point would be synthesized into a whole. The operations he described were complex, effective and brilliant.

Again, especially in teamwork he preaches: patience, practice, preparation and the basic knowledge of what is to happen.

After detailing the three possible kinds of two-person teams, between men and women, Mulholland offers that there must only be one trickster leader and one assistant. When the sex of the trickster is changed, the role of the assistant is changed dramatically. He gives an explanation based on social custom. Were a man and woman working in collusion to "play a trick" on a second woman, the following scenario would be acceptable to custom.

If the woman victim were to desire a cigarette, it would be customary for either the other man or woman to offer the cigarette, but one woman would not light the cigarette for another – that would be the man's job according to custom. Hence, in this scenario, the woman who offered the cigarette would be the assistant, while the man is the "trickster" who lights the cigarette, and covertly gives the victim a drug without the victim being aware of it.

Mulholland is very explicit when discussing the role of the assistant when it comes to pulling off a "trick." Basically, the trickster has to signal the assistant to bring forth a package of cigarettes and offer one to the victim. This can be done by blinking to get the assistant counting "one great big chimpanzee, two great big chimpanzees" in repetition with the trickster's own counting in the same manner. On the count of three, the trickster would blink again. The number three would have been transmitted silently by the trickster to the assistant. The assistant looks at the clock, and sees that the time is 2:57pm. The assistant realizes that the trickster would like the offer of a cigarette to the victim at 3 o'clock.

He wrote, "the assistant must follow the trickster and resign himself that he cannot know too much about what he is doing at any time." Paradoxically Mulholland explains how the use of an unknown assistant is very effective deception. In this instance, an agent would be sent to find a victim, perhaps at a bar. The trickster would require the assistance of a person to slip him the correct package of matches he needs for the operation. But prior to going to where the victim is and the operation is to take place, the agent has no idea of who will be the assistant to hand him the crucial pack of matches at the right time.

The meeting of the operator and the assistant was often done through the most secret channels of all clandestine work. The word "clandestine" means "secret," "covert." Therefore, the arrangement of a partner in an operation was often through a coded hello or a gesture. The partners not knowing who they would be working with in advance led to greater believability in operations. This seemingly loose affiliation was actually key to the mystery perpetrated. Dunninger, the great mind reader, used this technique. He was supplied answers to questions from his audience by his manager, Harold von Braunhut. That Dunninger honestly did not know how his manager got correct information added to the believability that he genuinely read minds. Along the same lines, when operators of Mulholland's methods worked in concert with one another, without prior knowledge of whom they were working with, this led to a greater believability for what they were doing in the eyes of subjects on whom tricks were played.

Mulholland counsels that when working as a mixed-sex team, there can only be one leader, "The man leads, and the woman follows."

Another method: The trickster stands on a train platform waiting for an arriving train with the victim. The agent (trickster) apparently is seeing his friend (victim) off. Actually what happens is an accomplice (trickster's assistant) on the arriving train will ask the victim if he knows what time it is. The victim will have to brush back his left coat sleeve to see the time. Just prior to the train's arrival, the trickster has stuck a pin in the sleeve that will be moved back to reveal the time, and also make a slight scratch in the process. The simplicity of the operation belies any notion of a method inherent in the operation. It is hiding in the most casual of all behaviors.

Or, an assistant suggests that everyone might enjoy a smoke. All the attention is on the assistant opening a crumpled pack of cigarettes. The assistant offers one cigarette to the female victim, and one to the trickster. The trickster offers a light to the lady victim.

Who is the lady going to suspect of covert action? The man who brought up cigarettes and provided them to smoke, or the man who offered a light that lasted less than two seconds?

The point Mulholland made was that once an action was completed by the brain, such as the cigarette lighting after a match being offered; there would be no attention, interest or suspicion of an almost-not-moving, unseen left hand holding a "harmless" pack of matches. Mulholland also encouraged the agent's success by also noting, "Remember, two hands are harder to watch than one, and besides, up close you see far less than were you to observe a stage." At this time, as a magician of forty years experience with close-up wonders, he knew of what he wrote. In 1941 he knew of his friend Dai Vernon's (a celebrated close-up magician), trouble in presenting his sleight of hand on a stage in a theatre that sat 6,000.

Bolder methods of distraction were also reviewed. Such practices included having an assistant pound on a table's edge in complaint to draw attention (which the magician wrote was "very effective"), or the vaudeville joke of spitting a drink (specified as wine, water or coffee) to distract a victim at the right time. Broad misdirection was something in which Mulholland was expert. He understood how the human mind worked, and he was able to defeat the logic brains normally apply to common situations by thinking several steps ahead, like a game of chess.

Above all, he maintained that these operations were delicate and that there must be a duet, not two soloists involved in "successful team operations." He wrote, "No matter how talented, two soloists are bound to have trouble." He adds that "often unlike individuals will, in this work, find that their differences, will make their task easier and compliment the other."

He concludes with the admonition that, "Having such knowledge (of what to do in a deception) makes rehearsal time important in team work just as it does for the individual."

These additional chapters on women and working as a team were written by Mulholland shortly before Frank Olson ingested LSD. Further, Mulholland's suggestions describing team work to the manual were accepted and funded by Gottlieb a short five days after Olson died.

Mulholland was offering a cleaner way of "doing business" and Gottlieb was taking him up on it in light of the fact one of their agents had just died from falling ten stories from a building in New York City the day after Thanksgiving! The death of Frank Olson was so conspicuous that it possibly followed established Agency procedure for being something other than what it appeared to be.

Declassified manuals on CIA operative assassination technique code named "executive action" specify making deaths look accidental or the result of a suicide. The portents of suicide bear no resemblance to the details contrived by the government men who sought in their manual to create this dark scenario to cover an actual assassination.

The key to any suicide is not motivation, but individual history, or to put it clinically, "conditioning." Historically Frank Olson never exhibited suicidal indications; there is a great hole in the assumption that he self-destructed, even in the aftermath of ingesting LSD. In a memorandum dated January 19, 1954, Robert H. Cunningham, the CIA Director of Special Security, refers to the "cover story," Olson's affiliations, and specifically states that the CIA wanted to avoid any investigation by insurance companies.

Further, on February 10, 1954, CIA Director Allen Dulles wrote to Dr. Gottlieb that he personally reviewed the files concerning the case of Dr. Olson and notes:

> *"...in recommending an unwitting application of the drug to a group of individuals and in recommending the unwitting application of the drug to your superior, you apparently did not give sufficient emphasis to the necessity for medical collaboration and for the proper consideration of the rights of the individual to whom it was being administered. This is to inform you that it is my opinion that you exercised poor judgment in this case."*

Gottlieb added his touch to fighting the Communist enemy during the Cold War. The CIA was investigating everything that it was alleged Hitler's Third Reich had investigated: astrology, witchcraft, ESP, black magic, occultism and psychic phenomena. This included conjuring up ghosts and energy fields, and trying to discover if there was "one mind" to the cosmos, and, if there was, how to tap into it for an advantage against the enemy.

The notion of "magic" has since been relegated into the worlds of children's fantasy and movie fiction.

However, if one stops and considers the genuine nature of awesome control over the forces of nature, one begins to understand the desire of the American government at this time. While generals and others may have scoffed at the firepower of the witch's broom and the crystal gazer's prophesy, the mere fact that the Soviet Union and the Chinese laid heavy significance on these ideas was something for the Americans to consider. Given that Gottlieb approached the world of magic and "magick" through hard neuro-science, the notion of controlling the mind's capabilities became less storybook fiction and more a tool of warfare.

Research was conducted any way the CIA desired. This was largely due to the predilections of "Wild Bill" Donovan the first head of the OSS. Donovan brought forth consultants as varied as John Ringling North the circus magnate and others from as diverse fields. If they had to open a brothel, give the "girls" methods of offering their compact to another and thereby injecting LSD (or other drugs), and then observe the victim in a place of ill repute, then so be it. Any person getting doped up in a whorehouse would never make the accusation anyway since he or she would not want to admit where the drug had been experienced. Whores on the CIA payroll regularly worked to dose those prostitutes who were not thought to be involved in ESP tests.

Lashbrook, Olson, Gottlieb, Bortner and deFlorenz were all extremely knowledgeable men. However, the clan knew nothing about psychological deception. Therefore they employed an expert in John Mulholland.

If you already have several prostitutes on the payroll, there does not seem to be anything so wild to also having a magician on the payroll. Many who commented on Mulholland's involvement with the CIA mentioned that it was to the Agency's credit that they had a magician in residence such as he. After all, Mulholland taught the Agency officials that everything the human mind sees are divided into real and unreal and that two thirds of what the mind perceives to be true is actually false.

The kind of game the government was running on the magician can be deduced. Although unlikely, if an upcoming mission went poorly, Mulholland could be considered the "fall guy." But this hypothesis does not hold to government practices. In CIA work there were no "fall guys." (At the time there was only a scientist who fell from a window.) In practice there was simply a shut down of information leading up to the investigated incident and the policy to deny everything. The Agency was also not above blackmailing their own agents with compromising situations to ensure their loyalty. Former CIA agents and directors that have written memoirs, such as directors William Colby, William Casey, Richard Helms and former agents Victor Marchetti and Philip Agee, write about this extensively.

Because the repetition of certain phrases might have included coded words (such as the word "universal") in his text and letters to the Agency heads, Mulholland is extremely detailed about his requests for not a word of his writing to be changed by a government secretary typing up his writing. This may have shown Mulholland's dogmatic magicianhood, and his awareness of Morse Allen's ARTICHOKE team that competed with Gottlieb's MK-ULTRA team. Largely, Allen's team proceeded without supervision, and were later criticized as "untethered cowboys." He was obviously scared of agents screwing up delicate operations because somebody decided to change his text.

Often in Agency work, a directive would be given without an operative knowing who was giving the directive, though the directive was clear. The CIA at this time believed that secrecy in the ranks was imperative. Some times this secrecy became confusing. Other times, it worked as if the devil himself was running the show.

Mulholland probably knew as much as he needed to, and nothing more. It is likely that he never saw his manual once he submitted it. He knew that this was part of government work, and he appreciated a veil of secrecy attendant to government matters. Whether he suspected deeper reasons than protocol is unknown.

In addition to seeking out better ways to interrogate and to develop truth and amnesia-inducing drugs, the CIA was looking for the nature of power, whether of human origin or not. The U.S. wanted to study Hitler's rise to power and the CIA scientists sought a solution that was, in part, metaphysical. Consequently, research topics and methods Mulholland lacked belief in, the government took most seriously.

It is likely that Mulholland also saw real danger in the mystical aspects of reality altering the pursuits of the United States government. If Mulholland felt that the men in the CIA were ill equipped to deal with phenomena beyond their understanding, then he wanted to be their teacher of what was illusion and what was not.

An episode of the TV program *The X-Files* makes use of Mulholland's techniques in action. One of the characters is stopped in a hallway at the FBI, where he works. When he is stopped and asked directions, another character very briefly touches the victim. When this contact is reviewed on videotape and the action frozen, the poisoning is uncovered. The creators of this episode might as well have been reading straight out of the manual written for the CIA by John Mulholland, while not providing the misdirective elegance detailed by the scholarly magician. (Other episodes of *The X-Files* have concerned "mind control" by government agents for assassination and the hallucinogenic effect of wild mushrooms.)

In magic there is a corny old joke concerning the request for a volunteer to assist the magician. The magician says, "May I have a victim, err, I mean...a volunteer." The point is that this joke was well known to Mulholland, who grew up in the era of the joke's usage. The word "victim" is a word magician's use with humor. In the manual Mulholland wrote he does not add any humor when he refers to people receiving drugs without their knowledge as "victims." Mulholland used words the way a surgeon uses a scalpel.

His writing in his last book, *The Magical Mind*, substantiates this. He states, "The distinction between the terms victim and subject is not arbitrary—nor is it being used as propaganda for education (a kind of propaganda with which we are flooded these days)."

Mulholland makes particular note of the word "victim" in his first book *Magic in the Making* (1925) on page 15. In his last book (1967) he also explored the use of and meaning of this word, on page 120.

From files released via the Freedom of Information Act, it was learned that the CIA had set up brothels, which had prostitutes administer drugs to the clients without their knowledge. Under the observation of two way mirrors (a natural for a whore's bedroom) the agents could observe how a man would respond to a drug dosage over a period of time. The whorehouse ruse was clever and may be alluded to in Mulholland's correspondence when he refers to "the girls" in writing to Gottlieb. The other key concept is that these "victims" were also "unwitting" or not aware of what was happening.

Especially frustrating to the CIA researchers were the "controls" of ESP experiments. A "john" (a whore's client) dosed on LSD in a covert manner by the prostitute agent schooled in Mulholland's techniques, was not aware that he had been dosed. The whore or agent would begin thinking of a place or song title in the adjacent room, while watching the two sexual partners through a two-way window.

If the "john" suddenly started saying aloud the name of the song, or humming a song thought of by the agent, for example, in the adjacent room, there would be statistical inquiry into whether the dosed "john" was exhibiting telepathy without awareness of it.

All the "john" would remember was going to a whorehouse, having sex, maybe getting drunk, and leaving. At no time would whorehouse clients believe they were the test subjects in a covert, telepathic experiment by the Central Intelligence Agency of the United States. This "experiment," was monitored, and reported on at times by one man deep in the shadows. This was crucial to the continuing success of the operation.

The experiment was risky, but brilliant in design. One researcher said, "The Agency was very likely interested in a pill that enhanced ESP." Frequent users of minor hallucinogens that induce a heightened state without outright hallucination have reported many instances of telepathy and clairvoyance. Greater claims of physical manifestations – sometimes called "apportments" – have been reported, though such information is suspect from a hallucinating subject. At the same time both police and news reporters know well the value of the "hunch." This is sometimes referred to as a "gut feeling" or intuition. Both professions esteem this value.

While Mulholland catalogued coincidence and dissected it, he also employed devious methods to ascertain information. He knew how

171

powerful a supposed revelation of hidden information was. In his *Beware Familiar Spirits* he details an instance where he knew of a man's origins in China before coming to the U.S. He asked the man to think of four numbers (which John Mulholland had surreptitiously obtained). When he made the revelation, he wrote the numbers the man thought of in Chinese, as if he had been in a trance. The man believed he had actually read his mind because of the revelation of his origins in China, a fact he believed impossible for Mulholland to know.

The magician pointed out how details like these made the story and "psychic" revelation more believable. Because of his extreme command of such details, Mulholland was rarely off his guard. He also used his replication of the effects of supposed psychic phenomenon to act as a control against uncritical thought.

Our emotions take hold in the details of "evidence." The magician is aware of this and uses this tendency for his own purpose. This "power of perception" aided the scientists at the CIA in determining what was genuine and what was not. Mostly they found charlatans attempting to gain part of the sizable budget dedicated to this clandestine, parapsychological research. One man familiar with both Mulholland and these tests observed Mulholland's contribution by stating "If you are going to play cards with the boys, you might want to know who 'the boys' are."

In a highly charged atmosphere of sex and drugs, in combination with the magical component of surreptitious behavior and intoxication (on many levels), the pursuit of paranormal phenomenon is not a great stretch.

This is where the magician was so effective. He'd either scoff at such barbaric tests, or statistically answer and give an erudite opinion of genuine psychic phenomena. It takes a trickster to understand the trickster-like phenomena of psi, or psychic phenomenon, which is theoretically supported by applied experiments in quantum physics. The results of such tests designate that neither time nor space matter in the realm of thought.

Skeptics largely railed against quantum physics as "a theoretical argument." However, concerning the quantum nature of the world, the physicist David Bohm stated "Science has shown scientists something they do not want to see because it changes the basic rudiments." Changes in "basic rudiments" are what the mind-kontrol-ultra scientists were interested in exploring.

The ability to harness telepathy would be extremely valuable in the cult of intelligence. To control the mind to think an enemy's thoughts before they were acted upon was a secret of the Cold War valuable enough to kill for.

This program was referred to as "Operation Midnight Climax."

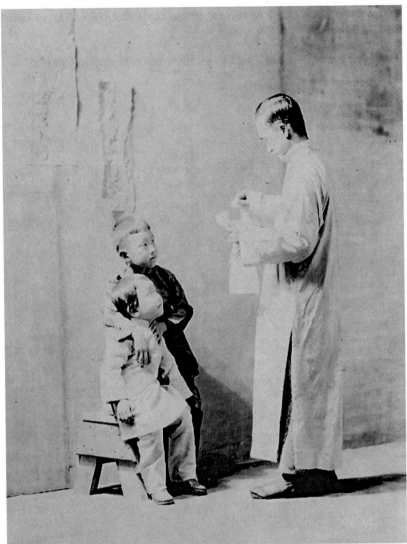

These two photos of a genuine Chinese magician were taken by John Mulholland during his 1923 trip to China. While most likely posed, considerable work went into capturing the images, that were reprinted in his first published book. (Courtesy of Richard Hatch.)

VIII. CIA, LSD & ESP

"The American intelligence business makes use of many sources and methods in order to arrive at a reasonable picture of the truth in a given situation. No one source provides all the answers, but taken together they contribute to a clearer picture of what is going on."

– Ambassador Joseph Wilson, *The Politics of Truth*

The use of unwitting subjects was paramount to the government's cause as the enemy would also be an "unwitting subject;" this is why such tests had to be carried out on unsuspecting, innocent citizens. (It was brought out in the Rockefeller Commission hearings investigating these matters that an unwitting dosing of LSD became an occupational hazard.) It was found that such tests were also used on convicts and mental patients in England. Olson knew this, and it may have been the cause for his admission to his wife of a "terrible mistake," meaning inhumane acts. The experiments on such subjects were conducted under the heading of "Project ARTICHOKE."

Mulholland's duties were not only writing at his desk to detail the deployment of drugs to unwitting subjects. He was also utilized as an on-site consultant to the CIA's experiments in parapsychology. The MK-ULTRA team of Gottlieb, Lashbrook and the members of the Technical Services Staff were interested in "real magic" or the study of parapsychology. Gottlieb was hired as head of the operation because he took a more academic approach than his ARTICHOKE predecessor Morse Allen.

Consequently, to investigate this area, under the rubric of "powers of the mind" they hired "a complete, unconventional magician" to quote Mulholland's friend George Gordon. Mulholland was an intellectual at heart, and like many of their agents, a former educator.

He was hired to help navigate the CIA's way through the world of ESP, clairvoyance and telekinesis (the ability to move objects with the mind alone). One paradoxical goal of the Agency of the time was to "brainwash" the U.S. agents so they could not be brainwashed by enemy countries. The delusion of paranoia took a foothold.

What was feared became the cause of acts that were potentially dangerous to the men hired to enforce national security.

In his *Search for the Manchurian Candidate* John Marks writes: "Most case officers prided themselves on being able to play their agents like a musical instrument at just the right tempo." Another man approached by the Agency during the 1950's related, "One should be very careful when entering the world of espionage. Operatives are disposable. Human life takes a back seat to the greater cause. Always." Marks notes that transcendental goals, such as mind expansion and developed clairvoyance, came later. This is incorrect. Documents in Mulholland's hand from 1954 found in his private papers (unseen by Marks) clearly show that the parapsychological goals concerned the MK-ULTRA scientists from the beginning. These goals were the most hidden of all the program's priorities.

```
Dr. Sidney Gottleib
Clark Thorpe

December 3rd
United Air Lines -- flight 621
La Guardia 8 A.M. arrive Chicago 10:25

Meet U.A.L. lobby meeting

Br.Robert Lashbrook
District 7 - #1334

Mr.Bortner -American Air Lines - Flight 269 - 10:15  (Daylight Mercury)
               (will bring papers)

Armour Research Foundation   Administration Building
35 West 33 Street, Chicago       Mr.Clark Thorpe
33rd and State

Kenneth Miller, Chairman
```

John Mulholland's notes on travel for the Agency.

Mulholland showed Gordon a paper he wrote for "an intelligence agency" and of that paper, Gordon remarked, "John's work for the CIA was not esoteric or strange. The CIA had been presented with a man who said he could send and receive thoughts or codes long distance by mental telepathy. So, they employed John to tell them if this was the real McCoy. And this man was no more a mind reader than fortunetellers can tell fortunes. The man was simply using tricks that magicians use to give the illusion of being able to read minds of others. John wrote how the charlatan was trying to take the CIA for a ride."

Mulholland's report titled *A New Type of Experiment in Parapsychology* dated November 11, 1953, is extensive regarding Dr. H. K. Puharich's experiments for "The Round Table Foundation." Dr. Puharich was also the same doctor who "verified" the controversial Hungarian-born Uri(ah) Geller as being a genuine psychic in the 1970's. Puharich changed his first name shortly after their initial meeting, possibly to obscure his past.

Mulholland was firm in his recommendation that the government was wasting money on parapsychological experiments without solid controls. In others words, they were throwing money after experiments that could have deceptive results due to out and out cheating by doctors and subjects who were shielded by Faraday cages.

The Faraday cage was used to block out all electrical influences to the "sensitive" subject being tested. The scientists who were unfamiliar with the ways of deception, assessed irrational findings through a rational locus. This tested the magician's ire. The general test was that a psychic test subject would know when an electrical current passed though the Faraday cage during 90-second intervals. The professional magician Mulholland was particularly virulent when he assessed scientists' findings:

> It seems to me that the report was too obviously written in the psychic researcher's four-dollar word double talk. This type of writing purportedly is done to be truly "scientific," but the results are more as if it were written for "Science Fiction" or one of the pulps in which the "scientific wonders" of the year 2000 are disclosed.

After filing this report from New York to Washington D.C., on November 11, 1953, Mulholland traveled to Chicago on December 3rd and 4th to meet with Mr. Clark Thorpe and Dr. H. K. Puharich of the Armour Research Foundation and the Chairman of the Foundation, Kenneth Miller. Dr. Robert V. Lashbrook and Dr. Henry Bortner, who later took over the Special Operations Division of the CIA, also traveled from Washington to Chicago on American Airlines Daylight Mercury[9]. All four then traveled to the Armour Research Foundation Administration Building at 35 West 33rd Street (33rd & State) in the Windy City. The CIA has said that they sought operatives in the field that are "the best actors, politicians and can think on their feet." This was clearly in evidence during the magician's trip to Chicago when reviewing the policies of the Armour Research Foundation.

Mulholland's report makes a special note that Clark Thorpe was unknown to the receptionist at the address the team was sent to. Only after much haggling was Thorpe discovered on the premises, whereupon the entire team was taken to another building.

The magician's assignment was to assess the value of research by Thorpe and company. Mulholland "respectfully submitted" a very detailed two-page report back to Washington stating that *The Literature Survay* (sic) *on Thought Transference* was "most Pollyanish in (its) make-up." He was probably accurate in his assessment as he found Dr. Puharich particularly sycophantic.

Apparently when a certain doctor's name was brought into the conversation, Puharich was quick to bring up a multitude of references concerning that doctor. Ever the watchdog of peculiar behavior on the part of the Armour Research Foundation parapsychologists,

Mulholland thought to test Puharich's assertions, and writes in his report:

> I was somewhat surprised by the Doctor's comparative youth. It is unusual to find a sincere believer in things psychic who has not passed through life's meridian. Mr. Thorpe took the Doctor and me on a tour through the Foundation's various departments. Our conversation was on what we were shown and was very general. After about an hour, I discovered that within five minutes of the time Mr. Thorpe mentioned a name or scientific discovery, the Doctor would mention the name or scientific data in some other connection. He seemed to be attempting to show familiarity with everyone and everything mentioned. So, I spoke about a Professor and the Doctor seemed to be quite familiar with his work. This interested me as I had just made up the name of the professor and what he had been doing. In my judgment, the doctor is using things psychic as a means to meet and mingle with people he otherwise would have no opportunity to know.

Mulholland wisely counsels his Washington contacts that such behavior of the parapsychologist's was based on ambition so strong that it would lead to trickery. He wrote, "I trust that I am wrong, but I am fearful that I am not." Mulholland's intuition was in line with what the Agency has said is a skill that cannot be taught. Special Ops agent Chase Brandon declared in the late 1990's that the goal of training was "To discern what is real and what is not. To listen to the intuitive voice in one's head. A voice that is not recognized by most people."

Mulholland proved that it does indeed take a deceptionist to catch a deceptionist. Deceptionist though he was, he also had an open mind and stated quite categorically in a letter "I do believe in extra-sensory perception of sorts. But, most certainly do not believe awareness of events that haven't yet happened, or precognition, though the policeman's intuition or newsman's hunch bears close scrutiny for their accuracy and how much information they had beforehand." Mulholland's open mindedness was an asset valued by the MK-ULTRA scientists. He was a careful, educated mix. He also had what he wrote of as the rarest of gifts – common sense.

After his Chicago trip of December 3-4, 1953 (just one day after Gottlieb approved his continuing to write new material for the manual) he toiled with expanding his original outline. In handwritten and typed formats, Mulholland sketched notes regarding the secretive deployment of drugs:

1.	Background Discussion of Deception
2.	Pills
    a.	About 1/4 size of aspirin.) (1) Standard shapes.
    b.	b. Aspirin Tablet. (2) Unusual shapes.
    c.	Alka Seltzer tablet.
3.	Liquids
    a.	One drop.
    b.	1cc (20 drops, about 1/5 teaspoonful)
    c.	5cc (about 1 teaspoonful)
4.	Solid material in loose form (like salt)
    a.	one speck up to about 1/5 teaspoonful
5.	The Theory and Practice of Free Choice
6.	The Theory and Practice of Picking Up Things
7.	Concealment
8.	The Proper Time and Place.

Chapter 7 became the chapter about women, and Chapter 8 became the section about teams putting into practice the operation designed by the magician. At the bottom of the typed list is Mulholland's handwriting indicating that this outline was submitted to Dr. Sidney Gottlieb and Dr. Robert V. Lashbrook with Lashbrook's phone number penciled at the bottom. (In one handwritten missive from Lashbrook in Mulholland's private papers, Lashbrook counsels the magician "Don't take any wooden nickels, John!") He didn't. In fact, the magician dissected his previous work to find clues and characteristics that might help agents working together. His rough notes on these procedures show not only the method, but also the situation in which his deceptive practices would be employed:

1.
    A.	Roles
    B.	Meet at Bar
2.
    B.	open tables - restaurant, large receptions - while holding drink
3.	Compartment on train in which B. rides
4.	B's home (family & servants) same as 1
      1. Impression of key
      2. A visits factory or conducted tour
      A works in factory of different department
      3. Papers

On this same sheet are random notes in the margins mentioning "magician's wax" and the ability to obtain things using tacks and pockets.

Mulholland was utilizing a principle that every professional magician knows well concerning the appearance of objects – a holding device to secure an object prior to its "reveal," as magicians call it; yet, a device that allows a quick release of the object that will "appear." Mountain climbers are familiar with such devices as carabiners. For this purpose magicians use a substance called diachylon, or "magician's wax." Mulholland synthesized the use of this wax to secure a tablet on the back of a common twenty-five cent piece. Hence, when one agent went to make a phone call with a drink in hand (while at a restaurant or bar as Mulholland describes), the agent could surreptitiously obtain a pill or tablet to be dispensed to an unwitting subject (such as the doomed Dr. Olson who was given LSD) without anyone being the wiser. Further instructions were written in his notes concerning the absorption of chemicals through "filed" fingertips. Mulholland knew that 19th century mind readers often depended more on the properties of lemon juice when applied to paper to discover secret information than actual telepathy and precognition. Hence, practicality and simplicity pervaded his suggestions for covert operations.

1. The John Mulholland "dope coin" made from a 1922 Liberty dollar coin. Work began in early 20's on this prop.

2. Typical to the "hidden humor" of Mulholland, he utilized the word "peace" to press to open the coin.

3. The word "peace" is pressed by a simple move of the thumb.

4. The coin is shown by the side with the thumb and forefinger holding it in position to open.

5. A slight pressure is exerted and the coin opens on a beveled hinge hidden inside the coin. The coin was usually loaded with several grams of a drug dispensed surreptitiously.

6. Another view of the coin opened. The beauty of this prop was that it was a one handed manipulation that was easy for agents to do, and took but seconds.

In 1960 U-2 bomber pilot Frances Gary Powers carried another magician's device. On his ill-fated covert flight over the former Soviet Union, he carried a drill bit coated with a deadly shellfish toxin concealed within a silver dollar. A coin that opens, or has a secret compartment, is an underground secret even among magicians. More the province of diabolical gamblers, this coin is known among card "mechanics" and smugglers as a "dope coin." The hidden compartment was used to contain a mirror, which aided dealers who cheated at cards, or addicts who carried contraband such as cocaine[10].

It is well known through intelligence communities that concealment devices for transporting information are lessons in cleverness. Prior to the digital age, the concealment of a drug in a coin or a book on a microdot of film was considered science fiction or Hollywood drama, but in fact, it was actual technology. This writer has been quizzed about the use of microdots in connection to the captured Russian double agent Robert Hanssen. Actually the allusion to a microdot was a fictional piece of humor – but serious enough to invite government scrutiny.

The clever "dope coin" that Mulholland machined for the Agency in 1953 is made from a 1921 silver dollar and opens when the word "peace" is gently pushed between thumb and forefinger. Mulholland charged fifteen dollars in machine fees when he submitted his bill for the presentation of this highly secret tool. Apparently Mulholland was no stranger to this device. He had been working on such a prop since his early 20's. This is noted in a letter to him by the well-known magic manufacturer in Philadelphia, Carl Brema. In his letter of March, 1922, Brema details that he had worked from a sketch of a coin that opens up, provided to him by Mulholland, and had failed with Plaster of Paris to get a working model, but felt that a metal coin could be machined to the magician's specifications. Why Mulholland required such a prop while still a teacher at the Horace Mann School for Boys is a mystery, except that his specialty was coin magic.

All of the deceptions detailed by Mulholland are ruled by the magician's axiom: Hide in the obvious. After all, to make a phone call, you would have to put your hand in your pocket to obtain some coins. The phone call might also appear innocent. However, if a prearranged assistant placed the call, then the role of the assistant was crucial to the trickster's timing. No one would think that a common coin could dispense a lethal drug by an unrecognized assassin, who would poison a victims' drink, during a simple phone call. Surely this was primitive deception, but no doubt worked as well as anything the fictional, infamous "Q" devised for James Bond.

Mulholland was careful about his own calls. His phone bill regarding calls to "The Company" is included in Mulholland's private papers and indicates that during January and February of 1954 he spoke with his associates in Washington fourteen times from his small vacation home, the Mulholland "Hide-a-Way" in Newtown, Connecticut.

He was reimbursed for the $15.00 he spent in long distance charges. His reimbursement was not inflated. In fact, he was very careful about his expenses, which ultimately brought him a little trouble with the Internal Revenue Service for declaring his income from a covert agency. While he admitted in later years that he "probably made more money than any other magician" he was clearly doing work that came without recognition, or the public praise to which he was accustomed.

		Subject to	
	NEW YORK TELEPHONE COMPANY **Toll Calls and Telegrams**	15% Tax	25% Tax
MON 2 8763			
JAN			
21	NEWTN	1	40
27	PLEASANTVL		30
28	WASHN	3	20
FEB			
5	NEWTN		40
6	"		45
8	"	1	20
6	FROM NEWTN		45
11	NEWTN	1	00
12	NEWTN		60
12	"		45
14	"	1	20
16	"		50
13	FROM NEWTN		45
20	NEWTN		40

Total U. S. Tax (*Tax Schedule on reverse*) 3 00

Total Carried to Bill 1500

A-1380   11-51

Phone record of calls made re "the work."

Chemrophyl Associates
P.O. Box 9174
Southeast Station
Washington 24, D.C.
February 23, 1954

Sherman C. Grifford

Mr. John Mulholland
600 West 115 Street
New York 25, New York

Dear John:

    According to my records, payments so far have been as

follows:

Date of Payment	For Period	Amount
April 13, 1953	March 1-17	150.00
May 5	March 18-April 13	150.00
June 17	May 11-18, 25-30, June 1-8	450.00
July 10	weeks begin June 15 & 22	300.00
August 12	weeks begin July 13 & 20	300.00
August 31	weeks begin July 27, August 3 & 10	450.00
October 24	weeks begin August 24, 31, Sept 14	450.00
October 22	weeks begin Sept 21, 28, Oct 4, 11	600.00
December 10	weeks begin Oct 19, 26, Nov 2	450.00
January 21, 1954	Nov 11-Dec 9	270.00

                                   $3,570.00

    In addition, payments for direct travel expenses were
$37.51 and $126.81.

                   Sincerely,

                   SHERMAN C. GRIFFORD

SCG:mk

Everyone kept tabs on expenses.

Mr.Sherman C.Grifford
Chemrophyl Associates
Washington,D.C.

Expenses incured during 1953 for which tax deductions were
not claimed. Reimbursement for excess income taxes.

Income received from you during 1953 $3300.
Standard 10% deduction   330.
22.2% tax on $330.   73.26

I certify that no deductions whatsoever were claimed for
the amount received from you although for the remainder
of my income itemized deductions were made,

Summary of actual expenses:

   Stationary $5.00
   Telephone   50.00
   Research
     (lunches-taxis   150.00
     Techines,books   50.00
   Model
    (shop and labor) 75.00
              $330.00

                          John Mulholland

Mr.Sherman C Grifford
Chemrophyl Associates
Washington.D.C.

Expenses...............................$73.26

                          John Mulholland

John Mulholland's accounting of CIA money.

IX. SAME PEOPLE–DIFFERENT NAMES

Concerning President Nixon's use of known CIA operatives used to burglarize the Democratic National Head Quarters in June, 1972:

"They bugged, they followed people, false press leaks, fake letters, canceled Democratic campaign rallies, investigated Democratic private lives, they planted spies, stole documents, and on and on. Now don't tell me you think this is all the work of little Don Segretti.

You done worse than let Haldeman slip away. You've got people feeling sorry for him. I didn't think that was possible. In a conspiracy like this you build from the outer edges and you go step by step. If you shoot too high and miss, everybody feels more secure. You put the investigation back months... It was a Haldeman operation. The whole business was run by Haldeman, the money, everything. It won't be easy getting at him, he was insulated. You'll have to find out how. Mitchell started doing covert stuff before anyone else. The list is longer than anyone can imagine. It involves the entire US Intelligence community. FBI, CIA, Justice. It's incredible. Cover-up had little to do with Watergate. It was mainly to protect the covert operations. It leads everywhere. Get out your notebook, there's more. Your lives are in danger."

– "Deep Throat" to Bob Woodward,
ALL THE PRESIDENTS MEN, 1974

What a company Grifford/Gottlieb and Wittstock/Lashbrook were!

In 1955 Mulholland was all of a sudden reporting to a seemingly different crew, the company of: Granger Research Inc. After he had submitted his manual, and its operations were under way, the people he worked for changed the name of their company.

Interestingly enough, the Sherman C. Grifford (of Chemrophyl Associates) who wrote to Mulholland on November 17, 1954, mentioning a cashier's check by number and amount, became a fellow named Samuel A. Granger, who also wrote to Mulholland on March 4, 1955 mentioning a Union Trust Company check by number and amount in a similar manner. Samuel A. Granger also had a conspicuously similar signature to Sherman C. Grifford. Of course, both were Sidney Gottlieb, the man whose obituary said, "took LSD to the CIA."

It seems that those who worked for the CIA had a penchant for changing their names with some regularity. In fact, it was standard Agency policy that no agent with TOP SECRET clearance was addressed by his or her real name – especially in correspondence.

From documents made available by the CIA concerning MK-ULTRA Gottlieb's signature matches that of Sherman C. Grifford and (not surprisingly) Samuel A. Granger. While John Marks in his *Search for the Manchurian Candidate* originally revealed the name "Sherman Grifford," the device of repeating initials was given no significance. The Granger name was not mentioned. Having solved this puzzle independently, I met with Assistant District Attorney Steven Saracco in New York; he told me he liked my persona. Guys in the other room, he said, "wanted a piece of him."

It makes sense that if a scientist were going to have a "spy name" then he would at least want familiar initials. The remarkable thing about the documents of Gottlieb's organization is that they appear so simply as one thing, when in actuality, they are quite indicative of something else. In fact when Mulholland's CIA materials were offered as part of a lot for auction, they were passed over as meaningless pieces of paper, given they did not have a sexy picture of a magician with red devils. And thus buyers missed the most interesting red devils of all!

It is likely that Mulholland knew that these men were in the business of deploying drugs covertly, and he kept a paper trail concerning what interaction he had with them. This was against Agency doctrine.

Whether or not Mulholland trusted his employers is a matter of conjecture. The first time "Grifford" wrote to Mulholland, the letter is addressed to the magician's mother's house. This is curious.

Mulholland had already lived as a married man several blocks away for over ten years. It is a possibility that Mulholland did not want the government scientists to know where he lived when they first met. Mulholland was a keen collector who never threw anything away and if he ever wrote something, he kept a copy. It can be seen that when he wrote something for the CIA, the Agency requested his carbon as well. Distinct to his private papers is correspondence more detailed *prior* to his Oath of Secrecy being signed.

Date of Payment	Period	Amount
January 21, 1954	November 11th to December 9th	$270.00
March 19, 1954	Weeks of January 11th and 18th, February 12th and 19th, and March 1st	750.00
June 11, 1954	March, April and May	750.00
September 30, 1954	Weeks of July 18th and August 23rd	300.00
November 22, 1954	September and October	300.00
		$2,370.00

I have not been able to locate the bill you gave us in December,
so I would appreciate it if you would send me another one.

Please note my new address. Please send future correspondance
to the address as it appears on this letterhead.

Sincerely yours,

Robert V. Wittstock

RVW:bg

Upon completion of his assignment, it might be thought that such official, detail-oriented government employees would have some document of closure. None exists in the extremely well kept files of John Mulholland. Grifford's Chemrophyl Associates seems to simply disappear, only to be replaced by the somewhat more officious Granger Research, Inc. However, there may be one tell tale document that indicates this metamorphosis. Shortly after August 19, 1954 Mulholland received a letter from a man who signed his name only as "Bob L." telling him that he had a new phone number, and that he would not accept any collect calls!

But Sidney Gottlieb's alter egos, Sherman C. Grifford and Samuel A. Granger, now had a title. He became the President of Granger Research. The Vice President, noted on the company stationary was a fellow named Robert V. Wittstock. Funny that Sherman C. also worked with a Robert V. Lashbrook. Perhaps being on a first name basis had more significance than one would imagine. One letter from Lashbrook/Wittstock is unidentifiable as to who wrote it because the author simply signed it "Robert V."

Lashbrook's handwritten letter to John Mulholland.

It appears that the spies in Washington were in desperate need of lessons in deception by a pro like Mulholland. Any junior sleuth would be able to see through their very lacking "blind." Like Chemrophyl Associates, Granger Research also occupied a post box at Southwest Station in Washington D.C. It also seems that though Dr. Sidney Gottlieb and Mulholland were well acquainted, Gottlieb never wrote even a short memo to the magician (that is, under his own real name).

Two years after Mulholland had been on the hefty government payroll, on May 5, 1955 (5/5/55), Sidney Gottlieb wrote a two-page memo concerning the war department's use of LSD. He detailed the uses of the drug as:

1. Substances, which will promote illogical thinking and impulsiveness to the point where the recipient would be discredited in public

2. Substances which increase the efficiency of mentation and perception

3. Materials which will prevent or counteract the intoxicating effect of alcohol

4. Materials which will promote the intoxicating effect of alcohol

5. Materials which will produce the signs and symptoms of recognized dementia in a reversible way so that they may be used for malingering, etc.

6. Materials which will render the induction of hypnosis easier or otherwise enhance its usefulness

7. Substances which will enhance the ability of individuals to withstand privation, torture and coercion during interrogation and so-called "brain washing"

8. Materials and physical methods which will produce amnesia for events preceding and during their use

9. Physical methods of producing check and confidence over extended periods of time and usable of surreptitious use

10. Substances which produce physical disablement such as paralysis of the legs, acute amnesia etc.

11. Substances which will produce pure euphoria with no subsequent let down

12. Substances which alter personality structure in such a way that the tendency of the recipient to become another person is enhanced

13. A material which will cause mental confusion of such a type that the individual under its influence will find it difficult to maintain a fabrication under questioning

14. Substances which will lower the ambition and general working efficiency of men when administered in undetectable amounts

15. Substances which promote weakness or distortion of the eyesight or hearing faculties, preferably without permanent effects

16. A knockout pill which can surreptitiously be administered in drinks, food, cigarettes, as an aerosol etc., which will be safe to use, provide a maximum of amnesia and be suitable for use by agent types on an ad hoc basis

17. A material which can be surreptitiously administered by the above routes and which in very small amounts will make it

impossible for a man to perform any physical activity whatsoever

Clearly a powerful drug with such an agenda was useless without the covert means of deployment. Mulholland's role was not solely as a scholarly researcher and a world authority on deception. Mulholland and the methods he designed might well be metaphorized as a pilot to the plane delivering the bomb in combat.

By 1955, Mulholland had been paid another $2,370 plus expenses of $52.14 for his labors. His employers were explicit about where receipts should be mailed for their very detailed and prompt payments. Never more than two weeks passed without the magician receiving a cashier's check for the average sum of $200 a week, which sometimes skyrocketed as high as $750.

As of 1956 Mulholland was making an average of $1000 a year from the office of Granger Research in Washington. While he corresponded with and billed his contemporaries in Washington D.C. five times in 1956, there seems to be a year-long gap in his employment between September of 1956 and September of 1957. One clue to Mulholland's lack of documentation may come from an intimate and hidden source. In January of 1957, a fictional character named Frank Joglar (actually a nom de plume of Milbourne Christopher) added to his "News & Notes" column for a magician's magazine, that "John Mulholland is home and on the mend after an operation at University Hospital."

Unfortunately, even though Mulholland extends the "standard 10% discount" to his employers, and was explicit in stating that no taxes had been deducted from his checks, there is little record in Mulholland's extensive documents concerning what his discounted work entailed. The only clues he left are mysterious references to "the girls" and "the women in Maine." It is likely that these people were psychic test subjects who attempted to read maps while blindfolded at a distance. Possibly he was referring to the prostitutes employed by the Agency for the deployment of their new drugs. Both operations existed simultaneously.

Another possibility is that the women he referred to were split personality subjects who were being experimented on to become unwitting assassins. These were actual "Manchurian Candidate" drones, which in fact was not fiction as edified by the following report document dated January 7, 1953. This report describes the experimental creation of a multiple personality in two 19-year-old girls:

"These subjects have clearly demonstrated that they can pass from a fully awake state to a deep hypnotic controlled state by telephone, by receiving written matter, or by the use of code, signal or words, and that control of those hypnotized can be passed from one individual to another without great difficulty. It has also been shown by experimentation with these girls that they can act as unwilling couriers for information purposes." (Document CIA Mori ID 190684)

What has only come to light via this inquiry is that the magician and the CIA found something via their "research" that the magician had been looking for all of his life; but never expected to find: evidence of real magic, or psychic phenomena. Mulholland was oblique when he admitted that psychic Eileen Garrett was never caught cheating throughout her career. Hence, Mulholland might have accepted that Ms. Garrett had "the real thing." Again, maybe not.

Substantiating such a claim is difficult historically as the nature of psychic phenomena is immediate and extremely transitory. Thousands of books have been written confirming and denying the existence of such phenomenon. However, if one considers that the CIA seriously undertook their study, one is hard pressed to deny that in 1952 two important events occurred simultaneously: the accepted discoveries of the quantum "zero point field" and the publication of Carl Jung's 20-year-old theory of meaningful coincidence, which he called "synchronicity."

Given that both the fields of psychology and physics came to similar conclusions about the nature of space, time and mind, it is extremely likely that not only did the CIA take notice, but that they also sought to control, or utilize the chaotic nature of the phenomenon for their efforts during the Cold War. With drugs and hypnosis and "electroshock therapy" as a gateway to other powers, or states of mind, the U.S. government realized it was 20 years behind the Soviets and Chinese in this research. Their consultants repeatedly claimed the U.S. was lacking in serious investigation in this regard.

This point was dogmatically fought over. A very detailed three-page letter was addressed to the MK–ULTRA scientists on June 22, 1954 and titled "The Military Application of Hypnotism." It deals with the unknown authored, hand-written note mentioned earlier: the unwitting hypnotically-induced courier of information. The letter claimed that the messenger would have no memory of being hypnotized, nor any knowledge of the contents of the message he carried. The recipient of the message was able to trigger the message from the courier by signals or phrases. The "theoretical hypnotic authority" as the author calls himself, is also somewhat dramatic in his claims, stating: "The hypnotic messenger will never, under any circumstances by a slip of the tongue divulge the true nature of his mission." He later writes, "Once, every month, or at such time is advisable they will be contacted by a member of our intelligence department, hypnotized, and as loyal American (sic) will tell what they know. This sounds unbelievable, but I assure, you, it will work."

The writer's conclusion was surely designed to create desperation and a job for his claims: "In closing, may I make one very significant point. The Russian literature is hard to get and carefully avoids any mention of the topic in question. Those Russian articles which I have been able to get leave no doubt about the fact that the Russian is just as conservative about the field of hypnotism as are we."

The man making the grand claims was not without his critics. Each claim was open to careful scrutiny and deliberate criticism by Mulholland who reviewed the claims and reported:

> *"The idea of a courier that has been hypnotized is not new and I am absolutely certain that (blanked out by the government) did not invent this idea. We ourselves have carried out much more complex problems than this and in a general sense I will agree that it is feasible. However, there is no proof that the hypnosis cannot be broken by another competent hypnotist, and the actual test has not been subjected to field conditions."*

Mulholland called the claim that the hypnotized courier would have no knowledge of his mission or having been hypnotized, "debatable."

At best Mulholland was, to use his own words, "lukewarm" on the notion of hypnotism, and wryly observed in 1935 in an article, "Yet there is always someone at the end of my show who says 'Mr. Mulholland, you magicians do really have a power. I mean it *is* hypnotism, isn't it?' "

Like most things the CIA has ever been up to, for obvious reasons it denied the existence of such inquiries. To their credit, they employed Mulholland as a vital control, to pursue the real thing, and listened carefully to his opinions to guard against fraud. In addition, to *purposely fake* parapsychological phenomenon was also a very desirable goal of the Agency. Presenting the ability to use real clairvoyance ("clear seeing") in matters of intelligence is a concrete course of action, regardless of opinion.

Scientists theorized that one way to excite the phenomenon of seeing great distances through psychic projection for spying efforts (called "remote viewing") was to expand consciousness and open the mind. Sidney Gottlieb knew that not only was LSD a tool for interrogation, but also that unexplained physical phenomenon was a likely occurrence of LSD-influenced thought. The problem is that the use of LSD seemingly invalidated any real data on psychic phenomenon because of the unreliable state of hallucinating mind. However, by 1963 the men involved in MK-ULTRA had sampled everything from palm reading to subliminal perception and were satisfied they had not overlooked anything in the field of human perception. Terence McKenna, often considered the successor to Timothy Leary, and his brother Dennis McKenna, both tackled "hidden realms" of the mind while influenced by hallucinogens. Reports of psychic manifestations were debated because of the unreliable state of mind perceived by non-hallucinating observers. In 2004, research continues in this realm funded by individuals concerned with dissecting the genuine nature of reality. Such research is not folly, is given a classification outside U.S. laws, and conducted at the highest levels of the Department of Defense.

By June of 1956 Mulholland's work seems to have encompassed everything from Astrology to Zionism. (Simple word systems seem to have been as common a practice with this group of scientific spies as the changing of last names.) The magician recounts in letters his "unaltered opinion" of scientific attainments by bogus witch doctors and characters he describes as just plain "nuts."

Although the money was good, Mulholland seems agitated in some of his correspondence that the Agency should be spending money, and his time, investigating the claims of astrologers, faith healers and things that go bump in the night. In one letter, while expressing appreciation for Grifford's secretarial typing, Mulholland is positively adamant that not a word of his writing should be changed or deleted without his consent. He wanted to guard against the politicizing of his opinions for bogus ventures. As a "watcher" of such "fringe" activities such as astrological conventions – Mulholland was understandably annoyed that his expert opinion might become diluted by ignorant desire or rampant paranoia that seized the collective mind of the government researchers. "Science" often was tainted by collusion of test subjects looking to make easy government money, and the hunger to develop *psychic warfare.*

Later, when Operation Stargate was finally disclosed in 1995, the CIA admitted only to spending 10 million dollars on psychic research between 1975 and 1995. The final conclusion: nothing much was found. Given the hard copy in this writer's possession, this admission is incorrect.

In January 1957 John Mulholland survived an operation on his stomach at the University Hospital. He received all of his condolence letters at his Sphinx office which became "the office of John Mulholland" when he closed the magazine in 1953 shortly after his new duties for the CIA began.

The magician had received nearly $1600 more and wrote to Samuel Granger on October 3, 1957 that he needed more time to work on his current assignment. It seems that whenever he needed more time to do a thorough job, it was not a problem; nor was payment for that time.

The last receipt in his personal files is from January 31, 1958. Another $400 was paid for more investigation by the magician into the weird practices of psychics and clairvoyants. Little is known about his investigations.

As well, in 1973, when Sidney Gottlieb claimed to purposely destroy many of the documents relating to these experiments, he was also burying in secrecy a fantastic tale. Gottlieb knew that he'd be reprimanded and also receive condemnation for exorbitant waste of funds on such a ridiculous topic as "real magic" or, as he put it, "the unlocking of the nature of coincidence."

In 1999 the CIA declassified several documents concerning John Mulholland, his involvement in MK-ULTRA Subproject 4,19 and others. The status of declassification is not an open admission of anything. Once the Freedom of Information Act is invoked, it can still be a matter of years before a heavily redacted document is offered for inspection.

Like the magician's paradox, sometimes what is not seen is more telling than what is. More importantly, the results of Mulholland's inquiry are still marked "Classified."

June 22,1956

Mr.Samuel A.Grander,
Granger Research Company
Washington,D.C.

Dear Samuel.

       Herewith is additional material having to do with
Astrology. The book list is one of a large number of similar catologs (my name is listed as a collector of occult
material) and none of them has listed a book having to do
with the particular phase of our interest.

       The convention program gives the names and addresses
of a considerable number of astrologers who claim to be very
much on the up and up. I spent a good part of one day at
the convention trying to size up the membership of the organization. My opinion remains unaltered and their claims to
scientific attainments did not impress me. However, the
members of the organization are supposed to be the most re-
putable in the field. I believe that you will want the
program for your files.

       The organization came out with a condemnation of all
newspaper horoscopes as being without value (which Heaven
knows is true) but it seemed that their reason for so doing
was entirely a business reason. If a person finds in his
daily paper a guide to his conduct as indicated by the stars
he does not have to pay a high fee to an individual to find
what the stars have instore for him. And the pronouncement
by the organization had the furthur objective of showing
how active the membership is in decrying the work of the
"unscientific" who write the newspaper columns. Their purpose is to xdvxxtxgx advance astrology as a "real science."
While one is with them they sound most convincing.

       With the hope that all your research projects are
progressing in the way you wish and with best regards,

          Sincerely yours

John Mulholland's letter re astrology.

X. INVISIBLE MEN

"How did John meet Sidney Gottlieb? I don't know. I really don't. But I am not surprised. John knew a lot of people from all walks of life, and as I got to know him, the ever-pouring cornucopia of his affiliations was constantly astounding."

– Dr. George N. Gordon

Were it not for John Mulholland's initials, address and phone number found in Robert Lashbrook's address book, Mulholland's role in MK-ULTRA might never have come to light. These are the details that slip through the cracks of time and ultimately tell volumes. The fact that John Mulholland kept practically every scrap of paper throughout his life, prompting his wife to write after his death, "I am sick of living in a warehouse" has led this researcher to uncover names associated with the MK-ULTRA that previously have been unexplored. Though the information is scant, the "Ultra" portion of the plan is seen a little more clearly. Another notion also becomes tantalizingly prominent:

THOSE THAT DEAL IN SECRETS DO NOT LIKE TO BE WRITTEN ABOUT AND LITTLE IS WRITTEN ABOUT THEM.

So little in fact that only brief biographies of some of the players can be put together. The indication, however is that Mulholland was familiar with a larger portion of the program than has ever been suspected. Just as John Mulholland's initials appeared in Robert Lashbrook's address book, a number of important names appeared on Mulholland's contact sheet in his files.

Understanding the intelligence world is kind of like looking through the wrong end of a telescope. Everything is in focus, but it is far away and hard to read.

Such is the case with affiliations in this field, and therefore the word "cult" is well applied. The definition of a cult is like-minded souls who follow a set path for a common goal. Therefore, given the tendencies we have observed concerning operatives' nature, almost anyone from the "old Grotonian world" might be a candidate to "help the Company." George Gordon's astonishment of who John Mulholland knew was well taken. One character who came into focus late in this researcher's adventure does not appear on this list is Dr. DeWitt Stetten, Jr. Magic historian Dr. Edwin A. Dawes met Stetten once at a biochemists' convention in New York City in the early 1970's. Having been told by Mulholland of Stetten's appreciation of magic,

Dawes quizzed the famous biochemist as to whether or not Mulholland taught him any tricks. "Yes, four" he replied. But, he was no longer able to present any of Mulholland's legerdemain.

Born in New York City on May 31, 1909, DeWitt Stetten Jr. attended the Horace Mann School for Boys while Mulholland taught woodworking skills, called at the time, industrial arts. Stetten's parents enjoined Mulholland to help their son overcome his extreme shyness by coaching him as a young magician.

Stetten Jr., known as "Hans" throughout his life, became stuck with his passion as an amateur magician for the remainder of his life, and his contributions to his vocation were considerable. The National Institute of Health Museum of Medical Research in Bethesda, Maryland, was named as the DeWitt Stetten Museum for his vast accomplishments in the field of biochemistry.

Schooled at Harvard in 1930, then receiving his M.D. and Ph.D. from Columbia in 1934 and 1940 respectively, Stetten is lauded for his extreme skill as a negotiator, his pervasive good humor, and hard work ethic. He authored over one hundred significant scientific papers, and became the first Dean of the Rutgers Medical School.

So how does Stetten fit into this story? Only by being close to the magician, having been chaperoned to Europe by Mulholland on one occasion, and being in a hotbed of research that might have put him in contact with such a character as Sidney Gottlieb. Both were experts in their fields, and in 1954 Stetten was appointed director in charge of the intramural research program concerning Arthritis and Metabolic Diseases at the National Institute of Health. What was discovered about diseases and their common cause was a topic of interest by the chemists at the CIA. Stetten seems as likely a source to have joined John Mulholland and Sidney Gottlieb as anyone in this universe of academics and government researchers. But, he is not mentioned in the private files of John Mulholland concerning his involvement with the CIA.

DeWitt Stetten Jr. died, after refusing to be slowed down by blindness, on August 28, 1990.

Equally impressive, Mulholland's notes do detail the involvement of another character from a similar background that would ultimately become the United States' first Ambassador to Cambodia, Robert Mills McClintock (a name he very typically misspells as "McClintook").

Robert Mills McClintock was born in King County, Washington, August 30, 1909. Ivy league trained, he was a Foreign Service Officer in Finland, 1942; Foreign Service Officer, Vietnam, 1953; U.S.

Ambassador to Cambodia, 1954; U.S. Ambassador to Lebanon, 1957; US Ambassador to Argentina, 1962-1964; U.S. Ambassador to Venezuela, 1970. He died age 65, in 1976 in a guardedly unknown location. The reason for the cloaking of his burial site has been met with knowing smiles and silence upon several inquiries. The general belief is that this was a man so involved in international affairs that he may have created enemies who would wish to desecrate his last resting place.

A U.S. "Chief of Mission" include Ministers, Charges d' Affairs, Diplomatic Agents and US Ambassadors also known as "Ambassadors Extraordinary and Plenipotentiary, or, AEP's." The ambassadors from the U.S. tend to be a mixture of career foreign service officer, patronage appointments and those that distinguished themselves by giving large amounts of money to an elected party. McClintock is mentioned in *Uncloaking the CIA*, as "the first Ambassador to Cambodia, and known to be an experienced CIA man."

Little is known about McClintock's activities in Cambodia and Viet Nam, but the time he was there, commensurate with his involvement with the CIA would have made him a convenient investigator of methods the U.S. was actively seeking defense against. At this time, Cambodia had recently won its independence from France.

McClintock's depiction as an "experienced" Agency man also tells us that he was likely practiced in the ways of developing relationships so as to ultimately undermine, and potentially create blackmail scenarios concerning sensitive information. He could have developed confidences, which ultimately would be betrayed. The thriller idea that an operative deals in guns, sexy women and the constant race against time is a misnomer.

Intelligence historian Keith Melton has pointed out that those involved in intelligence betray their duty once bullets start flying. The act of "intelligence" is to lead a double life: appearing one way, and actually seeking the means to an entirely different purpose. The ambassador's position is a matter of grace and confidence. Relationships formed for the good of two (or more nations) appear to seek the classic "win-win" situation. In the operative-ambassador position however, the reduction of, say, an import tax may hardly be the actual cause...surveying locations and setting up nearby "watch posts" for neighboring lands may be of utmost importance. This is where Mulholland came in.

As a magician of many faces, guises and talents he was often called upon with the task of creating a scenario ripe for illusion. Given his world travels, particularly to Burma, and his affiliations with the street entertainers of New Delhi and the upper aristocracy of England, he knew social customs all over the world. In his manual *Some Operational Applications of the Art of Deception*, he is even clear to mention what is appropriate given social custom. More importantly, he was able to advise the use of deception in social circles based on current social custom all over the world. In certain parts of Southeast Asia, at dinners and other ceremonial events, for example, it is common for servers to wear a new pair of gloves when offering each plate. Jewelry is often hidden by gloves, but not when encountered by a magician-trained operative. The "language of the hands" is something an expert magician would know and react to unlike the untrained diplomat.

Knowing this custom gave the magician "entry points" where some of the methods he created might come into play. Or, something as harmless as asking the age of a finger ring, might tell him hidden information about where the ring was purchased and by whom and therefore pinpoint when a man was in Geneva, when his story notes that he lived in Berlin at the time. Getting information is one thing. Getting information surreptitiously at a state dinner is quite another. Knowing that McClintock was an official put people on their guard, so an offhand table trick might break tension and loosen up partygoers.

When his affiliations with Cambodian Ambassador Robert Mills McClintock is inspected, Mulholland's role seems to be more specific. A compatriot of Mulholland's was a newspaperman who traveled the Far East in the 1940's via a commercial freighter. Only later, via the Freedom of Information Act, did this reporter learn that the newly born CIA wanted to exploit him (their words) because of his appointments to interview heads of state. Similarly, Ambassador McClintock exploited the knowledge he gleaned from his associations.

With an ambassador in place, and accepted over years, Mulholland would often be able to plan a portion of the operative's movements in circles to obtain objectives while the ambassador was able to present themselves and their cause as completely legitimate. Because of his knowledge as a magician, he would be able to create the suitable artifice to mask and integrate essential clandestine components already in place.

For instance, were an operative aware that a man he would soon be meeting had a slight stutter, the magician would counsel the operative to also affect a slight stutter this would bring familiarity to the meeting. Like the trick where Mulholland made the revelation in Chinese, he was able to find inroads in conversations and social situations which would create opportunities to meet and associate with another operative or with a "target."

In the case of McClintock in Cambodia in the middle 50's, Mulholland never came in direct contact with him (they would meet years later at a Washington correspondent's dinner). However, being briefed on the Ambassador's movements made it possible for the magician to assess and deduce possible scenarios where McClintock could be used. Most of the work McClintock carried out was filtered through his liaison Archibald J. Sampson.

Another character among the notes of John Mulholland's private CIA files is Dr. Robert Goodenow. He was with the Department of Genetics at the University of California at Berkley. His address was listed, which often indicated a face-to-face meeting. Agency policy, at the time was that little was written down, and only on a need-to-know basis was something written. And, if things were written down, it was later denied, as in the case of Gottlieb testifying that he destroyed all written records. If that were true, there would have been nothing to find.

While Goodenow's prowess as a scientist is not elaborated on when dealing with the MK-ULTRA consortium, it does not seem so unusual that another science was considered by Gottlieb and crew. The notion of the "ultra" part of their program meant, "all encompassing." Given that Hitler's Third Reich was heavily involved in the creation of a Master Race, the quest was to leave no stone unturned to find out if particular genes and ethnicities led the pack in certain abilities. One question nagged at the scientists: were those who lived at high altitude more capable of telepathy? Lab testing in this regard was futile. The search for telepathy never ascended to the heights sought.

On the same sheet as McClintock, Sampson and Goodenow, Mulholland notes Robert H. Dabney. Again, Dabney is a mystery man who doesn't seem to have any connection to this world through academia or as a field officer. Obviously, if his name was included, he was a member of "deep cover." Again, "deep cover" is not to suggest something pernicious. But, it obviously dealt with an area that was sensitive and indicated that this individual was an essential part of a team working to solve a problem, or to gain some particular knowledge. In fact, a person who seems "invisible" may have also been an object of attention – a person whom a covert plan involved, but without his or her knowledge. A person taken into this world would often relate certain findings which may be used for ends completely alien to their perception, much like a magician getting a person to look in the wrong place at the right time. This becomes a very important factor when deducing threats to national security. It also induces paranoia, as those taking up the mantle to defend the American way of life often feel threatened because of their built-in feeling that a threat is always lurking.

One person with whom Mulholland came into contact while employed as an Agency analyst and about whom a great deal is known was John Hays Hammond.

Born in 1888, he died in 1965. Hammond was an American inventor of radio-operated control systems. He is noted for being whimsical and practical. He enjoyed cooking, electronics and torpedoes! Born to privilege, family friends included Thomas Edison who advised him to patent everything and get a good lawyer. He also knew the Wright Brothers.

Hammond attended the Sheffield School of Science at Yale, concentrating on radio dynamics and was graduated in 1910. His father advanced him a quarter million dollars to found his own company. By 1916 he earned appreciation of the U.S. War Dept. for his work on jamming signals and a target seeking system. He was also a pioneer in frequency modulation (FM) broadcasting. He had some eccentric inventions as well: a magnetic bottle cap remover, a "pan-less stove," and a failed cure for baldness. Hammond especially enjoyed his ten-thousand pipe organ in his castle in Gloucester, Massachusetts.

He was a world famous traveler and a respected engineer, entrepreneur and inventor. John Mulholland wrote to Sidney Gottlieb on November 11, 1953 and stated, "My informant states positively that he (Hammond) is a 'nut.' " Mulholland using the term "informant" is significant. It shows dedication to his new job. He was a master deceptionist and employing an informant is not far removed from the world of clandestine intelligence work.

The importance of these affiliations is that they were not show biz acquaintances: Ambassadors, inventors, philanthropists, doctors of genetics, government officials; the men noted here as "invisible" were men who worked in the shadows of government research, sometimes without their knowing with what they were involved.

One man who definitely knew what was going on was Dr. Clarke Thorpe, a man Mulholland would travel to meet in person on several occasions. The purpose of the magician's visit was clear. He was testing the doctor to see where his allegiances lay and deduce if the government money was well spent on his research on behalf of the so-called Armour Research Foundation. In a report filed a short week after the Olson death, Mulholland reports to Gottlieb:

> "I understand that Dr. Thorpe's original interest in these experiments was because of his interest in making tests in thought-transference. He pointed out that there was one spot in the spectrum of electrical wavelengths, which covered waves about which there

was no knowledge scientific or otherwise. He felt that it would be worth while to make a study to determine whether there was a possibility that the human brain could emit these 'unknown' rays and by such means cause contact with another mind."

Clarke Thorpe was one player in the Armour Research Foundation; Dr. Kenneth Miller was another. References to Dr. Frederick Marion and Dr. Karlo Marches are also noted in tandem with the major players of Gottlieb, Lashbrook, and deFlores (actually Luis DeFlorenz).

And the last invisible man was someone simply referred to as "Cornelius."

He remains invisible.

XI. MULHOLLAND'S CAREER & THE FATE OF HIS PRICELESS COLLECTION

John Mulholland first lived in New York City in the 80's near Riverside Drive. After his father's "disappearance" mother and young son moved to 507 West 113th Street. From 1919 to 1921, while he taught at the Horace Mann School for Boys and Columbia Teachers College, he lived as a bachelor at 306 West 109th Street. Shortly after Mulholland began his career as a full-time professional magician in 1923, he took up residence at: 535 West 111th Street. In the 1940's he moved to (and lived for the rest of his life at) 600 West 115th Street, apartment #112, in New York City. His mother lived nearby at 628 West 114th Street as late as 1942, shown on a membership card she held with the New York Zoological Society. His office was on the tenth floor of 130 West 42nd Street. He kept that office address for better than thirty years.

John Mulholland
130 WEST FORTY-SECOND STREET · NEW YORK 18, N. Y.

CONFIRMATION OF ENGAGEMENT

Patron

Date

Time

Place

Program

Fee   *(To be paid to Mr. Mulholland on day of appearance)*

Correspondent

Sample of simple John Mulholland contract.

Beginning in the late 1920's, Mulholland was managed in the lecture field by William B. Feakins Inc. who had offices close by at 42nd Street and Broadway and across the country at 1200 Taylor

Street, in San Francisco. The Feakins agency also managed the bright light of the lecture world, Carl Sandburg. Mulholland "performed" six different lectures that filled the vast halls of the Brooklyn Academy of Music and the Minneapolis 5100-seat Northrup Auditorium. He was adept at portraying magicians of various cultures in their native garb. In May of 1941 he appeared as the last act in the second section of a program at Radio City Music Hall as a Chinese wizard performing the magic classics: the linking rings, and the appearance of a two gallon bowl of water filled with swimming goldfish. His summer house sported an authentic Tang dynasty figurine of a magician (allegedly smuggled out of China by his friend Long Tack Sam). The performer gave Mulholland this gift to commemorate Mulholland's appearance at Radio City performing the celebrated Long Tack Sam water bowl production (albeit without somersault).

He was a skilled woodworker who built a considerable amount of the "Mulholland Hide-A-Way" on Dinglebrook Lane in Newtown, Connecticut. When his massive collection (he began collecting as a boy of eight) was housed at his beloved Players club on Gramercy Park in New York City, he built the showcases where props from magic's past were displayed. The lectern he traveled with included secret moving parts. For a magician it is a wonder to behold. It is pragmatic, clever and intriguing, much like the wizard himself.

In addition to being a consultant for Chemrophyl Associates and Granger Research, Mulholland generously gave benefit performances for such causes as the League of Women Voters in his summer hamlet of Newtown, and the Hammond Museum in North Salem, Connecticut. The scholarly magician, with an easy-going and unaffected style of performance, was profiled in *The New Yorker*, *Vanity Fair*, and *The Times* of London, among many newspapers and magazines. It is a fair assessment of Mulholland's career that he was written about or had an article appear under his byline almost every two weeks in the popular media between 1920 and 1969.

At age 16, John Mulholland was the youngest magician ever admitted to the Society of American Magicians. At thirty he was vice president of the organization. His wry sense of humor pervaded his life. Once in Pittsburgh he remarked after a crash backstage, "Oh, don't worry, they are just bringing in my salary."

He often made himself the subject of a humorous story. He related a tale of performing in his early twenties where he asked for the loan of a ring from a member of the audience. His trick was to smash the ring, load the shattered pieces into a gun, fire the pieces at a box, and open the box to find the ring restored and attached to a bouquet of flowers. A toddler approached him with the desired ring. When Mulholland apparently smashed it, the child bellowed, "Now that was a hell of a thing to do!"

As a teen he was performing in New Hampshire and was requested to do something spectacular. He decided to make himself vanish.

He worked out his miracle by jumping out of a window, falling twenty feet and then running around the theatre to the entrance. However, his disappearance encountered one problem he had not prepared for during rehearsal: rain. Upon his leap from the window he fell into a barrel situated to catch rainwater, making a big splash. He was not hurt, but completely soaked and ran around the building encountering the town sheriff in the process. The policeman said, "Son, you must have run twenty miles to get that wet." The magician made his reappearance, which the audience appreciated and laughed at. The magician did not think it was as humorous.

The writer, Hendrik Willem Van Loon, lauded the tall, thin conjurian with the quote Mulholland thought well enough of to reprint next to his 1930's publicity:

> "John Mulholland is so good (now get this straight for it is complicated) that when he does a trick and I know perfectly well how it is done I don't know how it is done when I see him do it. Which I can also say of Kreisler and Paderewski and the late Rembrandt van Ryn for their craftsmanship is such that the impossible becomes the completely natural and when that has been achieved there is nothing more for us bunglers to do but sit very quietly and accept what we get like very small and happy children and sort of grin to ourselves for we have (rare occasion) come face to face with something that is really perfect."

Van Loon was also a confidant of the magician and was written about and quoted in Mulholland's *Beware Familiar Spirits*. Like the magician, Van Loon did not believe in ghosts, but loved mystery as entertainment.

Detailed programs from his performances in the New York City area from the 1930's show him holding the stage for about ninety minutes performing a wide selection of wonders. He began with the mysteries of the Indian jadoo wallah (street performing magician) and then metamorphosed into a dapper magician attired in evening tails. He closed with a recreation of a Chinese magician's performance. Doane Powell made the masks for his jadoo-wallah and Chinese impersonations. His depiction of the Indian magician was explained as "genuine" in his theatre programs from the 1930's. This was because he was adopted by a Moslem family of Indian magicians named Bakhsh. The mask Mulholland wore portraying the Indian magician was almost a replication of the younger Bakhsh, pictures of which show the father and son performing authentic marketplace miracles such as the appearance of little baby birds from a previously shown empty basket. He was also an honorary life member of the Indian Magicians Club.

JOHN MULHOLLAND
130 West 42 Street, New York City

Confirmation of Engagement

With

Correspondent

Auditorium Location

For

Date

Hour

Fee   (To be paid to Mr. Mulholland on day of appearance)

Remarks

John Mulholland modified contract.

Mulholland was intimately familiar with the conjurations of the Eastern mystic. He wrote extensively from personal encounters. In 1930 he was quick to capitalize on his rare, first-hand notes by writing for *Theatre Arts Monthly* an article titled "Eastern Magic." He writes of seeing a live decapitation and restoration in Burmah (sic) and writes with authority and detail of the magic of the Javanese, Malay, Japanese, Chinese, Indian, and Korean counterparts to the western conjuror. Mulholland was authentic in recreating the performance of the Indian street entertainer. He used a rattle-drum and gourd pipe to attract his audience the same way his friends in New Delhi had outdoors.

He carried the props for his full stage show in several lightweight cases. In *Quicker Than the Eye* Mulholland related how he once fell asleep on a train and bypassed his station where a committee of women was waiting for him. He decided to throw his bags off the train and jump, and wondered if the women thought all magicians made such an eccentric entrance. He was good-natured, never taking himself too seriously, except when being questioned as an authority on his subject.

In his final years, Mulholland confided to a close magician friend that he was always amazed how large circulation articles produced no bookings, while meeting a man at a party once brought him a thousand dollar fee for doing just one trick (the cut and restored rope). One clipping from the 1960's notes that he once charged an amateur magician in Cincinnati, Ohio $5,000 for two days of consultation on a fifteen minute act.

During his peripatetic career, he performed before the Sultan of Sulu at the Sultan's rustic home, which was a cross between an army bunker and a ranch. Mulholland, clad in a white tourist outfit made knots disappear from a handkerchief while the Sultan looked on in an eccentric combination of Eastern and Western dress. On his first swing around the globe he entertained the seven-year-old King Michael of Romania in the palace at Sinaia (in 1928), the Queen of Greece, the dowager Queen of Greece, Princess Helen (the King of Greece's sister), and the President of Mexico. Jealous of his contemporaries, he writes in *Quicker Than the Eye* that when Malini and Thurston exchanged stories about performing for royalty, Mulholland was chagrined he had not yet given a command performance. Had the magician only been gifted with true prophesy his anxieties would have disappeared. He appeared before the Roosevelts at the White House on eight separate occasions (which is probably an unchallenged record for a magician appearing there).

He was listed in *Who's Who in America* for 40 years and was constantly mindful that he was the only magician listed for many years (prior to the book becoming a place one could buy entry to). New York Governor Alfred E. Smith once asked Mulholland to perform at a settlement house on Christmas Day to spread good cheer. Mulholland recounted his tales of perception, deception and pretending between adult and children at Christmas time in an essay he published in *The New York Times* magazine in the 1940's. Good articles were always turned into promotional pieces and this must have led to his comment about large circulation articles.

When Houdini began what became his final tour in 1925, he made sure to enlist Mulholland to clean up his circus barker delivery for the lecture circuit. Houdini biographer William Lindsay Gresham noted, "The final Houdini, the personality remembered by the people who saw the last tour, was a personality largely sculpted by John Mulholland. Houdini always tried to overcompensate for his lack of formal schooling, and while largely self-educated, it was Mulholland who gave Houdini the polish he exhibited at the end." It is also possible that Houdini liked the idea of John Mulholland being a self-taught scholar, as Houdini presented himself to the public. While Mulholland was a genuine scholar, he also never was formally graduated from any institution of higher learning.

Albert Edward Wiggam of the editorial staff of *The American Magazine* wrote of the magician, *"I've seen all the magicians from Herrmann the Great down to the local wag who could do a couple of card tricks. Houdini was a good friend of mine and I knew his stuff from A to Z. But I have never seen any man tie an audience into knots, untie them and then tie them over again as John Mulholland did at our Dutch Treat club, which as you know is probably the hardest boiled bunch in America for an entertainer to go up against."*

Noted theater critic and radio personality Alexander Woollcott wrote of Mulholland, after a particularly humorous show at the Algonquin Hotel for the literati of the 1920's, "Pharaoh would have rejoiced in so good a tricker." Woollcott used words carefully and precisely. Though this was written in the 1920's it is a description that would facilitate the magician's understanding of "trickster-like practices" and resultant phenomenon much later in his career.

Mulholland's magnificent collection of books and antiquarian prints was first exhibited at the Grolier Club in New York City beginning March 18, 1927. He chose this place and this time to commemorate his return from his first world travels and also to help cross promote a series of articles in national dailies that would soon be turned into his book *Quicker Than The Eye* (which angered him for the mistakes included and for being selected by the Junior Literary Guild; Mulholland quietly snapped to friends, "This is not a children's book!").

Historian H. R. Evans singled out Mulholland's contributions, in his 1928 volume *History of Conjuring and Magic,* to making magic a cultural phenomenon. Another historian recorded that the Grolier Club exhibition was a history-making first, bringing magic an aura of esteem as a cultural art never-before-seen.

In 1928, the thirty-year-old magician wrote the accompanying booklet to an exhibition of conjuring books at the New York Public Library. His essay was titled, "Behind the Magician's Curtain." Typically this writing would be republished many times throughout his esteemed career.

In 1938 his collection of antiquarian prints and books was exhibited at the Chicago Public Library. He showed his growing collection for six months beginning in March of 1940 at the Museum of the City of New York. In the museum bulletin he contributed an article titled "Magic In New York." He detailed that while the famous city had played host to magicians it was mainly for one nighters and unlike London or Vienna, New York had never sustained a magic theatre (a conquest eluding Carter the Great, Houdini and others).

Mulholland noted the first magician to achieve success in the Big Apple was Joseph Broome who showed on March 18, 1734. Mulholland also noted the success of Ramo Samee, a troupe member of "superior Indian Jugglers" who swallowed beads and horsehair, later bringing up the beads threaded. When a theatrical manager suggested that the beads be replaced by needles, a magic classic was born, later brought to prominence by Houdini on the largest stage in the world, The Hippodrome. Mulholland worked feverishly to make this exhibit unique and to present magic as one of the great theatrical arts. The coup de grace was a false exhibit – a human-sized picture framed stage where the magician and his contemporaries took the small stage and brought the art to life as a living exhibit! Photos of this attraction convey a true sense of mystery. The illusion of art is brought full circle to living illusion.

In 1951 he exhibited rarities from his collection and rarities from the collections of Dr. Samuel Cox Hooker and Dr. Saram Ellison found in the New York Public Library.

Later, in 1965, he began work on a series of scripts for WPIX–TV in New York. "The John Mulholland Show" would have been a thirty-minute weekly TV show emphasizing the magician's good nature, his close-up magic talents, a section on magic history, and perhaps guest magicians. The program was never produced.

During his last years, Mulholland wrote for the *Encyclopedia Britannica* and was paid $150 per entry. He wrote to his friend George Gordon that he had received Gordon's book and that he intended on "studying, absorbing and finally to revel in." He reflects on himself when he writes about his friend's book, "Another detail which slows my reading is that at least once a page I have to stop to delight in knowing a scholar having so much knowledge and with the common-sense properly to correlate his facts in an understandable way."

Later he sadly informs Gordon that his arthritis is "raising hell" though this did not stop his updating his work on his famous essay called "Conjuring" for *Encyclopedia Britannica*. Later Mulholland's arthritis would "provide a hell of an attack" making him unable to eat. The magician lost twenty-five pounds. Finally, his situation warranted a ten-day stay at University Hospital, where he underwent a series of tests. He wrote "mostly quite mild. Everything was O.K. except me."

On October 27, 1967, New York Governor Nelson A. Rockefeller declared Halloween as "Magic Day" in New York State and cited Mulholland and Milbourne Christopher in the proclamation. Just six days earlier Mulholland appeared in New Haven Connecticut, near the Yale campus, with several titans of the magic profession: his old friends, Walter B. Gibson and Cardini. Seated in the front row of a group shot by magician/photographer Larry Shean, along with admiring local magicians in the background, Mulholland stands out as the gray-haired professor in conservative blue three-piece suit sporting a pocket watch with gold chain. Typical to the man, in his hand he holds one of his burning, unfiltered Phillip Morris cigarettes. He looks wise, almost like the Harvard Law School character Kingsfield from the film *The Paper Chase*.

In 1967, Mulholland published his last book with his friend and amateur magician, New York University professor Dr. George N. Gordon. In fact, Gordon and Mulholland had previously met several times.

Once in the 1930's when Mulholland enlisted a 12-year-old George Gordon on stage in a rope trick at the Princeton club in New York. Later, in 1944, during a USO show, following the great Ballantine, a comedy magician, at the New York Times Hall (later, Town Hall) in New York he involved the soldier Gordon in a card trick gone awry. The story Gordon tells has one detail that cements the truth of the event. The card Mulholland "forced" – meaning, make the audience participant choose while apparently having a random selection -- was the Two of Diamonds. John Mulholland favored this card because there was so much white space on the card, and a signature or other marking, could be seen in the last row. As stated, the magician was practical down to the smallest details.

Finally in 1965, Gordon booked Mulholland for a 10:30pm radio show aired on Friday nights called *The Lively Arts* (on the CBS network) and after Mulholland monopolized the 30-minute show as both artist and expert in his field (and thereby gaining twice the salary – one hundred dollars) he and the radio host Gordon soon collaborated on a book published less than two years later.

After the show, they walked from the CBS studios on 53rd Street to Scribner's Publishing on 5th Avenue where Mulholland got Gordon a copy of his 1963 volume *John Mulholland's Book of Magic*. As they spoke, Gordon remarked, "John we are wasting our sweetness upon the desert air. We may have something people might find useful." Gordon says of his dear friend, "It was simply a conversation that lasted five years. During the second year the conversation became a book I largely wrote."

Interestingly, the year Nelson Rockefeller gave Mulholland an award was also the year that Mulholland's fourteen years of association with the CIA was somewhat displayed in a book he co-authored with a college professor about propaganda, mind control and hypnosis. A mere coincidence?

What better place to "hide in the obvious" than to publish his work, roughly disguised as a book solely about "communication." Or, perhaps the magician was telling us what "communication" really entailed -- after all, he was an authority. Additionally Mulholland knew the paradox that the best place to hide a magicians' secret was to publish it in a book. "Hiding in the obvious" was almost a lifestyle choice for him.

Titled *The Magical Mind–Keys to Successful Communication* recycled part of the work Mulholland did for the CIA for mass consumption. The back page of the cover stated references to hypnotism, mind control and propaganda.

Nine years prior to this redemption of his work for the CIA, Mulholland published an article in an obscure magazine for the military called *Ex-CBI Roundup*, which covered the work of officers in China, Burma and India. He wrote in 1958, "I am convinced now that the process by which people come to believe in the Indian rope trick is akin to brain-washing." He made the conclusion after a careful examination of the myth and the psychology of the magician's performance where people often recount things they think the magician performed.

Mulholland's final book could have been a psychic redemption for his observations of human nature used as tools of warfare. Or, it may simply have been a rehash of material he found worthy of recapitulating for a popular audience. While Mulholland may have taught Houdini erudition, he learned the value of repeat promotion from the great escapologist. The paradigm of this: on the cover of his 1963 opus, the dust jacket bore his name repeatedly. Even Houdini never thought to have a book cover with his name repeated a hundred times as part of the design. Of course, Mulholland had the source material on which to draw.

In 1961 he would produce his most humble, yet most detailed literary effort: a book about puppetry. In *Practical Puppetry* he provided his typical scholarship and erudite display. Of the art of puppetry, he examined script writing and visibility, notions he also addressed as a magician. Mulholland knew his subject as many magicians added puppetry to their programs from the 16th century on. Through his own art, he knew another to the extent that he provided a very detailed treatise. In addition, he also keeps any mention of his career as a magician cleanly away from these pages – the consummate magician has disappeared from our vision, like the puppeteer, and we are not even aware of it. The portability of the props well described Mulholland's familiarity with practical and efficient theatre.

Mulholland's assertion that the magician's performance was 10% apparatus was clearly in affect here. When the book was released in Britain in late 1961 the publisher felt that solid promotion would yield a nice profit. However, the book disappeared into shelves. Just three years after his last known contact with the CIA, John Mulholland was writing about puppets, or was he?

One remembers the logo of the novel *The Godfather*, the hands of a marioneteer.

A puppet master.

A powerful man.

John Mulholland was, for a time, a clandestine puppet master to the CIA.

After all, the book prior to this, *The Art of Illusion*, was published seventeen years earlier in three separate editions including an Armed Services edition. Like his counterpart Jasper Maskelyne fighting the Desert Fox Rommel in North Africa, Mulholland was teaching the U.S. Armed Services to make magic at a closer range. Through a pocket manual of hand tricks, soldiers' attention was diverted from the tenets of war. He was a natural for the CIA to call when it came to using sleight of hand for intelligence during warfare.

From 1959 to 1967 he kept a prodigious writing career producing four books in eight years, at a release schedule of one new book every twenty-four months (November 1961, 1963, 1965 and 1967). After that, he was dogged by arthritis in his hands. A chain smoker for most of his life, cancer also set in.

In many group shots of magicians, he is almost always posing with a burning cigarette in hand. His over acidic stomach became worse. One must remember that while such a fast writing and publishing schedule seems almost superhuman, it was typical for the wizard Mulholland. He moved at this pace throughout his entire career. He had to. In a letter from 1969 to Joe G. Vitale, Mulholland described his life:

> "At various times, when the demand for a magician
> was small. (as when I was very young and during the
> great depression) I have been a salesman, a

216

schoolteacher, and editor ("The Town Hall Crier") – I
don't count "The Sphinx" as it was within the field of
magic) a writer, a lecturer in colleges, a machinist, a
cabinetmaker, and a librarian. In all these jobs my
training in magic was of the greatest aid."

The magician then admits readily that magic is a "precarious way
to make a living." While he has traveled widely and met many of the
greats of the world, it was not an income as providing as another more
"usual" line of work. John Mulholland did what it took to practice his
magic. For Mulholland, magic was a way of life.

On November 2, 1918, when John Mulholland was simply a 6'3"
twenty year old, he was noted in the following, obscure journal called
the "Society of American Magician Monthly":

Society of American Magician, Parent Assembly:
180th regular meeting of the Society was held at the Magical Palace, no. 493
Sixth Avenue[##], with the following members present:

M. Ill. (Most Illustrious) President Houdini, Ill. Vice President Heller.
Ill. Past Presidents Sargent, Teale and Hartley, Ill.: Treasurer Rulman,
and Ill. Compeers: Martinka, Hornmann, Toch, Raymond, Kline,
Meyenberg, Burrows, Irving, Kirch, Goodwin, Mulholland, Vincent,
Lenz and Hilliar. A special presentation by Jean Hugard on topics
abroad was a special presentation.

This shows that he associated with extraordinarily high level of
company at a very early age. He'd rather have done that with his life
than make a lot of money, even though he did make a lot of money at
times.

Mulholland was a philosopher always pondering magical questions
with other great thinkers. These exceptional men were also a veritable
Who's Who of twentieth century stage illusion, mind reading, side
show humbuggery, and retail magic.

John Mulholland's pride that he was listed in the *Who's Who* was
appropriate. He had fantastic affiliations all over the world. In fact, the
late Jackie Flosso said during the last TV interview given at the famous
magic shop (formerly Martinka's) on West 34th Street that it was
Mulholland, who recommended Jack's father, the famous Al Flosso, in
1960 to consult on magicians' technique when the producer from
United Artists called looking for a magician to consult on a little
known movie titled *The Manchurian Candidate*. Initially set for
release in 1962, the movie was held because of President Kennedy's
assassination, and the truth being too close to the film's fiction. Frank

---

[##] (Note, no. 493 was a magic store named "Martinka & Co." and can still be found in
business in 2008, after opening a hundred thirty years ago, at www. Martinka.com)

Sinatra owned the rights to the movie, and as a close friend of the Kennedys delayed the opening for several years. Mulholland, wisely, kept a distance from the production which was distinctly allied to the work he was involved in on behalf of Gottlieb's MK-ULTRA.

(Gottlieb was loosely portrayed by Patrick Stewart in the 1996 film *Conspiracy Theory* starring Mel Gibson and Julia Roberts. MK-ULTRA was also depicted with some creative license.)

In 1964 Mulholland's world-renowned collection of magic memorabilia (often described as priceless) was formally appraised as being worth seventy thousand dollars.

John Mulholland performing kuma tubes
at Sherry Netherland hotel, New York City, 1968.

In 1965, shortly before the conjuring periodical, *Genii* magazine, would feature Mulholland as the "most knowledgeable magician on Earth," Mulholland's secretary (and road companion) Dorothy Wolf died on June 19th. She had helped edit together and compile the lengthy tribute to the scholarly sorcerer. The issue was dedicated to her long service to Mulholland and to his long editorship of *The Sphinx*. (Which, by the end of its fifty-two years had been the longest running periodical on conjuring extant.) Her death shocked him greatly. He never forgot her, keeping nude photographs of her in his personal files, which his wife Pauline tolerated. When he met his wife Pauline, Dorothy Wolf had already been intimate with her husband to be for seven years. Pauline always said that when she married John, "Dorothy came along with the package." Pauline Mulholland seems to have had the feisty independent spirit often associated with Katharine Hepburn. She was a liberal thinker and many who knew her said that while she may not have particularly cared for magic, she did care for John and she wanted him to be recognized for his personal greatness.

In 1966 Mulholland's famous collection, comprising about eight thousand volumes, and several thousand magazines and posters relating to conjuring and allied arts began to take residence at his beloved club The Players. The installation of the complete volume would take another two years because of demands upon the magician's writing schedule and his woodworking on cases slowed by his ever painful arthritis.

On April 15, 1967 John Mulholland was the Honored Magician at the Society of American Magicians Parent Assembly Number One 65th Anniversary Celebration at the spacious Brooklyn Academy of Music. The large oversize program featured an illustration of a conjurer pulling a rabbit incorrectly by the ears from a silk top hat at a fashionable party. The illustration was by Charles Dana Gibson, earlier famous for the creation of "the Gibson Girl." Mulholland, singled out in the program notes as a celebrity magician alongside Thurston and Houdini, closed the first half of the program following the famous comedic manipulator Roy Benson. Photographs of this show by Irving Desfor at the Brooklyn Academy of Music show a tall, gaunt Mulholland attired in his Chinese robes producing a large quantity of silk from the innermost of two square wooden tubes. His authentic Chinese robes, veterans of thousands of performances all over the world, gleam in the stage lights, very well preserved. The live action photos convey a sense of fun, even as the magician of advanced years, suffering arthritis, moves about his show making a birdcage and canary disappear.

His very last performance took place on June 28, 1969 in an outdoor setting for the children of Dorothy and Tom Stix Jr., friends of many years. Amidst 98-degree heat the magician conjured and the audience was, as described by Ms. Stix, "absolutely enthralled." One trick did not make it to the performance however. Mulholland had planned to use a candle in his performance. Unfortunately, when the magician arrived at the show, he found that the candle had melted in the trunk of his car. When Mulholland died, Pauline Mulholland presented Mulholland's last cane and a few ties of her husband to the Stix family. The cane now resides in the collection of Ken Klosterman, provided to him by the author and the Stix family and mutual friends.

Three years after his collection took up residence at the Walter Hampden Memorial Library John Mulholland sold his priceless collection to The Players club for one half the estimated value, or thirty-five thousand dollars (to be paid in seventy weekly installments of five-hundred dollars). He wanted his treasures to remain for future scholars in the confines of the famous Edwin Booth town house on Gramercy Park. In a letter to John Henry Grossman he said that the Players would hold on to his books and other materials "as the Morgan

Library was set up." Pauline Mulholland said that her husband hoped the Mulholland Collection would repose within the Players' walls, faithful that the Players membership would treasure and use the collection to represent the art of magic amidst the other great theatre collections.

John Wickizer Mulholland, an inveterate cigarette smoker with habitual stomach problems, long suffering of arthritis, died of bone cancer at University Hospital in New York City on February 25, 1970 at the age of seventy-one.

His desire was that no memorial service be held. Milbourne Christopher wrote that this did not surprise him as "he had built a far more lasting monument with his great contributions to magic."

He was cremated and his ashes scattered at the Mulholland Hide-A-Way in Newtown, Connecticut, as were those of his wife Pauline, who died in 1987. However, there are markers for the couple next to his father's plot at Woodlawn Cemetery, in the Bronx in New York City. His headstone is along side his wife Pauline and mother Irene May Wickizer (formerly) and his fifty-eight year old father, also named John.

A fellow of The Players club (Mulholland's home away from home) Luis Van Rooten wrote the inscription on Mulholland's final marker:

> *The greatest magician of all has made John Mulholland disappear from before our eyes. Thoughtfully he has left his image in our hearts and minds.*

The veteran *New York Times* drama critic, Brooks Atkinson was a great friend of Mulholland. Upon his death, Atkinson wrote a lengthy appreciation, stating:

> *In addition to being a genius in magic, Mulholland was a profound student of magic. It was his ambition to convince the public that conjuring, sleight of hand, prestidigitation, whatever you want to call it is one of the performing arts, like acting and the ballet. The magician, he believed, must be an actor. Although Mulholland's attitude on stage was one of modesty and diffidence, he was acting. It must have been a great source of pride to him to be able to hold an audience so thoroughly and confound it with such virtuoso skill."*

In 1972 the Mulholland collection was again formally appraised as being worth $72,382.50. That same year Pauline Mulholland sold a portion of John Mulholland's printing plates to his beloved *Sphinx* magazine to Jeff Sheridan, the street magician who became famous for performing at the Sir Walter Scott statue in Central Park in the 1970's. Like other Mulholland artifacts, these were rescued from being abandoned in a dumpster in the early 1990's. Luckily many possessions of the great Mulholland have been preserved, even though they only hold real value for a small, admiring crowd of magic history lovers. Much of the memorabilia went to the great collectors Milbourne Christopher and Robert Lund, who was then planning his American Museum of Magic. When Lund insisted on paying what he felt were nominal fees for the Mulholland Indian and Chinese masks, Pauline responded by writing, "Please take them, I am tired of living in a warehouse."

On November 24, 1975, a magician named Chester Karkut bought over two hundred and fifty photographs of magicians and family pictures from Pauline Mulholland for five dollars, paid via a money order. Even by the day's standards, this is very cheap. These belongings have passed through two magicians hands since that time finally coming to rest with this writer so this story may be told in completion.

In 1977 Pauline Mulholland objected to The Players' news that it intended to sell the Mulholland Collection. While Mrs. Mulholland often noted in letters that attending magic shows put her to sleep, she clearly felt betrayed by the club's decision. She pleaded with the board of directors to honor the Mulholland name – especially after his dedicated service to The Players club for nearly forty years. "How could you do this to Johnny – who unhesitatingly gave his time and love to The Players? Please reconsider the monument left by your adoring member," she wrote.[11]

Pauline Pierce Mulholland left New York City after working for Planned Parenthood for twenty-eight years in the Bronx, New York. Pauline Mulholland, like her husband, was outspoken, and had a deliberate, off beat sense of humor. She retired to the Mulholland Hide-A-Way in Newtown, Connecticut in 1982 after being forced to leave her Manhattan apartment by an unscrupulous landlord.

When she was diagnosed with lung cancer, she sold her house and property to her husband's last literary collaborator, Dr. George N. Gordon and his Australian wife Nancy[12]. Shortly before her death she sold approximately fifty acres of their land, so it would be preserved as natural woodland. Gordon said in 2002, "This is a magical cottage. It is blessed by the Oriental and Occidental gods of magic and the magic of magic."

Pauline Mulholland died at her home in Connecticut in 1987. A solid gold rabbit in hat given to her by her husband, who had it made in replica of his famous logo, that she wore as a charm, was given to her adopted daughter, George Gordon's daughter. Dying of terminal cancer, Mrs. Mulholland euthanized herself and her cats at the same time, the check for their care being made out the morning of her death. She did not want to trust that her "children" would possibly be mistreated. Her cats were named "Cat" and "Deer."

In 1984 The Players club sold the Mulholland Collection to a banker named Carl Rheuban in California for $575,000. Milbourne Christopher's wife, Maurine, chairman of the Foundation in her husband's name, points out that The Players, "double crossed a dead man." Rheuban bought and expanded the collection with funds from the First Network Savings & Loan bank he controlled. He paid, as legal papers show, $48,000 to magician Ricky Jay for facilitating the deal between Rheuban and The Players club.

Ricky Jay was also appointed the Curator of the Mulholland Collection of Magic and Allied Arts. A Board of Directors was assembled including such well-known show business figures as playwright David Mamet and actor-comedian Steve Martin. During Ricky Jay's curatorship, another $1.5 million was used to build the Mulholland Collection of Conjuring and Allied Arts with more antiquarian conjuring rarities, including the automaton "the Singing Lesson" by Robert-Houdin (purchased from Madame Marteret in France) and the great Max Malini scrapbooks donated by Malini's son Oziar. The collection at the time of the disposition held approximately 15,000 books (5,000 added during this period) and a group of important 18th century playbills pertaining to Philip Astley, the founder of the modern circus.

In 1990 Rheuban's Savings & Loan Co. failed and the US government attached the collection. The Resolution Trust Corporation later sold it for $2.2 million dollars to a performer born David Seth Kotkin in Metuchen, New Jersey, who later appropriated the name of a Charles Dickens' novel.[13]

"David Copperfield" outbid the Library of Congress for the collection by one million dollars after it was seized as an asset of the Savings & Loan bank Rheuban (a member of the Hollywood Magic Castle) controlled. The Library of Congress complained that the public "lost" not having acquired the collection. He runs his massive acquisitions, as a private museum and has removed John Mulholland's name from the vast collection. He has purchased other impressive collections from Europe and elsewhere.

The bankruptcy court believed a cash offer was better than either Christies Auction House or Swann Auction Gallery who guaranteed $3.5 and $1.5 million (respectively) in sales if the collection were auctioned by their agencies. There was also another substantial cash offer – by the self-appointed "King of Pop," Michael Jackson (August 29, 1958 – June 25, 2009).

The vibrant collection, put together over sixty years, through thousands of friendships by John Mulholland, once used as an active archive to spread public appreciation of magic as an art, glorifying all the great practitioners of the profession, now sits in a temperature-controlled warehouse in Las Vegas, Nevada. Select scholars are allowed access by appointment. The owner has been criticized as purchasing the collection as a tax shelter. Responding to this charge, the owner points out he has spent nearly 10 million dollars on this collection with additions. "David Copperfield" has said on TV that he has "outdone Houdini" and that because he owns about half of what Houdini owned, relates, "I can tell you Houdini was a pretty cool guy."

Ricky Jay, described the Mulholland collection's current owner in the *New Yorker* as "an Elvis impersonator who has gone to live at Graceland."

The famous magic collector of materials as rare and expansive as the Mulholland collection, Ken Klosterman, creator of Salon De Magie, says of the current owner "He's primarily a businessman." The David Copperfield Collection was not used for this book.

Milbourne Christopher wrote, upon Mulholland's death that "he did more than any other magician of our time to convince the public that magic was a major art ...that its practitioners should be esteemed."

The New York Times quoted Mulholland's final words to his worldwide audience as:

> *You must leave your audience mystified if you want to leave them happy.*
>
> *Experienced magic-makers have agreed that one should never explain how a trick is done. As soon as you tell how the fooling is done, interest wanes immediately, and often someone feels cheated...*
>
> *The appeal of magic is mental, not visual. And the magician therefore must fool the minds rather than they eyes of his audience.*

The *Kansas City Star's* summation of John Mulholland's performance and knowledge of conjuring technique sums up this intriguing personality as a practitioner of "deception that is art."

EPILOGUE

John Mulholland utilized his sixty-five year passion for magic and magicians to help the U.S. government fight a silent war in the 1950's and 60's. The magician was an intellectual patriot who gave early operatives the know-how to kill with a handshake and the ability to ferret out the truth from professional liars. He cracked codes, developed silent methods of communication, and created complex means by which enemies of the State could be rendered useless to their governing body.

John Mulholland applied not only the magician's clandestine technique of sleight of hand, but essentially, imparted to operatives the magician's technique that human deception was based on: 80% psychology, 10% apparatus and 10% skill. This methodology translated into works of deception that became veritably unavoidable plans of attack, still in use in the 21st century – though less effective because of widespread publicity of magician's techniques. This is the least of what he did.

He succeeded in providing missing elements to *real national security*.

The levels of power involved in this bittersweet story — mind control, psychic research and perceived genuine psychic phenomenon, hypnosis, sex, hallucinogenic drugs, the White House, the CIA, the Pentagon, a Rockefeller, billions of dollars, and death — are some of the most formidable in history.

There is one additional force that was welcomed into this mix – the magician's deceptive arts and the concept of – m a g i c.

ADDENDUM

Just five days short of what would have been John Mulholland's 106th birthday a coincidental series of events concerning this story took place in Washington D.C. The CIA Director, George Tenet, who had served both the Clinton and Bush White House, resigned. While citing personal reasons, no doubt heavy criticism of intelligence failures prior to September 11th weighed on his decision.

Mr. Tenet was succeeded by a temporary acting director, who is an amateur magician, referred to in inter-Agency memos as "Merlin." His name: John McLaughlin[14].

John Mulholland, cancer-ridden though holding a cigarette, is seen at far right in the front row with Cardini in the center and Walter Gibson far left. Magic club men in back, October 21, 1967. Photo by Larry Shean. Used by permission of David Haversat.

AFTERWORD

I never met John Mulholland, but feel like I have. A thousand times I have heard his ghost whisper, "Go boy, tell the tale." Of course, John Mulholland did not believe in ghosts.

How then would he have explained the day I met with a Czechoslovakian film editor? She asked, while scanning images of Mulholland, "Tell me, did he ever perform in my country?" At that moment, a book laying flat upon a table fell off, surely propelled by an unseen force. The book, Mulholland's first, *Magic in the Making* from 1925, fell open to page 39. And on that page, you too will find that it concerns a trick titled "The Stolen Apple." The first line on that page reads: "This Czecho-Slovakian trick needs a little private preparation." The film editor did not talk to me for the rest of the day, clearly spooked. This is a true story.

I have spent time in his Connecticut "Hide-A-Way," read many of his letters, and known the people who bought the house in Connecticut from Pauline Mulholland. Milbourne Christopher once said to me, "Mulholland would have liked you." His wife Maurine added, "I think Chris (her husband) spoke to you the way John spoke to Chris." Mulholland's best friend said after meeting me, "John is with you now. I don't want to get all-metaphysical. But you've got it. You understand what he was about." John Booth, a confidant of the great Mulholland for over 50 years, and mine for over 20, obliged this project with his eloquent Foreword. Booth agreed I was the man for this job. Why?

From my earliest days studying magic in the late 1960's, Mulholland the man and the writer appealed to me. He revered magic as not just entertainment, but an art that gave individual notice of the human condition. How magicians were perceived; the stories they told; the adventures they had with the secret art – his writing consumed me and I was always left wanting more.

His perception was drawn from the entire modern history of magic dating back to records he owned, beginning shortly after the Italian Renaissance. He was frank about his successes and his failures. He was guarded about his beginnings just as his mentor Houdini had been. Mulholland provided a biography (see page 21) that was mis-interpreted by the editor of the Chicago Register, a society organization. If Houdini presented a mythic role of freedom to oppressed industrial workers of the early 20th century, Mulholland provided an intellectual model for conjuring to be revered as an art. Like his teacher John Sargent, Mulholland analyzed the practice of agreeable illusion.

In 1979, I visited with Mulholland's friend (and professional competitor) Milbourne Christopher. I noted the similarity between Christopher's essay on magic and misdirection in his 1977 *Milbourne Christopher's Magic Book,* and Mulholland's essay on conjuring at the end of his 1963 *Book of Magic.* Christopher, normally a reserved man, threw his head back in laughter and smiled approvingly at my literary instincts. He said, "Right you are, now if you only read all the texts to know where Mulholland got it!" Christopher, like Mulholland, was only too aware of what writers preceded him, and while amazed at my acumen, was somewhat shocked that at age seventeen I was well read enough to know what essays were derivative of another. (It was also at this meeting that I brought a picture of Mulholland seated with his secretary Dorothy Wolf while the great Cardini showed them both a small miracle. Christopher identified Wolf to me and then told me candidly that she was also Mulholland's mistress.)

For my birthday, a close friend, an associate of the great Mulholland and his wife, gave me John Mulholland's baby booties. Made of red leather, an artifact from two centuries ago, I wept when I held them. Silenced by time, the man who grew in those shoes has been my growing passion for nearly a decade of writing and nearly three decades spent finding the truth of the magician's life, my own and Mr. Mulholland's. I have had a wonderful time guided by luck and intuition.

I am honored to be the temporary curator of materials from the Mulholland family album, scrapbook elements from his tours, personal files of his secretary, and a good deal of his props, some that were seen by the audience, others that remained behind the magician's curtain.

His 1943 driver's license and his mother's teaching certificate provide a sense of intimacy usually found when searching for family artifacts in an attic by flashlight. Those documents, now well preserved, will one day be lovingly handed down mindful of a remarkable mother and son.

When these artifacts were part of a multimedia show I produced at Horace Mann, 81 years to the day of his last performance at Horace Mann, the students were staggered that I showed Mulholland's life from birth announcement to gravestone in one lovely film made by Jon Dix. Then after the hour recreation of his show, the lobby held a museum exhibit of what they had seen on stage and screen. John Mulholland lives surely as there is ink on this page!

His lectern sits atop a bookcase in my living room, crowned by a silk high hat he might have found in Germany from 1902. Papers found in his night side table when he died are now preserved among the other artifacts I have gathered from many countries and almost every state.

I have interviewed his best friend at length, and worked behind-the-scenes negotiating the truth of his most private assignment. Working directly with the office of New York State District Attorney I've attempted to expunge the record that John Mulholland could have had anything to do with the unfortunate death of Dr. Frank Olson.

Conclusively, John Mulholland was incapable of murder.

The meeting with Dr. Olson in November 1953 was simply a measure taken to quiet Olson's rambling, free-associating mind. There is no proof to the contrary; only sensationalistic TV producers who desire more blood to sell their wares. It is disquieting to see fabrication and conjecture attempt to ruin a life's work and reputation. Do not honor this activity, and you too instead will see honorable truth.

John Mulholland was a man so in love with his art that work he did for the U.S. Government was simply an assignment directed by his scholarly *patriotism*. Nothing more. He was paid well, and appropriately. He did nothing wrong by teaching covert operatives the world of sleight of hand. While he may have trained people to kill, he *did not ever* commit murder as alleged by an uninformed cable TV program that aired on the A & E Network. Extreme claims require extreme proof, and the producers of that show fell all over themselves with guesswork. They invited my participation. I declined.

There is not one shred of evidence to suggest that John Mulholland had anything to do with Dr. Frank Olson's death. One is innocent until proven guilty, and no proof exists. As his friend George Gordon summed it up when asked, "It is absurd to think that John had anything to do with that scientist's unfortunate end. He may have been placed in the position of 'fall guy.' But, the notion is absolutely absurd."

Our early 21st century is fraught with an almost celebrity-like coverage of terrorism. This is the murder of moral values, and the planted seed of unnecessary paranoia. As a magician Mulholland was sensitive to deception on every level. Clever like a fox, his last book points to human vulnerability reminding us "when you believe you can no longer be fooled, you have fooled yourself."

To me, the hotbed of Mulholland's adventure in the world of Gottlieb and MK-ULTRA makes the crimes of Watergate look like kindergarten. How typical that the magician should be part of a gargantuan story that remained hidden for almost twenty years.

Government deception is nothing new. Mulholland's work came under the rubric of psychological illusion. The magician provided visual and psychological lies that were created as measures of *counterterrorism*.

The wand he wielded was one of peace, humanity, family entertainment and charity. Above all, through intellectual means, he gave respect to an ancient art. To this, he dedicated his life. Think about that.

John Mulholland pursued experience, not money. Fame was an outgrowth of his experience, and his accomplishments deserved the recognition he received. Yet, the life of a magician is very hard. Spreading make-believe in a world of horrific impossibility (demonstrated on September 11th in my hometown) is at once needed and the hardest of gigs. John Mulholland chose the harder road, and never acted with regret. He had a fascinating life; one a book can only touch on.

The world needs more John Mulhollands. I will be delighted if this humble work gives breath to another true scholar; one more practitioner of illusion as art; a person, like the wizard himself, who stood tall, and defended his country and his art.

Ben Robinson
June 9, 2005
New York

*John Mulholland, shortly before
he died, December, 1969.*

NOTES

1

The Milbourne Christopher Collection was assembled by the Christophers through the greater part of the twentieth century. The duplicates of the vast holding have been partially auctioned in two record-setting sales, by Swann Galleries of New York: 1981 – grossing approximately $75,000 and 1997 – grossing approximately $325,000. The Christopher Collection is the most famous magic collection in the world, and the subject of several books and countless articles. While no longer the largest private collection, it is unrivaled in variety and rarity, boasting several books that are the only known copy. Like the John Mulholland Collection, it has been actively used by scholars and is the basis for most magic history written in America in the 20th century.

2

Prominent writing to inspect the role of "specialized" outside consultants to the CIA was published twenty years after-the-fact in two books and one newspaper article. In 1974 former CIA employee Victor Marchetti was successful in obtaining (through the Freedom of Information Act) over 16,000 pages of information from the CIA, most of which was argued against by the Agency for publication in his book, *The CIA and the Cult of Intelligence.* Of 363 deletions the Agency argued for, the U.S. Supreme Court ruled that only 167 were valid. After working with his friend Marchetti, author John D. Marks, then went further with his own 1978 volume *The Search for the Manchurian Candidate* published by Times Books. Six months prior to the publication of Marks' book *The New York Times* ran the brief article on August 3, 1977 titled as both: *MAGICIAN WAS BEHAVIOR GUIDE TO C.I.A.* and, *MAGICIAN WAS HIRED AS ADVISOR TO CIA.* The article by Joseph B. Treaster only told the minor facets of the intriguing story.

3

See: *The Autobiography of John N. Booth*, Chapter 312, *"John Mulholland: His Known and Unknown Life" The Linking Ring* magazine, December, 1997, p. 71-74. This article questions the validity of Mulholland's possibly surreptitious middle name. There is no mystery. Mulholland's middle name was his mother's maiden name, "Wickizer" as noted on her cemetery stone at Woodlawn Cemetery, the Bronx, New York. An original birth certificate shows his birth name as John Wickizer Mulholland, born to John Mulholland and Irene May Mulholland on June 9, 1898. A copy of the Mulholland family birth announcement is in the author's possession.

4

Mulholland attended DeKolta's January 1903 performance in New York City at the Eden Musee, a wax museum on Lower Sixth Avenue (bet. 18th & 19th Streets) in New York City. DeKolta died later that year in New Orleans and was buried in England.

5

The exact number of titles of conjuring books in the Mulholland collection circa 1919 is drawn from the magician's own typewritten bibliography which he circulated among friends.

6

See Edmund Wilson's essay *John Mulholland and the Art of Illusion* written March 11, 1944 included in his compendium, *Commercials and Classics*, published 1950.

7

See *MAGIC—A Pictorial History of Conjurer's in the Theater* by David Price, Cornwall Books, NY, 1985, p. 317.

8

In Marks' *Search for the Manchurian Candidate*, Mulholland is singled out as being employed by the Technical Services Staff (TSS), of which Gottlieb was the head. Papers attendant to the government's MK-ULTRA project note Gottlieb as the head of this project which dispersed drugs (primarily LSD) to have mind altering effects, and also to investigate altered behavior that may induce what is regarded as "telepathy."

9

This was flight #269 that left Washington D.C. at 8:18 AM, and landed in Chicago at 10:17 AM. Flight records are in the author's possession.

10

Mulholland's own dope coin resides in the author's collection.

11

Mulholland was a member of The Players club on Gramercy Park in New York City for 34 years. He was initially taken to the club by Columbia drama professor Brander Matthews. Mulholland was the second magician to join. Harry Kellar was first. Other magician-members have been Milbourne Christopher, Jay Marshall, Fred Keating and Dick Cavett. For further background of Mulholland at The Players, see Pauline Pierce Mulholland's January 11, 1982 letter to the club published in *The Players Book*, 1982.

Mulholland collaborated on his last published book, *The Magical Mind–Keys to Successful Communication* with Dr. George N. Gordon.

13

From 1969 to 1992, the Mulholland collection grew 62% in value. John Mulholland's name has been removed by the current owner. When the collection was owned by Carl Rheuban in the 1980's it was called *The Mulholland Collection of Magic and Allied Arts* and was under the curatorship of magic historian-actor, Ricky Jay. Court papers show that during this period a Board of Directors looked after the Collection's interests and cash bequests were made in the name of magic scholarship. Since then the collection has changed hands and is now housed in a Las Vegas warehouse where it forms the cornerstone of what the current owner has termed "The International Library and Museum of Magic."

14

Former Acting Director of the CIA, John Edward McLaughlin, a passionate amateur magician, wrote the Foreword to the reprinting of Mulholland's manuals for the CIA under the title *The Official CIA Manual of Trickery and Deception*, authored and edited by H. Keith Melton and Robert Wallace.

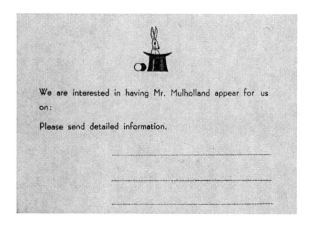

APPENDICIES

For this second edition of *The MagiCIAn*, both publisher and author felt it appropriate to let John Mulholland speak for himself. Therefore we offer six pages of his previously unpublished spy story called *SPY HUNT*. While incomplete, and rough, including his hand written corrections, we felt a taste of his fictional instincts might be of interest, especially since this was written thirteen years prior to his first official involvement with the CIA.

Secondly, we present three versions of his notable essay *The Christmas Conjuror*. Again, a product of his fertile mind in the 1940's, he wrote this piece no doubt to garner performances at this time of year. We present his initial typescript, the brochure he reprinted the final copy in, and the piece as it was published in *The New York Times Magazine Section*. Mulholland always wondered why large circulation articles did not produce the desired bookings, while meeting a man at a party once brought him a thousand dollars for merely performing one miracle.

Finally, the pageantry of one magician's output adorns our concluding pages. The variety of his output surely cements his status as one of the 20th century's most acclaimed and polished practitioners of illusion.

SPY HUNT

John Mulholland
130 West 42nd St.
New York City

SPY HUNT

Henry Miller sat in the dining car slowly drinking
his third cup of coffee in between puffs of the morning's
first cigarette. There was not one person in the car he
recalled having seen before he had climbed into his upper
the previous night. Miller knew very little about long
train trips and how cars were switched from one train to
another.

Miller was a young artist of considerable native
skill and a year of excellent training at an art school
in Chicago. Chicago, by the way, had been, up to this
trip, the furtherest he had ever been away from his small
town home in Central Indiana. After his art school he had
a commercial art job for a while in Great Bend. It hadn't
been much of a job and he had added to his capital by a
variety of other occupations.

Now he was on a train to New York, and had gotten as
far as Newark, as he could see by the station signs. The
world was before him and he had five hundred dollars in
his pocket to live on until the world became his. Five
hundred dollars was a lot of money, or seemed so to Miller
until he began noticing the advertised rates per day of the
hotels announced upon billboards between Newark and the
tunnel. He had no plan to spend any such sums for a room
and he didn't know how to find the name of a place within

his means. The old gentleman sitting across the table in
the dining car looked as if he might be a New Yorker, or
might know New York at any rate, and so Miller asked for
the name of a most inexpensive hotel somewhere in midtown
Manhattan. Miller knew that a majority of the advertising
agencies were in that part of the city, whatever that meant.
The old gentleman knew of no such hotel and suggested that
Miller ask at the Traveler's Aid desk in the station.

Miller asked where he might find the Traveler's Aid as
soon as he got off the train at the Pennsylvania station,
but did not get to the desk for some fifteen minutes for he
stopped time after time to admire the huge beauty of the
place. At the desk he described, at considerable length,
just what he wanted to find in the way of a hotel. He was
the only one making inquiries and the understanding manner
of the motherly lady in charge made him state his wants more
fully than he had any idea of doing. She went to a book on
her desk and wrote down the names of about a dozen hotels.
She told him that none of them was big, or a commercial hotels,
but that each was a rather small family establishment. He
took the list and thanked her.

Once outside the station he looked at the list again. As
no one name meant more to him than another he finally picked
one hotel by the simple method of reciting enie, menie, minie,
mo. He saw a policeman in the middle of the street and, at the
next green light, went out and asked him how to get to the
address given for that hotel. It was, according to the policeman, only a few blocks away. Taking a firmer grip on the two

large bags, in which were all his possessions not in his
pockets, Miller walked to the hotel.

The very old man at the desk seemed delighted that
Miller wanted a room and a price per week was named which
was quite suitable. The room was not very large, it was,
in fact, definitely small, but it was as clean and comfortable as it was small. Miller was quite satisfied but he
stayed in it for only a minute, as he was so anxious to get
out and spend his first day in New York trying to learn as
much as possible about this "Midtown Manhattan", in which he
was to make his fortune.

With his head buzzing with the memories of all that he
had seen his first day in New York, Miller got back to his
hotel about seven o'clock at night - happy, tired, dusty, and
exceedingly hungry. He decided to eat enough dinner to make
up for the lunch he had forgotten to have, just as soon as he
went up to his room and washed up. When he asked for his room
key at the desk, he was given his key and a letter. He had
heard that shops frequently get names from a hotel and write
letters soliciting patronage and decided that this must be
such a letter, for no one knew that he would stop at that hotel.
As he put the letter into his pocket, he laughed to himself
that he, even, hadn't known his adress until a few hours before.

After a quick wash, Miller went to the dining room and
made good his promise to himself by ordering everything offered
on the table d'hote dinner. After the waitress had taken his

238

order, Miller remembered the letter. He ripped open the
envelope and pulled out the two pieces of paper enclosed.
The first, to his surprise, was one page torn out of a
railroad timetable, the other a piece of hotel stationery.
The letter meant nothing to him at all, in fact it seemed
rather silly. He didn't know the writing, nor the signature. He then looked at the envelope again. The letter
was postmarked from a town,of which he had never heard,in
Maryland. He couldn't recall ever having met anyone from
that state. The name and address were right too. But no -
the name was Mr. H. Muller. That's right, it was a u not an
i. He carefully put the letter and piece of timetable back
into the envelope and decided to take it to the clerk at
the desk when he finished dinner.

All during dinner, he wondered about the letter. Somehow it worried him though he couldn't for the life of him
say why. After dinner instead of giving the letter to the
clerk, he decided to give it to the guest of the hotel with
the amazingly similar name. He asked the clerk if there was
a Mr. Muller stopping at the hotel.

"Why no," said the clerk, "there isn't and as I've been
here nearly all the fifty years this hotel has been open, I
can tell you that there never has been anyone here by that name.

That sounded so final that Miller didn't even take the
letter out of his pocket but just went up to his room. There
he read the letter through again and it still seemed rather
silly to him. But he was too tired to worry any more about it,
so he put it away in his dresser drawer and began to unpack his

bags. He took particular pains with the portfolio of the reproductions of his art work that he had done for the agency in Great Bend. That, he was going to take with him when he began to visit the advertising offices in the morning.

The next evening Miller came back to the hotel in an excellent mood for two of the firms he had visited were interested enough in his work to ask him to return to be interviewed by higher executives. His mood changed when at the desk he was given another letter. Again he could not tell why he felt queer but the letters annoyed him.

Miller waited until he was in his room to open the envelope. The second letter seemed even sillier than the first and he threw it in the drawer with the other and went down to dinner. Back once more in his room, he got both letters out again and read them over.

He began mumbling to himself. "They both read as if there were no really very good reason for writing them - well, then why were they written? The fellow wants me, or whoever was supposed to get them, to have them but he says nothing important - or does he say something I can't make out - boy, that would be code, now wouldn't it - well he's come to the right person. Didn't I go to art school and am I not trained to see every last detail there is to see? Sure I did and if there is anything to see I'm going to see it. But, why would anyone be playing games with me? Someone I don't even know? Well what do you care why, Henry, just get to work. You've got nothing else to do for a while."

#6

Dear Friend,

    Each town below Baltimore has been a lemon for
business. You had better know. My expenses are
sliced - right - the rub is not writing orders. Hope
sales are better in the next town. You and I are to
follow the stars it looks like. How about a letter?

    like always

        F.H.

Theo. Hardeen, Pres. • John Mulholland, Editor M.U.M.
Royal B. Vilas, Sec.
Eva Silber, Asst. to the Sec. • May Ward, Guest

John Mulholland
130 West 42nd St.
New York 18

The Christmas Conjurer

By John Mulholland

Using the straight forward and unencumbered logic of childhood, it immediately becomes apparent why Christmas and those days just before, and after, make up the most wonderful time of the year. Those few days out of the long year compose the all too short period when all adults act reasonably. Then, adults say "yes" more often than they say "no". On those days, they suggest second portions of ice cream, not needing the vestige of a hing, and even allow bedtime to go by without a word. Oh, there are a whole list of nice ways in which grown-ups act at Christmas time, and the really big thing is that they then not only seem to realize that pretending is sensible, but they themselves pretend. They pretend that the presents come down the chimney, and they pretend that they haven't the vaguest notion how the tree got trimmed. They even pretend that conduct has been excellent throughout the entire year, when conscious effort to be good has been made only since sometime after Thanksgiving. Adults become real people.

But, getting back to this idea of pretending; pretending, every child knows and every adult should remember, is a sort of home made magic. Magic, of course, is doing those things which should, but can't, be done. A real magician does them, and if you are not a real magician, you act as though they had been done - that's pretending. Of course, there is nothing that is as much fun to one who likes to pretend, as seeing a real magician. Christmas holidays (that means there is no school) is the time when everyone, old and young, plays pretend - therefore the Christmas conjurer.

I have been a conjurer, or magician, for over thirty years. It is a most pleasant occupation for three hundred and fifty days a year. During the extra days I am a Christmas Conjurer and that, as any magician will tell you, is something rather extra special. During these holidays everyone believes, and that makes everything nice;

243

scoffers belong only to a dreary world.

Ever since Christmas holidays have been the time when children and adults view things with complete (well almost complete) understanding, there have been Christmas Conjurers. These holiday performers usually appear under private auspices, though in England and some other countries, they also give special public stage performances of their mysteries. The magician at Christmas time in America is most frequently to be found at parties. True, some of these are gigantic affairs and run by clubs, and other organizations, but they are, nevertheless, parties. Many families for their private parties annually do as much to ensure the presence of the conjurer, as they do the presents of Santa.

Welcoming the Christmas Conjurer goes right back to the beginning of America. When New York City was still in a British Colony, the newspapers carried paid notices that the sleight-of-hand performer "will wait on any Gentlemen or Ladies at their own homes." These advertisements of a willingness to appear at private parties were always in greater number just before Christmas. Some of the oldest members of our oldest families cannot recall a Christmas without a party, where there was a magician with his marvels. It is quite usual for one performer of mysteries to go back year after year to one family until he begins to be the Christmas Conjurer for the second, and, even, the third and fourth, generation.

Any magician who has been a Christmas Conjurer during several years has learned that his feats of legerdemain must be most carefully chosen. Each mystery must, to put it in a sentence, be in the mood and humor of a fairy story. No deep mental marvels, no decapitations, no hilarious feats are to be included in a holiday program. Every wonderful occurrence should be the natural result of saying a magic word, tooting on a magic whistle, or waving the hands in quite the magically approved manner. A Christmas Conjurer should no more surround his magic with quips and jokes than should a publisher of fairy tales include in his book even the lagest funny stories.

244

There is fun and humor in the Christmas magic show but it is of a very special sort. It is the same kind of fun which comes through the lovely unreality of the fairy story. Those stories where you believe, and want to believe, and enjoy, knowing, way down deep, that they aren't true. The Christmas Conjurer isn't challenging your intellect. He is only trying his best to prove to you that the world of pretense is real.

Part of adult pretending is that a magic show at Christmas time is, primarily, for children. Therefore at least one or two children will be in the audience. The way it works out is that anyone may be considered a child whenever a person of an earlier generation is present. I have shown my magic before holiday audiences where most of the sons were bald headed and many of the daughters had silver in their hair.

There are a number of people who feel that a performance of mysteries should be so much a part of every child's Christmas holiday that they engage magicians and present their services at boys and girls orphanages and to the children's wards in hospitals. All magicians donate as much of their magic, as time will allow, for organizations dealing with underprivileged children.

I shall never forget the Christmas day show I gave many years ago at a settlement house, at the request of the late Governor Alfred E. Smith. For the occasion, I made up a special Christmas story to go with each bit of magic and I worked hard on those stories for the Governor impressed upon me how little those children had. The children were most enthusiastic about the magic, but listened to each story with expressionless faces. After the performance the kind director of the settlement house thanked me for my services and expressed pleasure with both the magic and the stories. "Those stories," she said, "were so charming it is really too bad there wasn't a child in the audience who understands English."

But we magicians have very few troubles in our role of Christmas Conjurer. It is a most satisfactory work. As a matter of fact, there is only one complaint we have.

#4 - John Mulholland

That is about the child who, just as we start to do a trick, calls out, "Oh! I know how that one is done. I got it for Christmas." It really doesn't bother us much for it never is the same trick. You see, Mr. Claus and the Christmas Conjurer work in very close harmony.

Published by
OFFICE OF JOHN MULHOLLAND
130 West 42nd Street, New York 18, N. Y.

Christmas Conjurer

By JOHN MULHOLLAND

USING the straightforward and un-encumbered logic of childhood, it immediately becomes apparent why Christmas and those days just before and after make up the most wonderful time of the year. Those few days out of the long year compose the all-too-short period when all adults act reasonably. Then, adults say "yes" more often than they say "no." On those days they suggest second portions of ice cream, not needing the vestige of a hint, and even allow bed-time to go by without a word.

Oh, there are a whole list of nice ways in which grown-ups act at Christmas

John Mulholland demonstrates "Christmas conjuring" for a group of children.

The Old, Old Magic

It blossoms anew at Christmas, when children and parents like to "pretend."

By JOHN MULHOLLAND

USING the straightforward and unencumbered logic of childhood, it immediately becomes apparent why Christmas and those days just before and after make up the most wonderful time of the year. Those few days out of the long year compose the all-too-short period when all adults act reasonably. Then, adults say "yes" more often than they say "no." On those days they suggest second portions of ice cream, not needing the vestige of a hint, and even allow bedtime to go by without a word.

Oh, there are a whole list of nice ways in which grown-ups act at Christmas time, and the really big thing is that they then not only seem to realize that pretending is sensible but they themselves pretend. They pretend that the presents come down the chimney, and they pretend that they haven't the vaguest notion how the tree got trimmed. They even pretend that conduct has been excellent throughout the entire year, when conscious effort to be good has been made only since some time after Thanksgiving. Adults become real people.

But, getting back to this idea of pretending. Pretending, every child knows and every adult should remember, is a sort of home-made magic. Magic, of course, is doing those things which should, but can't, be done. A real magician does them and if you are not a real magician you act as though they had been done—that's pretending. Of course, there is nothing that is as much fun to one who likes to pretend, as seeing a real magician. Christmas holidays (that means there is no school) are the time when everyone, old and young, plays pretend. Hence, the Christmas conjurer.

I have been a conjurer, or magician, for over thirty years. It is a most pleasant occupation for three hundred and fifty days a year. During the extra days, I am a Christmas conjurer and that, as any magician will tell you, is something rather extra special. During these holidays everyone believes, and that makes everything nice; scoffers belong only to a dreary world.

EVER since Christmas holidays have been the time when children and adults view things with complete (well, almost complete) understanding, there have been Christmas conjurers. These holiday performers usually appear under private auspices, though in England and some other countries they also give special public stage performances of their mysteries. The magician at Christmas time in America is most frequently to be found at parties. True, some of these are gigantic affairs and run by clubs and other organizations, but they are, nevertheless, parties. Many families for their private parties annually do as much to insure the presence of the conjurer as they do the presents of Santa.

Welcoming the Christmas conjurer goes right back to the beginning of America.

DO NOT FORGET THE NEEDIEST!

When New York City was still in a British colony, the newspapers carried paid notices that the sleight-of-hand performer "will wait on any gentlemen or ladies at their own homes." These advertisements of a willingness to appear at private parties were always in greater number just before Christmas. Some of the oldest members of our oldest families cannot recall a Christmas without a party where there was a magician with his marvels. It is quite usual for one performer of mysteries to go back year after year to one family until he begins to be the Christmas conjurer for the second, and even the third and fourth, generation.

ANY magician who has been a Christmas conjurer during several years has learned that his feats of legerdemain must be most carefully chosen. Each mystery must, to put it in a sentence, be in the mood and humor of a fairy story. No deep mental marvels, no decapitations, no hilarious feats are to be included in a holiday program. Every wonderful occurrence should be the natural result of saying a magic word, tooting on a magic whistle, or waving the hands in quite the magically approved manner.

A Christmas conjurer should no more surround his magic with quips and jokes than should a publisher of fairy tales include in his book even the latest funny stories. There is fun and humor in the Christmas magic show, but it is of a very special sort. It is the same kind of fun which comes through the lovely unreality of the fairy story—those stories you believe, and want to believe, but enjoy knowing, way down deep, aren't true.

Part of adult pretending is that a magic show at Christmas time is, primarily, for children. Therefore, at least one or two children will be in the audience. The way it works out is that anyone may be considered a child whenever a person is an earlier generation is present. I have shown my magic before holiday audiences where most of the sons were bald-headed and many of the daughters had silver in their hair.

There are a number of people who feel that a performance of mysteries should be so much a part of every child's Christmas holiday that they engage magicians and present their services at boys' and girls' orphanages and to the children's wards in hospitals.

I SHALL never forget the Christmas Day show I gave many years ago at a settlement house at the request of the late Gov. Alfred E. Smith. For the occasion I made up a special Christmas story to go with each bit of magic and I worked hard on those stories, for the Governor impressed upon me how little those children had. The children were most enthusiastic about the magic, but listened to each story with expressionless faces. After the performance the kind director of the settlement house thanked me for my services and expressed pleasure with both the magic and the stories.

"Those stories," she said, "were so charming it is really too bad there wasn't a child in the audience who understands English."

But we magicians have very few troubles in our role of Christmas conjurer. It is a most satisfactory work. As a matter of fact, there is only one complaint we have. That is about the child who just as we start to do a trick, calls out "Oh! I know how that one is done. I got it for Christmas." It really doesn't bother us much, for if never is the same trick. You see, Mr. Claus and the Christmas conjurer work in very close harmony.

13

BOOK COVERS

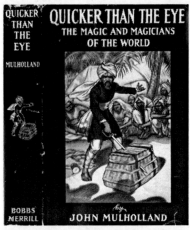

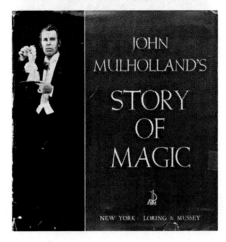

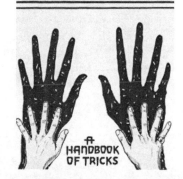

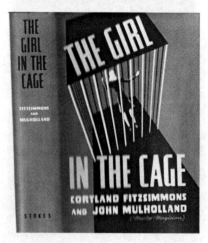

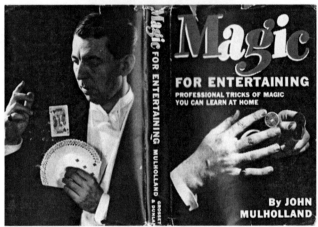

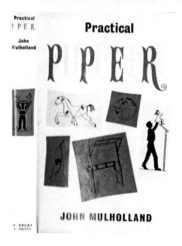

This bibliography is the result of many researchers working for several decades to help provide an insight into John Mulholland's life, celebrity, magical technique, scholarship and the period in which he lived. Notably, the New York Public Library, the Lincoln Center Library of the Performing Arts, the Milbourne Christopher Collection, the Collection of Christian Fechner, the American Museum of Magic and Salon de Magie – the Collection of Kenneth Klosterman – were of great assistance. Primary help was provided to the author by: Special Agent A. Anderson, Ted Bogusta, Edwin A. Dawes, Gabe Fajuri, the Gordon family, George P. Hansen, Richard Hatch, David Haversat, Harrison Kaplan, Louis Rachow, William V. Rauscher, Daniel Stashower, An R. Trotter, Bill Vande Water, information officers at the CIA, and one who prefers anonymity.

Chronological Bibliography

By John Mulholland

Magic in the Making: A First Book of Conjuring, with Milton M. Smith, Charles, Scribner's Sons, New York, 1925.

Quicker Than The Eye, Bobbs Merrill & Co., New York, copyright 1927, published in book form, Junior Literary Guild, 1932.

Behind the Magician's Curtain, The New York Public Library, 1928.

The Story of Magic, Loring & Mussey, New York, 1935.

Modern Magician—A Handbook of Tricks, Introduction by Lowell Thomas, Danbury Printing Co., 1937.

Beware Familiar Spirits, Charles Scribner's & Sons, New York, 1938.

The Girl in the Cage, with Cortland Fitzsimmons, Frederick A. Stokes Company, New York, 1939.

The Art of Illusion, (also titled "Magic for Men to Do" Armed Services Division, 1944) Charles Scribner's, New York, 1944.

Magic For Entertaining, (Professional Tricks of Magic You Can Learn at Home), (formerly *The Art of Illusion*), Grosset and Dunlop, New York, 1944.

The Early Magic Shows, Office of John Mulholland, New York, 1945.

Some Operational Applications of the Art of Deception, Office of John Mulholland, Prepared for the Central Intelligence Agency, 1953-1954. Property of the Office of New York District Attorney, NY State.

El Prestidigitator Moderno, A Manual of Secrets, Introduction by Lowel (sic) Thomas, Translated by A. Gallardo Mendez, Mexico City, D.F. Ediciones, Ciceron, 1952, 1954. (Spanish version of 1937 booklet.)

Practical Puppetry, Herbert Jenkins Limited Publishers, London, Arco Publishing, New York (trade paperback), 1961.

John Mulholland's Book of Magic, Charles Scribner's & Sons, New York, 1963.

Magic of the World, Charles Scribner's & Sons, New York, 1965.

The Magical Mind–Keys to Successful Communication (with Dr. George N. Gordon), Hastings House, New York, 1967.

Concerning John Mulholland (partially annotated)

Pre 1900-1929:

The Discovery of Witchcraft – proving that the Contracts of Witches with Devils and all Infernal Spirits of Familiars are but Erroreous Novelties, and Imaginary Conceptions by Reginald Scot, 1665 version of the 1584 volume.

Robert-Houdin, The French Magician, by Brander Matthews, *Harper's Young People*, Volume IX, No. 434, February 21, 1888, p. 290-291, Vol. IX No. 435, p.307-308, Vol. IX No. 436, p. 316-317.

Black & White, Egyptian Hall program reference, London, June 27, 1891.

HYPNOTISM — A Correct Guide to the Science and How Subjects are Influenced by Carl Sextus, The Page Company, Boston, 1893.

Hypnotism – How it is Done; Its Uses and Dangers, by James R. Cocke, M.D., Arena Publishing Co., Boston, 1894.

Isn't It Wonderful? by Charles Bertram, Swam Sonnenschein & Co.,Ltd., 1899, p. 280.

A Wonderful Conjuror, *The New York Dramatic Mirror*, June 3, 1899.

Program of the Eden Musee, January, 1903.

Say John Mulholland Owes $1,400,000 -- International Finance and Development Company Admits Charges, *The New York Times*, November 7, 1903, p.1.

Letter to Samuel C. Hooker by S. Ansbach, Hillsdale, NJ, February 16, 1906, three pages.

Smoke & Bubbles by John William Sargent, pictures by Nella Fontaine Binckley, Saalfield Publishing, Akron Ohio, 1906, presentation copy to John Mulhollland, on his birthday June 9, 1918.

Society of American Magicians Monthly, New York, November, 1918.

Letter to Jane and Mrs. Howard Thurston by Howard Thurston, February 26, 1919.

Annual Commencement Program of the Horace Mann School for Boys, June 3, 1919.

New Light on the Bullet Catching Trick by Harry Houdini, *MUM* magazine, August, 1919.

Letter to John Mulholland by Harry Houdini, January 20, 1921 written from Boston, collection of Robert Rossi.

Letter to Harry Houdini by Harry Kellar, January 31, 1921, two pages handwritten.

Letter to John Mulholland c/o American Consul, Vienna, Austria by Dr. Milton A. Bridges, September 6, 1921, one page.

The Horace Manniken, published by The Horace Mann School, Riverdale, New York, Editions: 1919 – 1925.

Letter to Samuel C. Hooker by John Mulholland, December 1, 1921, one page.

Letter to John Mulholland by Carl Brema, one page relating to the creation of a Mulholland prop, March 4, 1922, private collection.

Letter to A. M. Wilson by Harry Houdini, June 22, 1922, one page typewritten.

Renowned Magician Arrives in Mexico, appearance at "Regis" covered, np, nd, early 1920's.

John Mulholland, American Wizard, *International Herald Tribune*, Paris, France, nd.

Mulholland Would've Been Buried Alive –Those who failed to see this modern medicine man will always regret it, *The Daily Sketch*, England, nd.

The Art of Magic – An American Conjurer's Demonstration, *The Manchester Guardian*, nd.

Letter to John Mulholland by Gus Fowler, May 8, 1923, one page.

Thurston's Easy Pocket Tricks (Book Number Seven) by Thurston World's Master Magician, printed by the magician, New York, 1924.

Practical Lessons in Hypnotism by Wm. Wesley Cook, Candid Institute, New York, 1924.

Horace Mann School for Boys, Assembly Program #16, Friday January 11, 1924, John Mulholland magic show.

Conjurer and Pedagogue by John Mulholland and Milton M. Smith, *The Journal of Educational Method*, February, 1925, p. 253-256.

Scribners present John Mulholland and Milton M. Smith in Magic in the Making, a promotional announcement by Leo Rullman, New York City, 1925.

Scrapbook of John Mulholland's first world tour, handwritten notes, April, 1925 – November, 1926, private collection.

Smith College Yearbook, 1926, p. 83.

New York, Day By Day, by O. O. McIntyre, 1926.

Houdini on Spiritualism, text of final lecture, presented Princess Theatre, Wednesday, April 21, 1926. Eight pages accompanying slides. Courtesy of Arthur Moses.

The Sphinx, March 1927, Volume XXVI, no. 1., John Mulholland and Dr. Milton A. Bridges on cover, though names and photos are regrettably switched. Mulholland's mounting influence is seen in the magic world.

Advertising brochure of John Mulholland by William B. Feakins Inc, Times Building, New York City, 1927, one page folded, one of a kind.

Grolier News, news of Mulholland exhibit, March 4, 1927.

Books on Magic Exhibited -- 300 Volumes May be Seen at Grolier Club Until April 9, *The New York Times*, March 18, 1927, p. 24.

Letter to Robert Sherms by John Mulholland, New York City, August, 1927.

Revoking Venders of Wipes, Flukum, Googs and Cornpunk Demand Their Rights (Alagazam, Dear Reader! Pitchmen Tip The Office on How to Get the Cocoanuts by Robert Golden, *The World*, October 16, 1927, private scrapbook on "Ballyhoo" of Jean Hugard.

Hypnotizing Patients So They Won't Feel The Surgeon's Knife, *The Chicago Herald and Examiner*, Sunday, January 15, 1928.

History of Conjuring and Magic, by Henry Ridgely Evans, The International Brotherhood of Magicians, Kenton, Ohio, 1928.

Behind the Magician's Curtain, An Exhibition of Books and Prints Relating to Conjuring by John Mulholland, on exhibit at the New York Public Library, 1928.

The Magician Waves a New Wand by Bella Cohen, *The New York Times*, January 29, 1928, p. 126.

Behind the Magician's Curtain by John Mulholland, *New York Public Library Bulletin*, Vol. 32. No. 2. February, 1928.

Letter to John Mulholland by H.M. Lydenburg, from the New York Public Library, May 3, 1928.

Milton A. Bridges by John Mulholland, *The Sphinx*, August 1928, Volume XXVII, No. 6, p. 249.

Letter to John Mulholland by Dr. Milton A. Bridges, September 8, 1928, one page.

The Sphinx, November 1928, Volume XXVII, No. 9. Important photo of Mulholland on cover with Oswald Williams and Jasper Maskelyne. Important notation on JM, p. 403. An 18 yr. old John Booth also contributes a trick envelope and a silk wonder. This issue portrays the subculture at its finest.

Old World Wizards and Wizardry by John Mulholland, *The Sphinx*, (Mulholland on cover) November, 1928, p. 418-419.

Academy of Denistry Program, New York City, biography of John Mulholland written by the magician, 1929.

PS. Straus Back, Lauds N.Y.U Work, *The New York Times*, June 5, 1929, p. 37.

Letter to John Mulholland by Fulton Oursler, July 1, 1929, one page.

Letter to Oscar Teale by John Mulholland, January 24, 1929, one page.

Letter to Oscar Teale by John Mulholland, February 24, 1929, one page.

Magic in America by John Mulholland, *The Institute Magazine*, Columbia University, vol. 1 number VI, March, 1929, 8-9, 26.

Magic in America by John Mulholland, *The Philadelphia Forum Magazine*, May, 1929, p. 31.

Magic For Magicians by John Mulholland, *The Sphinx*, No. 28, June 1929, p. 62-63.

Believe It or Not by A.M. Wilson, *The Sphinx*, no. 28, June 1929, p. 144-145.

Gossip and Gimmick by John Mulholland, *The Sphinx*, no. 28, June, 1929, p. 63.

Things That Never Were, *The New York World*, June 16, 1929.

Letter to John Mulholland by Burling Hull, July 3, 1929, one page.

Letter to John Mulholland by Howard Thurston, November 1, 1929.

Mulholland Does a Few Tricks — and in Between Explains How Mind Reading Depends on Magic, *The New York Sun*, Friday, December 20, 1929, p. 20.

1930-1939:

Brochure of the William B. Feakins Agency, Inc. 1930's.

Vanishing Prop Through Magic, exclusive to the *Detroit Times*, nd, probably 1930's.

Nothing Up The Sleeve by Fred C. Kelly, *Readers Digest*, nd, probably 1930's.

NY Day by Day by O. O. Mc Intyre, nd, probably 1930's.

Nicola Extends a Yule Gladhand to Mulholland, *Variety*, nd, probably 1930's.

The Dutch Treat Club by Frank Sullivan, nd, probably 1930's.

Letter to John Mulholland by S. S. Henry, nd, probably 1930's, three pages handwritten.

The Master Magician by Lowell Thomas, (about John Mulholland), no pub, nd, probably early 1930's.

Good Money No Good, So He Coined His Own, Collector Has Magician's Coin by Edmund Leamy, *The New York Times*, nd, probably 1930's.

Mulholland Performs Magic for Rotary Club Lunches; Reveals Death Bed Plea Made Him an Editor by Clyde B. Davis, *The New York Times*, nd, probably 1930's.

John Mulholland, Magician Mystifies Large Audience at Uptown Clubhouse — Magician Fascinates Members of Women's Club With Tricks, Santa Barbara, CA, nd, probably 1930's.

Mulholland Opens Bag of Tricks to Show Hand is Quicker Than Eye, (*Scholarly Magician Matches Modern Masters of China, Japan, India in Amphitheatre*), nd, probably 1930's.

Peter Carter Says, News column syndicated, nd, probably 1930's.

Sorcerer (profile of John Mulholland), *The New Yorker*, 1930's.

Notes of Social Activities in New York and Elsewhere, *The New York Times*, January 24, 1930, p. 28.

A Living Wizard, *My Life of Magic* reviewed by John Mulholland, *The New York Times Book Section*, February 9, 1930.

Detailed description of John Mulholland's show by Edward J. McLaughlin, Clinton, Iowa, February 11, 1930, three pages typewritten.

Detailed description of John Mulholland's show by Edward J. McLaughlin, Caleb Mills Hall, February 28, 1930, three pages typewritten.

The Equipment of the School Theater by Milton A. Smith, *Bureau of Publications*, Teacher's College, New York, Columbia University, 1930.

Eastern Magic by John Mulholland, *Theater Arts Monthly*, Vol. XIV, #3, March, 1930, p. 211-217.

Letter to Robert W. Lull, Esq., by John Mulholland, April 14, 1930, one page typewritten.

Presto! Magic Puts Kibosh on Seers' Racket, *Chicago Daily Tribune*, May 29, 1930, p. 5.

A Skull Shows Its Brain to The Magicians, *Chicago Daily Tribune*, June 1, 1930, p. 17.

Letter to Oscar Teale by John Mulholland, July 14, 1930, one page.

Letter to Oscar Teale by John Mulholland, September 26, 1930, one page.

Vanity Fair, November, 1930, p. 55.

Letter to T. Nelson Downs by John Mulholland, November 4, 1930, one page typewritten.

The Science of Hypnotism, compiled by L. E. Young, Franklin Publishing Co., Chicago, 1931.

CIGAM (Magic as Presented by Modern Magicians) Edited by Walter A. Schwartz, Hartford, CT, 1931, p. 9-10.

Letter to C. E. Brooks by John Mulholland, Great Barrington, MA, February 25, 1931.

Smart Folks are Easy to Fool, *The American Magazine*, March, 1931, p. 50-51, 157-159.

Letter to John Mulholland by Chris (unknown), from Grand Rapids, April 6, 1931, one page typewritten.

Magicians in Meeting Ignore Natural Laws, *The New York Times*, May 27, 1931, p. 19.

Hits Telling of Fortunes – John Mulholland, Magician, Warns Audience of Menace in Future "Readings," np, April 6, 1931.

Letter to Tom Boyer by John Mulholland, August 21,1931, one page typewritten.

The Sphinx (An Independent Magazine for Magicians) John Mulholland editor, Rotogravure Section, June, 1931.

Magician to Fight Fortune Tellers, *The New York Times*, July 15, 1931, p. 21.

If So John Mulholland Magician and Physician Will Cure You, John Mulholland profiled in *Bumblebee*, by Edward P. Harrison, pub. by the Rochester Ad Club, Vol. XVIII, Aug. 27, 1931-Sept. 3, 1931, no. 47-48.

Forecasters of the Future Who Flourish in New York by Rebecca Hourwich, *The New York Times*, September 6, 1931, p. 106.

Magician Mulholland Fools Ad Clubbers Without Fuss or Feathers by Dwight Greenfield, np, September 10, 1931.

Letter to Thomas Worthington by John Mulholland, September 10, 1931, one page.

Modern Merlins Perform for One Another – Even Let a Ventriloquist Do His Stint, *The New York Times*, November 13, 1931, p. 21.

The Magic and Magicians of the World, pamphlet published by John Mulholland promoting his book *Quicker Than The Eye*, 1932.

Profiteering Prophets by John Mulholland, *The American Magazine* (also published In *Esquire Magazine*), January, 1932.

Magician Explains Rules of Deception, *Detroit Press*, 1932.

Fooling the Public and Making Them Like It by John Mulholland, *The Boston Herald*, Sunday, April 3, 1932.

The Trade of Trickery – Trees Grow While You Wait, *New York Herald Tribune*, Sunday, April 3, 1932 & Sunday, April 10, 1932. Reprint of first chapter of *Quicker Than the Eye*, "Peddlers of Wonders."

Following Trade of Trickery, *The Sunday Star* (Washington D.C.), April 3, 1932, part 7.

Magician Explains Rules of Deception, John Mulholland's Book Says Many Tricks Are Based on Old Psychological Data, *The New York Times*, April 20, 1932, p. 21.

Transcript of Lowell Thomas Radio Broadcast featuring John Mulholland, guest. May 9, 1932. 1-page typed.

Shivering in the Dark (with Jean Harlow), by Anthony Abbot, *The Illustrated Detective Magazine*, May, 1932, p. 26-93.

John Mulholland, profiled in *The New York World Telegram*, May 3, 1932.

Letter to John Mulholland by Howard Thurston, Kansas City, MO, June 11, 1932.

Ghost Girl by Anthony Abbot, *The Illustrated Detective Magazine*, June, 1932, p. 32-92.

Magic is a Hobby of Noted Magician – 29 Years of Study Behind Practical Psychologist, *The Birmingham News-Age Herald*, Sunday, July 11, 1932, p. 7.

Letter to Will Goldston by John Mulholland (written from Mexico), August 25, 1932, one page typewritten.

An English Magician Sees America by Stuart Drayton Raw, *The Magic Wand*, October, 1932.

Comment on deviant magicien, The Paris - soir, 1933.

Wizard with the Cards, American Puzzles London Magicians, *The Evening Standard*, April, 1933.

Le Prestidigitateur, (official organ for the Syndicate of International Artist Prestidigitateurs) Mai, 1933. No. 173, p. 1527.

Dinner to Mr. John Mulholland, MIMC, *The Magic Circular*, publication of the Magic Circle, London, Vol. 27, no. 309, June, 1933, p. 129 -132.

Interview with John Mulholland, *The World Telegram*, July 1, 1933.

Letter to Will Goldston by John Mulholland, August 7, 1933, one page.

Letter to Dr. Jules D'Hotel by John Mulholland, August 8, 1933, one page.

Le Prestidigitateur, (official organ for the Syndicate of International Artist Prestidigitateurs) *Roberta's Views on Women Magicians*, September, 1933. no. 165, p. 1454-1455.

Black Magic by John Kieran, *The New York Times*, September 17, 1933, p. S2.

Les prestiditateurs francais ont recu un manipulator d'Amerique by Serge, Comedia, Jeundi 4 Mai, 1933.

Magician to Show Old Chinese Trick, Mexico, 1933.

John Mulholland Uno de los illusionistas mas famosos del mondo esta en Mexico, *The Universal Grafico*, Mexico, 1933.

The Hand is Not Quicker Than the Eye by John Mulholland, *The New York Times* Magazine, October 8, 1933.

Letter to Thomas Worthington by John Mulholland, October 18, 1933, one page.

Letter to John Mulholland by Will Goldston, October 18, 1933, one page.

Letter to Will Goldston by John Mulholland, November 8, 1933, one page.

The Wide-Spread Appeal of Magic, *The Literary Digest*, December 9, 1933, p. 22.

Who's Who in Magic by Will Goldston, Will Goldston Ltd., Aladdin House, London, 1934. Copious Mulholland biography on pages 71-72, noting his favorite book, magician and trick.

How's Tricks? An Interview with a Famous Magician by Harriet Thorndyke, *The Family Circle*, Volume 4, No. 2, January 12, 1934, p. 14, 15, 18, 22.

The Faculty Club presents World Renowned Magician John Mulholland (program) March 8-9, 1934, one detailed page of a two-night stand in two different auditoriums.

Letter to John Mulholland by John Macrae, President of E.P. Dutton & Co., August 9, 1934, one page.

The Impossible Trick, *Oil Power* magazine, publication of Soccony-Vacuum Oil Co., September, 1934, vol. IX, #8, p. 116-121.

Letter to John Mulholland by Fetaque Sanders, December 19, 1934, small postcard.

Ship in a Bottle? That's Nothing Much, The Old Magician Put Pigeons There, *The Detroit News*, 1935.

The Audience Fools Itself by John Mulholland, *The Stage*, April, 1935, p. 44-45.

Letter to Phil Thomas by John Mulholland, October 2, 1935, one page typed, private collection.

Dr. Samuel Hooker, Chemist Dies at 71, *The New York Times*, obituary, October 14, 1935.

Letter to John Mulholland by John E. Low, October 26, 1935, one page.

Letter to John Mulholland by Brunel White, January 15, 1936, two pages.

Stoopnocrats Plan a Valentine Party – Charity With Hilarity, *The New York Times*, February 9, 1936, p. N3.

Letter to John Mulholland by Fred Keating regarding Howard Thurston's death, April 14, 1936, two pages.

Program of the NY Junior League, annual gala, John Mulholland featured entertainer, April 17, 1936.

Hundreds Attend Jubilee of League, *The New York Times*, April 18, 1936, p. 12.

Magicians Shelving Their Big Gimmicks (Turning Back From Elaborate Stage Spectacles to Intimate One Man Shows), *The New York World*, April 23, 1936, p. 18.

The Sphinx, vol. XXXV, number five, July, 1936, p. 142.

Volumes on Magic Given to Library, Valuable Collection of 1,000 Works Presented by Heirs of Dr. Samuel Hooker, *The New York Times*, August 5, 1936, p. 21.

An American Doctor's Odyssey – Adventures in Forty-Five Countries by Victor George Heiser, W. W. Norton & Co., New

York, 1936. An account of Mulholland's performance for the Sultan of Sulu, p. 148-149.

Detroit Institute of the Arts, notice of Mulholland lecture, 1937.

The Encyclopedia of Cigarette Tricks by Keith Clark, with a Preface by John Mulholland, published by the author, New York and Paris, 1937.

Cups and Balls Magic by Tom Osborne, including *The Oldest Trick* by John Mulholland, Kanter's Magic Shop, Philadelphia, 1937.

India's Rope Trick Bunkum, *The Sunday Oregonian* (Portland), January 10, 1937, p. 2.

Do You Believe in Magic? by John Mulholland, *The Commentator*, April, 1937, p. 97.

Letter to John Mulholland by Horace Goldin, from England, September 10, 1937.

Genii, *The International Conjuror's Magazine*, October, 1937.

Fete For Children's Home – Benefit Entertainment to be Held in Brooklyn, *The New York Times*, November 21, 1937, p. 87.

The Business of Miracles by John Mulholland, *Nation's Business*, December, 1937, p. 48-50.

Mystery Cloaks Magicians' "Trial," *The New York Times*, December 5, 1937, p. 45.

Greater Magic by John Northern Hilliard, 6th edition, Carl Waring Jones Publisher, Minneapolis, MN, 1938.

San Francisco Town Hall Lecture program, John Mulholland presents "Adventures in Magic," January 25, 1938.

Advertising flyer for John Mulholland, Veteran's Auditorium, Wednesday, January 26, 1938. (Oddly noting that Mulholland is a Columbia University Professor!) 1-page printed.

Advertising Brochure for John Mulholland, Woman's Club of Hollywood, Friday, January 28, 1938, Los Magicos Proudly Presents Mr. John Mulholland in "Adventures in Magic." 1 typeset page.

Letter to John Mulholland by H. M. Anderson, Ed. *The New York Sun*, April 7, 1938, one page.

King of Magicians, *Coronet Magazine*, July, 1938.

Letter to Norman Todd by John Mulholland, September 1, 1938, one typewritten page.

Skill and Spirits by Edmund Gilligan, *The New York Sun*, November 2, 1938.

Mulholland's Cavalcade of Spirits a profile of Mulholland's *Beware Familiar Spirits*, by Charles Poore, Books of the Times, *The New York Times*, December 21, 1938, p. 27.

How's Tricks by Gerald Kaufman, Introduction by John Mulholland, Frederick Stokes Publishing Co., New York, 1938.

My Day by Eleanor Roosevelt, Washington DC, United Feature Syndicate, 1939. Specific reference to John Mulholland's performance in glowing terms.

Letter to Ornum Skinner by John Mulholland, February 11, 1939.

Astral Fluid, a review, by John Mulholland, *Saturday Review*, April 29, 1939.

Letter to John Mulholland by Julien J. Proskauer, May 23, 1939, one page typewritten.

Whalen Now Magician – Society Honors Him, *The New York Times*, May 27, 1939, p. 9.

Letter to John Mulholland by Will Rock, October 8, 1939, one page handwritten.

Nate Leipzig, 66, A Prestidigitator, Former President of American Society of Magicians Had Appeared before Royalty, *The New York Times*, obituary, October 14, 1939, p. 19.

The First Reader by Harry Hansen, *The New York World-Telegram*, Thursday, December 21, 1939.

John Mulholland in Japan, 1923.

1940-1949:

Advertising brochure of John Mulholland by William B. Feakins Inc, 500 Fifth Avenue, New York City, circa 1940's, rare.

Original typescript biography by John Mulholland, circa 1940, submitted to the *Chicago Social Register* and misquoted to spread incorrect idea his last name was not Mulholland! Mother's maiden name was misappropriated as his last name. Actual type under magnification matches typescript pages of articles of same era. Mulholland's typewriting; editor's grave error.

Circus Saints and Sinners, nd, probably 1941.

Magicians Hail Kemal For Abolishing Magic, Constantinople Turkey, Associated Press, nd, probably 1940's.

Photo by Irving Desfor

Tricks of the Fortune Tellers by Forest Hills, *Popular Mechanics*, nd, probably 1940's.

Ladies Home Journal, *The Journal About Town*, nd, probably 1940's.

Letter to John Mulholland by John C. Greene, one page handwritten, nd, probably 1940's.

Plucks Cards From Air to Prove LaGuardia Will Win, (re Mulholland) np, nd: November 4, probably 1940's.

The Magician's Rings, Mulholland brochure-booklet, Office of John Mulholland, 1940, eight pages.

Psychic Investigator From Coast Gives Lunchers the Jitters by Burns Mantle, *The New York Daily News*, January 24, 1940.

Magic in New York, *Bulletin of the Museum of the City of New York*, March, 1940, p. 38-43.

Notice of Museum of the City of New York, Berthold Hochschild Architectual Gallery, March 12, 1940.

Social Activities in New York and Elsewhere, *The New York Times*, May 4, 1940, p. 20.

Letter to John Mulholland by Will Rock, written on Thurston stationary, May 17, 1940, one page typewritten.

Correspondence between John Mulholland and Ed Reno, August 6, 7, 9, 1940, three letters, each one page typewritten.

New England Convention of Magicians, souvenir program, Hotel Taft, New Haven, CT, September 21-22, 1940.

It's Fun to be Fooled—Even When You're a Magician, *Spot* (magazine), Vol. 1, no.2, October, 1940, p. 28-29.

The Girl in the Cage, by Cortland Fitzsimmons and John Mulholland, *The Philadelphia Inquirer*, Sunday, November 3, 1940. Illustrated by W. V. Chambers. A Gold Seal $2 Novel Complete. 19-oversize pages.

Conjuring by John Mulholland, Encyclopedia Britannica, first published edition, 1941. 5 reprinted pages in tri-fold presentation folder, signed to Bill Kuethe by Mulholland.

Letter to Jack Crimmins by John Mulholland, January 10, 1941, one page.

The Sphinx, Fortieth Anniversary Issue, Ed. John Mulholland, Vol. XL, No. 1, March, 1941, Editor's Notes, p. 64.

Magic is Also Regimented in Hitler's Reich – Mulholland Tells Plight of Colleagues Who Can't Use Food in Their Tricks, *The New York World Telegram*, March 7, 1941, p. 8.

Letter to Edward J. McLaughlin by John Mulholland, March 7, 1941.

Letter to John Mulholland by Harry Usher, March 3, 1941.

Secret Magic by Peter Finley, *New York Sunday Mirror Magazine*, April 6, 1941.

Finding Stage Neatest Trick of Magician, John Mulholland Admits He Fears Trapdoors on His Trips to Footlights by Irving Drutman, *The New York World Telegram*, May, 1941.

Radio City Music Hall, W. G. Van Schumers, Managing Director, week beginning May 15, 1941, program notes, with additional clips from *The NY Daily News, The World Telegram, The NY Post, The Herald Tribune, The Journal American.*

The Smarter They Are The Harder They Fall by Harry Gray, *LIBERTY magazine,* July 5, 1941, p. 39 & 48.

Letter to Charles C. Tillinghast by Dorothy Wolf, Horace Mann School, September 30, 1941.

Magic by Barrows Mussey, A. S. Barnes & Co., New York, 1942.

Keith Clark's Silks Supreme, Introduction by John Mulholland, Silk King Studios, Cincinnati, Ohio, 1942.

The Stage Calls All Hands to Entertain the Navy by Theodore Laymon, *New York Herald Tribune,* March 8, 1942.

Showplace Magazine of Radio City Music Hall, May 15, 1942.

Letter to Ralph L. Erlewine by Dorothy L. Wolf, September 10, 1942. one typewritten page.

Bookmen's Holiday by Harry Miller Lydenburg, The New York Public Library, New York, 1943.

Magic in the Library by John Mulholland, New York Public Library, 1943.

Artist profile: John Mulholland, Edison Business Club of Detroit, February 10, 1943.

Magic on Broadway, Saturday, *The New York Times,* May 5, 1943, p. 23.

The Sphinx, Vol. XLII #4, June, 1943, p. 72.

Everybody's Making Magic, *United Newspaper Magazine Corp.,* 1944.

John Mulholland and the Art of Illusion by Edmund Wilson, *The New Yorker,* March 11, 1944, p. 83.

Letter to John Mulholland by Servais LeRoy, November 29, 1944, May 17, 1940, three pages typewritten.

Tops Magazine, (Mulholland on cover), Abbott's Magic Manufacturing Co., Colon, MI, November, 1944.

Magic in America by John Mulholland, *The Linking Ring*, February 1945, Vol. 24, No. 12, p. 21.

A Dollar Well Spent by Henry Deane, Jr., *The Linking Ring*, February 1945, Vol. 24, No.12, p. 26.

My Friend John Mulholland by Silent Mora, *The Linking Ring*, February 1945, Vol. 24, No. 12, p. 30-31, 68, 71.

Children's Bookshop by John Mulholland, Printed as a souvenir of the Magic Party, Children's Bookshop, 293 Alexander Street, Rochester, NY, March 24, 1945.

Seeing Things – Miss Taylor's Return (review) by John Mason Brown, *The Saturday Review*, April 14, 1945. p. 34-36.

Everybody's Making Magic by Jerry Mason, *Dallas Morning News*, May 14, 1945.

Letter to John Mulholland by Joe Ovette, May 15, 1945, one page.

Letter to Joe Ovette by John Mulholland, May 17, 1945, one page.

Letter to Will Rock by John Mulholland, September 1, 1945, one page typewritten.

Letter to Sam Horowitz by John Mulholland, September 15, 1945.

The Christmas Conjurer by John Mulholland, original typescript, Office of John Mulholland, 130 West 42nd Street, New York City, 10018. 4-pages typed.   Written for *The New York Times Magazine*, December 16, 1945. Also reprinted as a small, yellow covered promotional booklet by The Office of John Mulholland, 130 West 42nd Street.

The Old, Old Magic by John Mulholland, *The New York Times Magazine*, December 16, 1945, p. 13.

Christmas Conjurer by John Mulholland, reprint, Office of John Mulholland (author's copy), 1945.

Conjeeveram—Conjuring by John Mulholland, *Encyclopedia Britannica*, 14th edition, 1945, p. 260-264.

Illustrated Magic by Ottokar Fischer, The Macmillan Company, New York, 1946.

Long, Long Ago by Alexander Woollcott, The Viking Press, New York, 1944. 2nd ed: Bantam Books, New York, 1946, p. 162-165.

Will G. Goldston, Magician, 67, Dies, *The New York Times*, obituary, February 25, 1946, p. 19.

Leo Rullman, Won Fame as a Magician, *The New York Times*, obituary, August 23, 1946, p. 19.

Letter to Joseph Sherman, Esq., by John Mulholland, October 29, 1946, one page.

It Was Hallowe'en and Good Times to Remind the Public of Phoney Mediums by C. M. Sievert, *The New York World Telegram*, November 1, 1946.

Correspondence between Bob Lund and John and Pauline Mulholland, covering February 8, 1947 - October 6, 1977. Fifty letters, property of the American Museum of Magic, Marshall, MI.

Letter to S. Leo Horowitz, by John Mulholland, March 3, 1947.

Ellison Collection Unearthed, *The Conjuror's Magazine*, April, 1947, p. 8-9.

Modern Hypnosis by Lesley Kuhn & Salvatore Russo, Psychological Library Publishers, New York, 1947.

Gems of Mental Magic by John Brown Cook and Arthur Buckley, Introduction by John Mulholland, Chicago, June 7, 1947.

These Are Strange Tales, by Anthony Abbot, (Futon Oursler) The John C. Winston Co., Philadelphia, 1948. Mulholland's copy with notes by JM inside.

John Mulholland's Wonders of the World, *Programme Magazine*, January, 1948.

There's a Trick to It column by John Mulholland, *Colliers Magazine*, March 27, 1948; April 10, 194; April 24, 1948; May 8, 1948; May 22, 1948; June 5, 1948; June 26, 1948; July 3, 1948.

New England Convention of Magicians, souvenir program, Hotel Kimball, Springfield, MA, October 15-17, 1948.

Profile of John Mulholland by Bob Lund, 1948, two pages typewritten.

Three Thousand Years of Espionage by Kurt Singer, Prentice Hall Publishing, New York, 1948.

Hypnotism by G.H. Estabrooks, E. P. Dutton & Co., New York, 7th ed., 1948.

About People, Helen Worden *The New York Herald Tribune*, December 20, 1948.

1949 Calendar created by John Mulholland.

Letter to Dr. Boris Zola by John Mulholland, February 1, 1949, one page handwritten.

Cyclopedia of Magic by Henry Hay, Editor, David McKay Company, Washington Square, 1949.

1950-1959:

How Magicians Mystify Their Audiences by John Mulholland, Compton's Encyclopedia, entry for Magic, nd, 1950's.

Carnegie Hall Presents a New Idea in Entertainment, Director, Helen Arthur, Notice of Mulholland's appearance on November 3, nd. Probably 1950's.

Our Mysteries, edited by Al Flosso, Introduction by John Mulholland, Flosso-Hornmann Magic Company, New York, nd, probably 1950's.

John Mulholland and the Art of Illusion by Edmund Wilson, (originally published in *The New Yorker* magazine, March 11, 1944), *Classics and Commercials; A Literary Chronicle of the Forties*, Farrar, Straus & Co., NY 1950, p. 147-152.

John Mulholland, Artist profile, *The New Yorker*, April 8, 1950.

Fakirs tricks Put a Hex on a Pixie by Paul Phelan, *The New York World-Telegram*, October 4, 1950.

Letter to Foster Fender by John Mulholland, December 19,1950, one page typewritten.

Letter to Milbourne Christopher by John Mulholland, December 19, 1950, New York, three pages typewritten.

Letter to C. Spencer Chambers by John Mulholland, February 19, 1951.

Later Magic by Professor Hoffmann, with a new Introduction by John Mulholland, E.P. Dutton & Co., 1951.

St. Nicholas Makes Annual Earlier Visit, *The New York Times*, nd, probably 1950's.

Magicians' Secrets Guarded At Exhibit, *The New York Times*, March 20, 1951, p. 46.

NY Historical Society announcement of St. Nicholas Day Festivities, December 6, 1951.

Letter to Milbourne Christopher by John Mulholland, March 9, 1951, one page.

The Mystery of Legerdemain, (unknown) *New York Magazine*, April 7, 1951.

The Sphinx Golden Jubilee Book of Magic, compiled by Milbourne Christopher, Introduction by John Mulholland, Sphinx Publishing Co., New York, 1951,p. 5-6.

Letter to John Mulholland by Fred Keating, January 17, 1952, one page.

Lincoln – Mercury Times, March-April,1952. Published by Lincoln-Mercury division of Ford Motor Co.

A Hypnotist Finally Got the Man Off the Ledge, *MKEE Standard*, Wisconsin, Associated Press, April 26, 1952.

Program of Stamford Fire Company, presents world renowned magician John Mulholland, May 17, 1952.

A Matter of Importance by Fred C. Kelly, *Coronet Magazine*, June, 1952.

Hocus Pocus by Bennett Cerf, *This Week Magazine*, July 20, 1952.

Magicians Scoff at Flying Saucers by John Mulholland, *Popular Mechanics*, September, 1952.

Coin Magic by J. B. Bobo, Carl W. Jones Publisher, Minneapolis, 1952.

Private file of CIA work by John Mulholland, 1953-1958, fifty-six pages, private collection.

Rabbit and Stein of Beer Pulled From Ballot Box as Magicians Elect, *The Herald* (NY), June 1, 1953.

Postcard to subscription of *The Sphinx*, June 1, 1953.

Letter to Readership of *The Sphinx* by John Mulholland, detailing the suspension of *The Sphinx*, June 29, 1953.

Magician Shares Stage At Concert, Mulholland Makes Pelletier's Baton Vanish, but Town Hall Youth Program Goes On, *The New York Times*, November 22, 1953, p. 87.

Magician At Concert, Mulholland Performs for Small Fry at Philharmonic Program, *The New York Times*, December 27, 1953, p. 63.

The Man Who Never Was by The Hon. Ewen E. S. Montagu, J.B. Lippincott Company, 1954.

Fred Keating Talks About The Magical Tradition by Robert Coleman, *The New York Mirror*, March 7, 1954.

Program of the Fogg Art Museum, Cambridge, MA, 50th Anniversary, June 16, 1954.

Hypnotism' Too Easy! by Stuart Johns, Australasian Post, January 20, 1955, p. 9-11.

The Pyramid, publication of the Quarter Century Club, Mulholland on cover, March, 1955.

Mulholland vs. Keating, *The Players Bulletin*, Spring, 1956.

Backstage with Frank Joglar, *Hugard's Magic Monthly*, January, 1957, p. 518.

The Dynasty by Arthur LeRoy "Out Of My Profonde" in Hugard's Magic Monthly Vol. 14, no 8, 9 January - February 1957.

How's Your Library by James B. Findlay, with a Preface by John Mulholland, Ireland Magic Co., Chicago, IL, 1958.

Life With Kalamazoo's TV Quiz Champ, *The Detroit News*, April 4, 1958.

The Great Rope Trick Mystery, *This Week Magazine* with The Detroit News, April 6, 1958.

Letter to John Mulholland by William F. Duhlmeir, Tyndall Air Force Base, Panama City, Florida, April 12, 1958, 8-pages handwritten, responding urgently to Mulholland's article in the *NY Times* "The Great Rope trick Mystery." Part fan letter, part crackpot.

Letter to John Mulholland by Neil L. Maurer, Co-Editor, *Ex-CBI Roundup*, April 17, 1958, 1 small page typed referring to the reprint of his famous article "The Great Rope Trick Mystery."

MK-ULTRA Sub Project 58, memorandum by Sidney Gottlieb, Technical Services Staff, April 18, 1958.

The Occult Cult Flourishes by Guy Talese, *The New York Times*, October 12, 1958, p. SM41.

The Great Rope Trick Mystery by John Mulholland, Ex-CBI Roundup, (reprinted from *This Week Magazine*) December, 1958.

The Manchurian Candidate by Richard Condon, McGraw Hill Book Co. Inc., New York - Toronto, 1959.

1960-1969:

Images of Tomorrow by D. Ewen Cameron, M.D., *American Journal of Psychotherapy*, Vol. 14, No. 1, January, 1960.

Among Friends #19, *Friends of the Detroit Public Library*, Summer, 1960.

M-U-M 50, Vol. 50, no. 7, December, 1960.

Sorcar on Magic by P.C. Sorcar, Introduction by John Mulholland, Indrajal Publications, Calcutta, India, 1960.

Letter From America, *Daily Telegraph and Morning Post*, February 23, 1961.

Charlie Rice's Punch Bowl, *This Week Magazine*, February 26, 1961.

Letter to Dr. Mitchell Gratwick by John Mulholland, The Horace Mann School, October 2, 1961, one page typewritten.

Houdini's Eve, *Staff News*, The New York Public Library, Vol. 51, November 9, 1961, no. 45.

Letter to Gerald Morice, Esq, by Herbert Jenkins Publishers concerning John Mulholland's British edition of *Practical Puppetry*, November 28, 1961.

Xmas Card by John Mulholland and Dorothy Wolf, 1961.

Unpublished Magic Books by John Mulholland, *The Magic Cauldron*, 1962, p.23.

Savvy Inside Stuff, Back on Abracadabra, *Variety*, April 17, 1962.

Founders Night, *The New Yorker*, January 19, 1963.

The Craft of Intelligence by Allen W. Dulles, Harper & Row Publishers, New York, 1963.

Pipe Night by Henry Fisk Carlton, *The Players Bulletin*, review of, Spring, 1963.

Magic Circle Magic, Edited by Will Dexter, Harry Clarke and The Magic Circle, England, 1963.

Library Journal, by Robert B. Jackson, *Sports and Pastimes, John Mulholland's Book of Magic* noted as an expanded version of *The Art of Illusion*, April 1, 1963.

You See, It Was Like This – Or Was It? by Norton Mockridge, *The New York World Telegram*, May 29, 1963.

Girl Shaking Off Effects of Hypnosis Act, *Kansas City Star*, MO, October 5, 1963.

Confessions of a Magician, *New Hampshire Sunday News*, Family Weekly, October 20, 1963.

The Invisible Government by David Wise and Thomas B. Ross, Random House Publishing, New York, 1964.

CIA: The Invisible Government by David Wise and Thomas B. Ross, *LOOK Magazine*, June 16, 1964, p. 37-49.

John Mulholland, *Genii Magazine*, Vol 28, No. 11, July, 1964.

Secrets & Spies, The Readers Digest Corporation, 1964.

Letter to John Henry Grossman by John Mulholland, private collection, September 29, 1965.

Letter to George N. Gordon by John Mulholland, collection of Diane Gordon, Newtown, CT, nd, 1960's.

World Renowned Magician – John Mulholland, *Genii Magazine*, Volume 30, No 3, November, 1965.

Ideas for Magic by John Mulholland, *Genii Magazine*, Volume 30, No 3, November 1965, p. 110-113.

John Mulholland – A Living Legend, *Genii Magazine*, Volume 30, No 3, November 1965, p.114.

John Mulholland – The Gentleman by David T. Bamberg (Fu Manchu), *Genii Magazine*, Volume 30, No 3, November, 1965, p. 118.

John Mulholland – The Lecturer by Arthur LeRoy, *Genii Magazine*, Volume 30, No 3, November, 1965, p. 120.

John Mulholland – The Writer, by Robert Lund, *Genii Magazine*, Volume 30, No 3, November, 1965, p. 121.

John Mulholland – The Editor by John Braun, *Genii Magazine*, Volume 30, No 3, November, 1965, p. 122.

John Mulholland – The Collector by Jay Marshall, *Genii Magazine*, Volume 30, No 3, November, 1965, p. 126.

A Magical Afternoon, The House of the Magic Rabbit, *The New York Times*, November 20, 1965.

New York Day by Day by Frank Farrell, *The New York World Telegram & Sun*, December 8, 1965.

Too Many Words Spoil the Magic Moment by Norton Mockridge, *The New York World Telegram*, December 23, 1965.

Announcement of Players Club, Pipe Night in Honor of John Mulholland, February 6, 1966.

The John Mulholland Magic Collection, by John Mulholland, *The Players Bulletin*, Spring, 1966, p. 14-16.

Magic, Mirth and Mr. Mulholland, *The Players Bulletin*, Spring, 1966, p. 3.

Program of the Hammond Museum, Georgian Fair, John Mulholland MC, 1966.

In Search of Magic, *The Daily Telegraph*, London, September 9, 1966.

Memoirs of a Magician's Ghost – The Autobiography of John Booth, Chapter 14, *The Linking Ring* magazine, November, 1966, vol. 46, no. 4. p. 35.

We Often See Things We Didn't See At All by Norton Mockridge, *The Baltimore Sun*, December 15, 1966.

Brochure of Communication Arts Books, Hastings House Publishers, New York, 1967.

The Greatest Magicians in the World by William W. Larsen, *Genii Magazine*, vol. 31, January, 1967, p. 219.

The Magical Mind, release from Ben Hall Associates, New York, February 14, 1967.

Variety, General news column regarding John Mulholland's new book, March 1, 1967.

The (NY) Morning Telegraph, review of *The Magical Mind*, April 14, 1967.

Society of American Magicians program, Oversize folded program featuring John Mulholland, April 15, 1967.

Proclamation of the State of New York "National Magic Day" by Governor Nelson A. Rockefeller, Records of The Rockefeller Archives, Pocantico Hills, New York, October 31, 1967.

Letter to Milbourne Christopher by John Mulholland, November 1, 1967, one page.

Cataloging Sleight of Hand by John Mulholland, *Library Journal*, April 1, 1968.

Teachers Who Earn Fortunes by Leslie Lieber, *The Baltimore Sun*, May 12, 1968.

Butcher Hams it up Computer Fashion by Norton Mockridge, *Detroit News*, September 30, 1968.

Letter to Barry H. Wiley by John Mulholland, November 21, 1968, 1-page typescript regarding Anna Eva Fay.

Card Tricks For Everyone by Ellis Stanyon, Foreword by John Mulholland, Emerson Books, Inc., Buchanan, NY, 1968.

HOUDINI: The Untold Story by Milbourne Christopher, T.Y. Crowell, New York, 1969.

Letter to Tom Stix Jr. by John Mulholland, circa late 1960's regarding Houdini, two pages, handwritten, undated.

Letter to Joe G. Vitale by John Mulholland, private collection, January 24, 1969, two pages typewritten.

Pistol Words (from Charlie Rice's Punchbowl), *This Week Magazine*, March 16, 1969, p.14.

Book Reviews, American Notes & Queries, *Houdini: The Untold Story* by Milbourne Christopher, reviewed by John Mulholland, April 1969, p. 126-127.

1970-1979:

NAME	
TITLE	
PUBLISHER	
PLACE	DATE
ILLUSTRATED	SIZE BINDING
NOTES	
	JOHN MULHOLLAND

Letter to George N. Gordon by John Mulholland, Newtown, CT, nd, 1970's collection of Diane Gordon.

Notes of Milbourne Christopher, private interview with John Mulholland, Dec. 1969; Jan, Feb 1970.

John Mulholland – In Memoriam by Milbourne Christopher, *Genii Magazine*, February, 1970, p. 279.

An Appreciation of John Mulholland on the Occasion of his Death by Brooks Atkinson, February 25, 1970.

John Mulholland (obituary), *The New York Daily News*, February 26, 1970.

John Mulholland (obituary), *The New York Post*, February 26, 1970.

John Mulholland, Magician and Author, 71, Dies, *The New York Times*, February 27, 1970.

Magician Dies at 71 (obituary), *Detroit Free Press*, February 27, 1970.

John Mulholland (obituary), *The Daily Variety*, March 4, 1970.

John Mulholland (obituary), *Newsweek* magazine, March 9, 1970.

The Stage (obituary), England, March 12, 1970.

Antiquarian Bookman, (obituary), March 16, 1970.

Genii Magazine, Vol 34, No. 8, April, 1970, p. 368.

Broken Wand (obituary), by John Henry Grossman, *M-U-M* magazine, May, 1970, p. 14-15.

JOHN MULHOLLAND by Milbourne Christopher, (obituary) *The Linking Ring*, May, 1970, p. 95 - 97.

Letter to June Barrows Mussey by Pauline Mulholland, February 4, 1972, one page handwritten. Reproduced in A MAGICAL UPBRINGING—June Barrows Mussey (Collected Letters and Articles) by Dagmar Mussey, Lybrary.com, 2008, p. 97.

Letter to June Barrows Mussey by Pauline Mulholland, February 21, 1972, one page handwritten. Reproduced in A MAGICAL UPBRINGING—June Barrows Mussey (Collected Letters and Articles) by Dagmar Mussey, Lybrary.com, 2008, p. 97.

United States Chiefs of Mission 1778-1973 by Richardson Dougall and Mary Patricia Chapman, Historical Office, Bureau of Public Affairs, Dept. of State, 1973, p. 92.

All The President's Men by Carl Bernstein and Bob Woodward, Simon and Schuster, New York, 1974.

The Hoffmann Collector, #2, Mulholland on Hoffmann, Edited by Thomas A. Sawyer, September, 1974.

Letter to Milbourne Christopher by Pauline Mulholland, March 9, 1975, one page handwritten.

Letter from Louis Rachow (librarian of The Players), to "Magic Enthusiasts," November 3, 1975.

The CIA and the Cult of Intelligence by Victor Marchetti and John D. Marks, Dell Publishing Co., New York, 1975.

Family Plans to Sue CIA Over Suicide in Drug Test by Seymour M. Hersh, *The New York Times*, July 10, 1975.

Inside the Company: CIA Diary by Philip Agee, Stonehill Publishing Company, New York, 1975.

Death Inquiry is Re-opened in LSD Case by Joseph B. Treaster, *The New York Times*, July 12, 1975, p. 55.

Destruction of LSD Data Laid to CIA Aide in '73 by Nicholas M. Horrock, *The New York Times*, July 18, 1975, p. 63.

Ex CIA Aide Took LSD as a "Guinea Pig" by Joseph B. Treaster, *The New York Times*, July 19, 1975, p. 37.

OLSONS REVEAL That Ford Told CIA to Yield Data -- Olsons Say Ford Gave Order by Joseph B. Treaster, The New York Times, July 23, 1975. p. 1, 73.

CIA Files on LSD Death Found to be Contradictory by Joseph B. Treaster, *The New York Times*, January 11, 1976, p. 29.

Memoirs of a CIA Psychologist by Maureen Orth, *New Times Communications*, June 25, 1976, Volume 6, No. 13, p. 19-24.

The Original Houdini Scrapbook by Walter B. Gibson, Corwin Sterling Publishing Co., Inc., New York, 1976. p. 181, 189.

Files on CIA Drug Testing Work Said to List "Prominent" Doctors by Nicholas M. Horrock, *The New York Times*, July 17, 1977, p. 61.

Private Institutions Used in CIA Effort to Control Behavior -- 25 Year, 25 Million Program reported by John M. Crewsdon, Nicholas M. Horrock, Boyce Rensberger, Jo Thomas, and Joseph

B. Treaster. Written by Nicholas M. Horrack, *The New York Times*, August 1, 1977.

Magician Was Hired As Advisor to C.I.A. (also titled *CIA Hired Magician in Behavior Project—Hired him to Write Manual as Aid in Secretly Giving Drugs*) by Joseph B. Treaster, *The New York Times*, August 3, 1977.

The CIA's Magician, Good Evening column, *The Evening Bulletin*, August, 3, 1977.

Magician Hired in CIA Brain Control Effort, *St, Louis Post Dispatch*, August 3, 1977.

Letter to Milbourne Christopher by Pauline Mulholland, August 4, 1977, one page.

CIA Used Magician as Research Consultant by Joseph B. Treaster, *The International Herald Tribune*, August 4, 1977.

Mulholland CIA Link Queried, *The Bridgeport Post*, Tuesday, August 9, 1977, p. 8.

CIA HAD A THEORY MAGICOS WERE FOR REAL, *Variety*, August 10, 1977.

CIA Head Offers Drug Test Files If Justice Department Has Inquiry by Anthony Marro, *The New York Times*, August 10, 1977, p. 1.

CIA Says It Found More Secret Papers on Behavioral Control by Jo Thomas, *The New York Times*, September 3, 1977, p. 1.

Files Show Tests For Truth Drug Began in O.S.S, Marijuana Derivative Reported Used, by John M. Crewsdon and Jo Thomas, *The New York Times*, September 5, 1977, p. 1, 33.

Ex CIA Aide Asks Immunity to Testify by John C. Crewsdon and Jo Thomas, written by Jo Thomas, *The New York Times*, September 7, 1977, p. 11.

Key Witness in CIA Inquiry – Sidney Gottlieb, *The New York Times*, September 19, 1977, p. 83.

Abuses in Testing Of Drugs by CIA To Be Panel Focus reported by John M. Crewsdon and Jo Thomas, written by John M. Crewsdon, *The New York Times*, September 20, 1977, p. 1.

284

Key Figure Testifies in Private on CIA Drug Tests by Jo Thomas, *The New York Times*, September 21, 1977, p. 1.

Letter to Milbourne Christopher by Pauline Mulholland, September 30, 1977, one page handwritten.

Letter to Milbourne Christopher by Pauline Mulholland, October 5, 1977, one page handwritten.

Letter to Pauline Mulholland by Allen Berlinski, December 7, 1977, one page handwritten.

Edmund Wilson – Man of Letter and Legerdemain by Edwin A. Dawes, *The Magic Circular*, no 72, May, 1978, p. 62-66.

Interview with Paul Draper, Carnegie Mellon University, Summer, 1978.

Letter to Diane Gordon by Pauline Mulholland, Collection of Diane Gordon, November 24, 1978, one page.

Search for the Manchurian Candidate by John Marks, New York Times Books, New York, 1978.

Uncloaking the CIA, Howard Frazier, editor, The Free Press, New York, 1978.

Conjurer Adds Magic to Christmas Party by Norton Mockridge, *The Evening Standard*, p. B4, probably 1970's.

Interview with Louis Rachow, Librarian at The Players club, Gramercy Park, New York, June-August, 1979.

1980-1989:

Theatre & Performing Arts Collections, Louis A. Rachow, Guest Editor, Volume 1, Number 1, Fall 1981, The Haworth Press, New York, 1981, p. 31.

Letter to The Players by Pauline Pierce Mulholland, *The Players Book*, January 11, 1982, p. 65.

The Notes of (Anonymous) Diary entry, 17-page description of an LSD trip handwritten under the influence over a 14-hour period, private collection. October 31 - November 1, 1982.

Letter to Ben Robinson from John A. Keel (re: Mulholland's lacking scholarship), July 25, 1983, one page typewritten.

Swann Galleries, F.P. Model & Co., Inc., news release concerning the sale of the Mulholland Collection, October 8, 1984, five pages.

Mulholland Magic Collection to be Auditioned (sic) **Off,** *Variety*, October 17, 1984, p. 47.

Swann Galleries, news release: "Mulholland Magic Collection, Sold to Private Buyer," November 8, 1985, four pages.

Magic Collection Sold to Unnamed Collector by Michael Schlesinger, *Variety*, November 14, 1984, p. 2.

Acid Dreams -- The Complete Social History of LSD, The CIA, and the Sixties and Beyond, by Martin AZ. Lee and Bruce Schlom, Grove Press, New York, 1985.

MAGIC–A Pictorial History of Conjurers in the Theater by David Price, Cornwall Books, New Jersey, 1985, p. 316-318.

Interview with Walter Gibson, May, 1985.

I Sold My Linking Rings by William V. Rauscher, privately published by the author, 1985.

Wonders of Magic by John N. Booth, Ridgeway Press, Los Alamitos, CA, 1986, p. 62- 65.

Spy Catcher--The Candid Autobiography of a Senior Intelligence Officer by Peter Wright, Viking Press, USA, 1987.

Illusion Show – A Life in Magic by David Bamberg, David Meyer Magic Books, Glenwood, IL, 1988.

Spotlight on Mulholland, Houdini and Maskelyne by Dr. John N. Booth, Chapter 226, Memoirs of a Magician's Ghost, *The Linking Ring*, Vol 68, No. 11, November, 1988, p. 65.

Journey Into Madness (Medical Torture and the Mind Controllers) by Gordon Thomas, Bantam Press, London, 1988.

Letter to Ben Robinson by Sydney Eddison, Newtown, CT, June 26, 1989.

The Mulholland Library of Conjuring and the Allied Arts presents the Conference on Magical History, (program booklet) November 2, 3, 4, 1989 at The Beverly Garland Resort Hotel, North Hollywood, CA, 1989.

1990-1999:

Creative World of Conjuring by John N. Booth, Ridgeway Press, Los Alamitos, CA, 1990.

Ownership and Disposition of the Mulholland Library of Conjuring and the Allied Arts, Memorandum by Katharine Warwick, January 21, 1990.

The Art of Honest Deception by Vincent H. Gaddis, *Strange Magazine*, Spring, 1990.

How One Savings Institution Fell Apart by Richard W. Stevenson, *The New York Times*, June 12, 1990, p. 1, C4.

The Trick: Turn Magic Into Money, *The Los Angeles Times*, October 12, 1990, p. A3, A25.

The CIA Catalogue of Clandestine Weapons, Tools and Gadgets by John Minnery, Barricade Books Inc., Fort Lee, NJ, 1990.

The Encyclopedia of Parapsychology and Psychical Research by Arthur S. Berger and Joyce Berger, Paragon House, New York, 1991, p. 452-453.

Centrist Cover The R. T. C's Shimmery Headache by Leslie Wayne, April 21, 1991.

A John Mulholland Secret By Robert Lund, MAGICOL, No. 100, August, 1991, p. 2-3.

US Bankruptcy Court Central District of California, Notice and Motion and motion for authority to sell interests in Mulholland Library of Conjuring and the Allied Arts free and clear of claims of interests and allocating proceeds of sale, October 15, 1991.

Expensive Magic, Newsmakers column, *The Detroit News*, October 24, 1991.

RTC to Make Magic Library Disappear for 2.2 Million by James Bates, *The Los Angeles Times*, November, 1991.

The Genii Speaks by William W. Larsen Jr., Genii – The International Conjurer's Magazine, November 1991, p. 25.

Mulholland Magic Collection Awaits Fate, *The Los Angeles Times*, Sunday, April 26, 1992.

True Hallucinations by Terence McKenna, HarperSanFrancisco, New York, 1993.

The Honest Deceiver, *USA Today*, March 29, 1993, p. D1, D2.

Fooled Again by Jim Steinmeyer, *MAGIC* magazine, January, 1994, p. 36-41.

Words About Wizards by Robert Parrish, David Meyer Magic Books, Glenwood, IL, 1994, p. 13-15.

The Catcher Was a Spy by Nicholas Dawidoff, Vintage Books, 1994.

Psychics and Spooks: How Spoon-benders fought the cold war by Gregory Vistica, *Newsweek*, National Affairs, December 11, 1995.

Spring 1996 Horace Mann Magazine, by Hon. Giles S. Rich (Horace Mann 1922), p. 22-23.

HOUDINI—The Career of Erich Weiss by Kenneth Silverman, HarperCollins Publishers, New York, 1996.

William E. Colby, Head of CIA in Time of Upheaval, Dies at 76 by Tim Weiner, *The New York Times*, May 7, 1996.

Master Creator of Ghosts is Honored by CIA by Tim Weiner, *The New York Times*, September 18, 1996.

Memoirs of the National Academy of Sciences by J. Edwin Seegmiller, DeWitt Stetten, Jr., no. 71, 1997, p. 332-345.

Aging Shop of Horrors: the CIA Limps to 50 by Tim Weiner, *The New York Times*, July 20, 1997.

John Mulholland: His Known and Unknown Life, The Autobiography of John N. Booth, Chapter 312, *The Linking Ring* Magazine, December, 1997, p. 71-74.

Letter to Ben Robinson by J. Kevin O'Brien, Federal Bureau of Investigation, U.S. Dept. of Justice., March 20, 1998. Regarding John Mulholland.

Letter to Ben Robinson by J. Kevin O'Brien, Federal Bureau of Investigation, U.S. Dept. of Justice., March 31, 1998. Regarding John Mulholland.

The Spy Who Came Back From the Grave, *The Mail on Sunday Review*, Kevin Dowling and Philip Knightly, August 23, 1998, p.11-13.

Meet Sidney Gottlieb – CIA dirty trickster by Sarah Foster, *WoldNetDaily.com*, Thursday, November 19, 1998.

Sidney Gottlieb, 80, Dies; Took LSD to C.I.A., *The New York Times*, March 10, 1999.

CIA Official Sidney Gottlieb, 80, Dies; Directed Tests with LSD in '50s, '60s, *The Washington Post*, March 10, 1999.

Terence McKenna Live, last public lecture, recorded by Jon Dix, HPX, Inc., Seattle, WA, April, 1999.

Writing Codes, Movies and Now a Book by Mel Gussow, *The New York Times*, July 17, 1999. p. B1,15.

2000-

MK-ULTRA documents declassified covering 1945-1975, Office of Information and Privacy including over 18,000 documents first released in part in 1975 by the Rockefeller Commission investigating improper use of power by the CIA regarding MK-ULTRA.

The Houdini Code Mystery – A Spirit Secret Solved by William V. Rauscher, Mike Caveney's Magic Words, Pasadena, CA, 2000.

A Cold Case, by Philip Gourevitch, *The New Yorker*, February 14, 2000, p. 42-60.

Tinker, Writer, Artist, Spy; Intellectuals During the Cold War, by Jeff Sharlet, *The Chronicle of Higher Education*, March 31, 2000, p. A19.

The Trickster and the Paranormal by George P. Hansen, X Libris Corporation, 2001.

Cord Meyer Jr. Dies at 80; Communism Fighter at CIA, *The New York Times*, March 16, 2001.

How the CIA Played Dirty Tricks With Culture by Laurence Zuckerman, *The New York Times*, March 18, 2001 p. B7.

What Did the CIA Do to Eric Olson's Father? by Michael Ignatieff, *The New York Times*, April 1, 2001.

The Sphinx & The Spy, The Clandestine World of John Mulholland by Michael Edwards, *Genii - The Conjuror's Magazine*, Volume 64, Number 4, April 2, 2001, p. 22-39.

For Your Eyes Only by Hank Schlesinger, *Smithsonian Magazine*, June, 2001.

What Went Wrong The CIA and the Failure of American Intelligence by Seymour M. Hersh, *The New Yorker*, October 8, 2001, p. 34.

The Mind Readers by William V. Rauscher, Mystic Light Press, Woodbury, NJ, 2002.

Stem Rust of Wheat: Ancient Enemy to Modern Foe by Dr. Roland F. Line and Clay S. Griffith, APS Press, 2002.

Agent Who Betrayed FBI Cites Its Laxity by Philip Shenon, *The New York Times*, April 5, 2002, p. A16.

Interview with George N. Gordon at the Mulholland-Hide-A-Way, Newtown, CT, May, 2002.

The Trenchcoat Robbers, *The New Yorker*, July 8, 2002, p. 34-39.

Interview with H. Keith Melton, July 13, 2002.

Once Secret And Now On Display by Phil Patton, *The New York Times*, July 17, 2002.

Literature Re-enlists In the Military by Mel Gussow, *The New York Times*, November 7, 2002, p. E1, E4.

Inclined Toward Magic by David Meyer, Waltham Street Press, 2003.

The Vanished Man by Jeffery Deaver, Pocket Books, New York, 2003.

Some Operational Applications of the Art of Deception by John Mulholland, *Genii – The International Conjurers Magazine*, Edited by Richard Kaufman, August 2003, p. 40-79.

How I was a Psychic Spy for the CIA and Found God (a profile of Russell Targ), by Doris Lora, *IONS, Noetic Sciences Review*, September/November 2003, p. 32-35.

Interview with CIA Officer Chase Brandon from the film *The Recruit*, Spyglass Productions, 2003.

Secrets Of the Scandal by Nicholas D. Kristof, *The New York Times*, October 11, 2003, p. A15.

Correspondence between Central Intelligence Agency and an anonymous researcher, December 10, 2003, one page typewritten.

The CIA's Anonymous No. 2 by Dana Priest, *The Washington Post*, January 9, 2004.

George Tenet Resigns, *The New York Times*, Op. Ed. Page, June 4, 2004.

A Quiet Man Takes Charge, John Edward McLaughlin by Joel Brinkley, *The New York Times*, June 4, 2004, p. A13.

CIA's New Acting Director Is Known for Analytical – and Magic – Skills by Dana Priest, *The Washington Post*, June 4, 2004.

Out of the Rich Cabinet by Edwin A. Dawes, a lecture delivered at the IBM convention, Cleveland, Ohio, July 1, 2004, p. 7.

The Men Who Stared at Goats by Jon Ronson, Simon & Schuster, New York, 2004.

Fears of Vacuum in Terror Fight, As Tenet and Aide leave, Some See Gap at C. I. A, by Douglas Jehl, *The New York Times*, June 5, 2004. p. 1.

Letter to Ben Robinson by Dr. John N. Booth, July 12, 2004, one page typewritten.

Empty Office Adds to Sense of Isolation At the CIA by Douglas Jehl, The *New York Times*, July 13, 2004, p. A9.

Can the CIA Really Be That Bad? by Michael O'Hanlon, *The New York Times*, July 13, 2004, p. A19.

White House and CIA Withhold Document on Prewar Intelligence Given to Bush by Douglas Jehl, *The New York Times*, July 14, 2004, p. A13.

Letter to Ben Robinson by Dr. John N. Booth, July 16, 2004, one page typewritten.

Eddie Albert, Character Actor, Dies at 99 by Margalit Fox, *The New York Times*, May 28, 2005, p. 22.

John K. Vance; Uncovered LSD Project at CIA by Joe Holley, *The Washington Post*, June 16, 2005, p. B8.

Private Spy and Public Spouse Live at Center of Leak Case by Scott Shane, *The New York Times*, July 5, 2005, p.1 & 12.

Letter to Ken Klosterman from Dorothy Stix, November, 2006, one page.

Interview with Dorothy Stix by Ben Robinson, December 9, 2006.

Romania's King Without a Throne Outlives Foes and Setbacks, by Craig S. Smith, The New York Times, January 27, 2007.

Next for the CIA's Least Secret Officer: A Quieter Life by Michael Powell, The New York Times, March 8, 2007, p. A 18.

Agent in Leak Case Sues CIA for Blocking the Release of Her Memoir, The New York Times, June 1, 2007, p. A 18.

John Mulholland, Collector by David Meyer, Magicol, No. 163, May 2007, p 3-8.

The Tenth Los Angeles Conference on Magic History, published and copyright Jim Steinmeyer, Los Angeles, CA, 2007.

A Magical Upbringing — June Barrows Mussey (Collected Letters and Articles) by Dagmar Mussey, Lybrary.com, 2008.

Mulholland's show at the New York Public Library
of rarities from his collection, 1940's.

INDEX

M

N

The Author

Ben Robinson became enamored with magic by watching Dutch master magician Fred Kaps follow the Beatles on *The Ed Sullivan Show*. Seven years later, he made his professional debut on his 14th birthday. He has since written a history of: Martinka & Co., the oldest US magical supply house, the vanishing elephant illusion, a pictorial history of the rabbit-in-hat icon, a short biography of the Marx Brothers grandfather-magician Laff Schoenberg, and the cult classic history of magicians killed attempting to catch bullets in their teeth: *Twelve Have Died* (1986). His life-long study of Buster Keaton's use of illusion was published in 2002 by the International Buster Keaton Society, The Damfinos. In 2008 he received a trophy from the International Brotherhood of Magicians for his writing on *Al Flosso: An American Original 1895-1976*.

He was first presented as a one-man surrealist magic show (*Out Of Order*) in a by avant-garde and Broadway producer Lyn Austin and her renowned Music-Theatre Group. His work was reviewed as "must see!" entertainment. He is the only one-man show ever presented in their history. In 1989 he trekked to the Base Camp of Mount Everest with the American Everest Team and entertained Sherpas, monks and climbers. Other one-man shows presented nationally: *After Magic?*, *Pyschodyssey*, *Time For Magic*, and in 2009 for the internationally renowned Belgian circus cabaret Spiegeltent he created the 90-minute wonder show *L'Art De La Magie*.

In 2005, he recreated John Mulholland's performance at Mulholland's alma mater, using some of Mulholland's actual props. Complimenting the multimedia presentation he produced a short film made from Mulholland's personal scrapbooks, and an exhibit of Mulholland's life. The show was presented 81-years to the day of Mulholland's last appearance at Horace Mann.

Ben Robinson is the only magician to have received both the Milbourne Christopher Foundation award and the Leslie R. Guest Award of Excellence from the Society of American Magicians. After his service following 9/11, the New York City Police Dept. presented him with an honorary shield. In 2010 he was honored by his alma mater Connecticut College in their Distinguished Alumni Series for his achievements as an artist. The following week he presented 21 shows in one week at Hollywood's famous Magic Castle. He was reviewed as "comedy magic at its finest" by *American Variety*.

As a producer he brought *STOMP* and rock'n roll to Lincoln Center, and he also co-founded the *Art Rock'n Roll Circus*. He has presented over 10,000 one-man shows internationally and across the U.S. For Metro Video Productions he has chronicled his experiences on CD, *Ben Robinson on Synchronicity* (2001), on home video *Ben Robinson Live in Central Park* (2002) and on DVD *Ben Robinson Live at Kafe AtmoZphere* (2003). Currently, he is found in the music scene as an opening act, working in concert with popular bands, emceeing and entertaining backstage. He also appears at special events worldwide. He and wife An live in Manhattan. They are owned by a 17-year-old Meyer's parrot – Stubby.

See: www.illusiongenius.com

Also by Ben Robinson

<u>Writing & Recording:</u>
Indian Magic
Twelve Have Died   (with Larry White)
Mouth Coil Magic   (with Ray Goulet)
Index for the John Booth Memoirs   (with Amy Janello)
The Magic Box   (with Daniel Stashower)
Ben Robinson on Synchronicity   (CD)

<u>One Man Shows:</u>
Out Of Order   (Music-Theatre Group, 1988)
After Magic?   (Theatreclub Funambules, 1989)
Psychodyssey   (appearances nationally, 1991)
Time For Magic   (The Neighborhood Playhouse, 2007)
L'Art De La Magie   (Spiegeltent, 2009)